The Law of Interdict

The Law of Interdict

Stanley Scott Robinson, M.B.E., T.D., S.S.C
Lately Sheriff of Grampian, Highland
and Islands at Inverness

London/Edinburgh
Butterworths
1987

United Kingdom	Butterworth & Co (Publishers) Ltd, 88 Kingsway, LONDON WC2B 6AB and 61A North Castle Street, EDINBURGH EH2 3LJ
Australia	Butterworths Pty Ltd, SYDNEY, MELBOURNE, BRISBANE, ADELAIDE, PERTH, CANBERRA and HOBART
Canada	Butterworths. A division of Reed Inc., TORONTO and VANCOUVER
New Zealand	Butterworths of New Zealand Ltd, WELLINGTON and AUCKLAND
Singapore	Butterworth & Co (Asia) Pte Ltd, SINGAPORE
South Africa	Butterworth Publishers (Pty) Ltd, DURBAN and PRETORIA
USA	Butterworths Legal Publishers, ST PAUL, Minnesota, SEATTLE, Washington, BOSTON, Massachusetts, AUSTIN, Texas and D & S Publishers, CLEARWATER, Florida

© Butterworth & Co (Publishers) Ltd 1987

All rights reserved. No part of this publication may be reproduced or transmitted in any form or by any means, including photocopying and recording, without the written permission of the copyright holder, application for which should be addressed to the publisher. Such written permission must also be obtained before any part of this publication is stored in a retrieval system of any nature.

This book is sold subject to the Standard Conditions of Sale of Net Books and may not be re-sold in the UK below the net price fixed by Butterworths for the book in our current catalogue.

British Library Cataloguing in Publication Data

Robinson, S. Scott
   The law of interdict.
   1. Injunctions – Scotland
   I. Title
   344.1107'77   KDC896

ISBN 0 406 10445 X

Typeset by Lin-Art, Ashford, Kent
Printed in Great Britain by Billings of Worcester

Preface

More than fifty years have passed since the publication of Sheriff Burn-Murdoch's scholarly and comprehensive treatise on the law of interdict in Scotland. During that period it has remained the universally acknowledged authority upon a subject which enters virtually every aspect of our law.

The present work does not attempt to emulate the philosophical and analytical approach of Burn-Murdoch. It does, however, endeavour in a practical way, to update the law of interdict particularly in the fields of domestic law, industrial relations, the protection of intellectual property, environmental control and the principles governing the vitally important matter of interim interdict. At the time of going to press, substantial amendment of the law of copyright and some amendment of patent law is forecast in the Government White Paper, *Intellectual Property and Innovation* ((1986) Cmnd 9712). The provisions of the Patents, Designs and Marks Act 1986 (which deals with the computerisation of the registers and related matters) were brought into force too late for inclusion in detail in the text but brief reference has been made to the Act in the appropriate footnotes.

The object of this book is to provide the practitioner and the student with a ready reference to the leading modern authorities bearing upon the use of interdict in the main branches of our law. Given such a wide canvas, it is inevitable that some cases may have been omitted and others perhaps dealt with superficially. If, however the result is to point the reader in the required direction for further research, the object will have been achieved.

I wish to acknowledge the help and advice given to me by many friends and colleagues in the preparation of the work. In particular, I must thank Professor Robert Black, Dr Hector MacQueen and Mr Douglas Brodie, all of the Faculty of Law at Edinburgh University for their respective comments on the chapters on Jurisdiction, the Protection of Intellectual Property and Industrial Relations. Their observations have saved me from several errors and omissions. The responsibility for any which remain in these and the other chapters rests entirely with me.

I wish also to thank Mr Andrew Gill, of the SSC Library for his kindly assistance, Miss Catherine Macdonald and Mrs Helen McAngus who, with admirable patience, typed the oft-amended manuscript, and the publishers Messrs Butterworth for their helpful advice throughout. Finally my thanks are due to my wife, Helen, without whose constant encouragement, this book would not have been written.

S Scott Robinson
Inverness
1987

Contents

Preface v
Table of statutes xv
Table of cases xx

Chapter 1   Nature of the remedy   1
   General principles   1
   Scope of the preventative process   2
   Negative interdict   2
   Completed and continuing wrongs   3
   Personal nature of interdict   3
   Judicial review of statutory functions   4

Chapter 2   Jurisdiction   5
   Under Civil Jurisdiction and Judgments Act 1982   5
   Domicile as the basis of jurisdiction   6
   Interdict as a protective measure   6
   Principals and agents as defenders   7
   Employer and employee   7
   Collective liability   8
   Interdict against corporate bodies   8

Chapter 3   Title to sue   9
   Interrelation of title and interest   9
   Heritable and possessory titles   9
      a Proprietors of heritage   9
      b Landlord and tenant   10
      c Joint proprietors   11
   Servitudes   12
   Title as regards corporeal moveables   12
   Title arising from patrimonial interest   12
   Title and interest arising under contract   13
   Title and interest of members of the public; *actio popularis*   14

viii   Contents

Chapter 4   Exclusion of the remedy   15
Where other common law remedies are available   15
In criminal proceedings   16
Interdicts excluded by statutory remedies   16
Interdict under Town and Country Planning Act (Scotland) 1972   17
Mora and taciturnity   18
Res judicata   18
Acquiescence   19
Immunity of the Crown   19

Chapter 5   Interdict against proceedings and wrongful use of diligence   20
1 Against legal proceedings   20
General principles   20
Abuse of process   20
Court of Session's power to control inferior courts and administrative bodies   21
Interdict against publication of proceedings   21
Restraint of proceedings in foreign courts   22
Restraint of statutory bodies   22
Decree taken in breach of contract   23
Arbitration   23
2 Interdict against wrongful use of diligence   24
General principles   24
Inhibition and arrestment   25
Wrongful use of sequestration   25
Interdict in liquidation proceedings   25
Diligence sought *periculo petentis*   26
Suspension and interdict of poinding   26

Chapter 6   Interdict against nuisance, encroachment upon heritable property, water rights and the foreshore   28
1 Against nuisance   28
Nature and categories of nuisance liable to interdict   28
Common law nuisance   28
Anticipated nuisance   29
Nuisance by animals   30
Nuisance by noise and vibration   30
Nuisance by pollution of water   31
Pollution of the air   33
Nuisance arising from misuse of the highway and foreshore   33
Miscellaneous common law nuisances   34
Nuisance arising from playing of games   35
Statutory nuisance   35

Conventional nuisance   35
2 Defences to interdict against nuisance   36
   Prescription   36
   Acquiesence   36
   Licence and statutory authority   37
   Coming to the nuisance   38
   Public interest   38
   Normal and familiar use of property   39
   Possibility of remedial measures   39
   Judicial undertakings to modify nuisance   40
3 Interdict against encroachment upon heritable property and rights of support   40
   The nature of encroachment   40
   Miscellaneous encroachments   41
   Encroachment on burial grounds   41
   Right of support   42
   Mining operations   42
   Rights not extinguished by prescription or acquiescence   45
   Support of pipe lines   45
   Operations under Pipe Lines Act 1962   45
   Support of adjacent buildings   46
4 Interdict against encroachment upon water rights and the foreshore   47
   Navigable rivers   47
   Rights in the foreshore   48
   Non-navigable rivers   49
   Right of access to water and streams in the countryside   50

Chapter 7   Interdict against trespass   51
   The nature of trespass   51
   Competency of interdict   51
   Claims for damages   52
   Examples of trespass   52
   Trespass by animals   53
   Trespass in execution of statutory authority   53
   Trespass in air space   54
   Rights under access agreements   54

Chapter 8   Interdict of company proceedings   55
   Rights of majority and minority shareholders   55
   Ultra vires actings   56
   Appointment and removal of directors   57
   Transfer of shares   57
   Interdict in winding up   58

Chapter 9 Protection of intellectual property including commercial, literary and artistic interests 59
1 Goodwill 59
2 Actions to restrain passing off 59
  Nature of passing off 59
  Descriptive names for goods 60
  Damages combined with interdict 61
  Fraud and fraudulent intent 61
  Examples of passing off 62
  Class actions for passing off 63
3 Protection of business and professional names and designations 64
  Professional organisations 65
4 Protection of the royal warrant 65
  Grant and restraint of abuse 65
  Queen's Award for Industry 66
5 Infringement of trade marks and service marks 66
  Trade marks 66
  General principles 66
  Nature of infringement 67
  Threatened infringement and threats against infringement 69
  Infringement arising out of contract 69
  Service marks – Trade marks (Amendment) Act 1984 70
6 Copyright 71
  Nature of copyright 71
  General principles of infringement 72
  Infringement of copyright in literary, dramatic and musical works 72
  Computer programs 73
  Interdict of breach of future copyrights 74
  Artistic works 74
  Infringement of artistic works 74
  Fair dealing 75
  Cases where copyright excluded on the grounds of public policy 75
  Miscellaneous exemptions from copyright 76
  Registered industrial design 76
  Published editions of works 77
  Copyright in sound recordings 77
  Cinematograph films 78
  Copyright in television and sound broadcasts 79
  Proceedings by way of interdict for infringement 79
  Proof of facts in copyright actions 80
  Crown copyright 80
7 Registered designs 81
  General principles 81
  Nature of infringement 81

Certification that validity has been contested 82
Infringement of unregistered trade designs 82
Similarity of designs 82
8 Patents 83
Definition and exclusions 83
Acts defined as infringement 83
Nature of interdict sought 85
References to the Comptroller of Patents 85
Assignation of patents and licences 86
Interdict of threatened infringement 86
Patents under international conventions 86
Interdict against threats of infringement proceedings 87
Withdrawal of privileges against self-incrimination in proceedings relating to intellectual property 87
Interim interdict in the protection of intellectual property 88

Chapter 10 Interdicts and exclusion orders under the Matrimonial Homes (Family Protection) (Scotland) Act 1981 89
General principles 89
Occupancy rights of spouses 89
Orders as to occupancy and protection granted by the court 90
Exclusion orders 91
Ancillary orders and interdicts attached to exclusion orders 92
Interim exclusion orders 93
Grounds for granting of exclusion orders 93
Grounds for granting interim exclusion orders 94
Matrimonial interdicts 95
Attachment of powers of arrest to matrimonial interdicts 96
Procedure on arrest and powers of police 97
Interdicts and exclusion orders affecting cohabiting couples 98

Chapter 11 Interdict in industrial disputes 100
Historical background 100
Immunity from legal proceedings 101
Vicarious liability of trade unions 102
Industrial action without ballots 103
Peaceful picketing 103
Acts in furtherance of trade disputes 104
Definition of trade dispute 106
Primary picketing 107
Legal rights of non-striking workers against picketing 108
Primary picketing operations which may be restrained by interdict 109
Secondary industrial action 109
Secret ballots before industrial action 111

xii   Contents

Restriction on compulsion to work   112
Ex parte interdicts   112

Chapter 12   Interdict against abuse of power and government Act   113
Restraint of the Crown and its Ministers   113
Interdict in judicial review   114
Acts ultra vires of statutory bodies   116
Abuse of power by public authorities and public bodies   117
Acts ultra vires of trade unions   119

Chapter 13   Interdict in personal relationships   120
Interdict against defamation or personal molestation   120
Interdict against contracting a marriage   120
Against removal of property in divorce   122
Right of wife to have abortion   122
Removal of children from the jurisdiction   122

Chapter 14   Damages for wrongful interdict   123
General principles   123
Interdict must have been wrongful   123
Invasion of legal right essential to claim   124
Recall of interdict   124
Damages for interim interdict   125
Inversion of present position   125

Chapter 15   Interdict against breach of contract and breach of confidence   126
General principles   126
Contracts in restraint of trade and employment   127
Contracts containing severable restraints   127
Distinction between restraints on employment and restraints on trading   127
Basis of validity   128
  Area, duration and public interest   128
  Geographical Area of restraint   128
Duration and nature of restraint   130
Protection of trade secrets under contract   130
Public interest   131
Interdict in miscellaneous contracts   131
Inducing a breach of contract   132
Interdict in breach of confidence   132

Chapter 16   Enforcement of interdict and proceedings for breach of interdict   135
   Geneal principles   135
   Misnomer of defender   135
   Defect of jurisdiction in interdict   136
   Duration of enforcement   136
   Induciae in breach of interdict   136
   Caution against repetition of breach and as a condition of interdict   136
   Procedure in defended cases   137
   Postponement of interdict order   137
   Procedures where breach admitted or proved   137
   Wilful disregard of court order   138
   Remission of imprisonment   138
   Enforcement where change of circumstances   139

Chapter 17   Interim interdict   140
   Nature of the remedy   140
   Prima facie case on declaratory judgment   141
   Competing titles to heritage   141
   Documentary evidence   141
   Affidavit evidence   141
   Question of competency   142
   Granted periculo petentis   142
   Factors affecting the grant or refusal of interim interdict   142
   Examples of cases where interim interdict may be granted   143
   Cases where interim interdict may be refused   145
   The balance of convenience   146

Chapter 18   Procedure in actions of interdict   147
1 In the Court of Session   147
   Commencement of the action   147
   Induciae   147
   Further procedure   148
   Special procedure for obtaining interim interdict   148
   Caveats   149
   Caution generally   149
   Juratory caution   150
   Productions in interim interdict   150
   Certificates of refusal   150
   Appointment to adjustment roll   150
   Decrees in absence   151
   Interdict against removal of children   151
   Interdict against infringement of patents and designs   151
   Breach of interdict   152

2 In the sheriff court   152
   Commencement of the action   152
   Citation   152
   Further procedure   153
   Interim interdict   153
   Caution   154
   Caveat   154
   Productions   154

Appendix   Digest of cases involving grant and refusal of interim interdict   159
   Cases 1 to 56   159

Index 197

Table of Statutes

	PAGE
Abortion Act 1967	122
s 1	122
Administration of Justice (Scotland) Act 1933	
s 6	147
(4)	135, 152
Administration of Justice (Scotland) Act 1972	
s 1	7, 87, 88, 148
Agricultural Holdings (Scotland) Act 1949	159
Agricultural Marketing Act 1931	114
Agriculture (Safety and Welfare Provisions) Act 1956	
s 10	53
Betting, Gaming and Lotteries Act 1963	38
British Nationality Act 1981	72
Burgh Police (Scotland) Act 1892	17
Burial Grounds (Scotland) Act 1855	42
Cable and Broadcasting Act 1984	
s 22	79
Sch 5	
para 6(7)	79
Child Abduction and Custody Act 1985	122
Civic Government (Scotland) Act 1982	
ss 5, 60, 99	53-54
Civil Aviation Act 1949	
ss 40, 41	31
s 76	54
Civil Aviation Act 1982	
Sch 1	
para 13	31
Civil Jurisdiction and Judgments Act 1982	5, 136
s 24(2)	7
27(1)	6, 7, 22
41(2)-(4), (6)	6

	PAGE
Civil Jurisdiction and Judgments Act 1982—continued	
s 42(1), (3)	6
Sch 1	
art 5(1)	6
(3)	5
Sch 4	
art 5(1)	5
(3)	5, 153
Sch 8	5
r 1	5
2(10)	5, 6
Clean Air Act 1956	35
Clean Air Act 1968	35
Coal Industry Nationalisation Act 1946	
s 48(1)	44
Coal Mines Refuse Act 1952	35
Coal Mining (Subsidence) Act 1950	
s 1	44
Coal Mining Act (Subsidence) Act 1957	44
Companies Act 1985	144
s 35	56
Conspiracy and Protection of Property Act 1875	
s 7	105
Control of Pollution Act 1974	17, 35, 166
s 54(4)	167
58(8)	167
Copyright Act 1956	71, 72, 73, 74, 76, 77, 78, 79, 80, 168
s 1	72, 73, 80
(1)	71
(2)	72
(5)(a), (b)	72
2	71, 73
(1)	71, 72
(2)	71
(3)	71, 72
(5), (6)	73

xv

xvi *Table of Statutes*

	PAGE
Copyright Act 1956—*continued*	
s 3	72, 73
(1)	72, 74
(a)	76
(5)	75
4	73
(2), (3)	75
5	73
(5)	73
6	73
(1)-(6)	75
7	73, 76
(6)	76
8	73
(1)	76
9	73
(2)-(4)	76
(8)	74
(9)	76
10	73, 76, 77, 82
11	73
12	77
(3)-(5)	77
(7), (8)	78
13	77, 79
(3), (5)	79
14	77, 79
(1), (2), (4)	79
ss 15, 16	77
s 17	80
(1)	167
(4)	76
(6)	167
19	80
(3)	80
20	80
21	79
24	80
31	71
37	74, 80
39	80
48	78
(1)	71
Copyright (Amendment) Act 1971	71
Copyright (Computer Software) Act 1985	71, 73
Countryside (Scotland) Act 1967	50, 54
s 11	50, 54
Crofters Holdings (Scotland) Act 1886	16
Court of Session Act 1868	
s 89	4
91	4, 114

	PAGE
Crown Proceedings Act 1947	
s 3	80
21	114, 115
(a)	19, 80, 113, 116
43	115
(a)	19, 80, 113, 116
Cruelty to Animals (Scotland) Act 1850	53
Debtors (Scotland) Act 1838	27
Defamation Act 1952	
s 10	170
Deposit of Poisonous Waste Act 1972	35
Design Copyright Act 1968	76, 82
s 1	71
Divorce (Scotland) Act 1976	
s 6	122
Docks and Harbours Act 1966	
s 32	53
Dramatic and Musical Performers' Protection Act 1958	78
s 1	78
Education Act 1944	172
s 1(1)	172
8	173
(1)	172
99(1)	173
Education (Scotland) Act 1946	
s 81	175
Education (Scotland) Act 1980	172
s 22D	172
Employment Act 1980	101
s 3	107
(4), (5)	103
16	103, 107
(1)	110
(2)	106
17	103, 110
(1)	109
(2)	103
(3), (4), (5)	110
Employment Act 1982	101
ss 12 to 14	104
s 15	101, 102, 138
(3)	103, 111
(4)	103
18	103, 106, 109
19(1)	104, 105, 106
(2)	102
Employment Protection Act 1975 Sch 16, Part III	
para 6	112

	PAGE
Employment Protection (Consolidation) Act 1978	101, 165
s 28	165
European Assembly Elections Act 1978	165, 166
European Communities Act 1972	
s 2	114
Execution of Diligence (Scotland) Act 1926	27
Family Law (Scotland) Act 1985	122
s 14(2)	96
18	122
Game (Scotland) Act 1832	
s 16	51
Gas Act 1972	53
Health and Safety at Work Act 1974	
s 19	53
Health Services and Public Health Act 1968	53
House of Commons (Redistribution of Seats) Act 1949	114
Independent Broadcasting Authority Act 1973	164
s 2	164
(2)	117
22	164
Industrial Relations Act 1971	100, 101
Law Reform (Diligence) (Scotland) Act 1973	27
Law Reform (Miscellaneous Provisions) (Scotland) Act 1980 Sch 3	154
Law Reform (Miscellaneous Provisions) (Scotland) Act 1985	3, 89
cll 8, 9	183
s 13(5)	91
15	87
(3)	87
(5)	88
19	87, 88
Licensing (Scotland) Act 1959	
ss 113 to 117	166
s 118	166
Licensing (Scotland) Act 1976	38
Local Government (Scotland) Act 1947	
s 356	17
Local Government (Scotland) Act 1973	42
s 63	163
(1)	163

	PAGE
Local Government (Scotland) Act 1973—*continued*	
s 69(1)	165
88(2)(a)	163
211	4
Marriage Notice (Scotland) Act 1878	
s 10	121
Matrimonial Homes (Family Protection) (Scotland) Act 1981	3, 89, 91, 93, 96, 141
s 1	89
(1)(a), (b)	89
2	98
3	89, 91, 99
(1)	90, 91
(c)	99
(2)	90, 91
(3)	90
(4), (5)	91
4	89, 93, 95, 96, 99
(1)	91
(2)	91, 95
(3)	91, 92, 95
(4), (5)	92, 93
(6)	97
5	99
13	99
14	89, 99
(1)	95
(2)	95, 96, 136
15	97, 99
(1)	92, 93, 96
(2)-(5)	97
16	99
(1)(a), (b)	97
(2)	97
17	99
(2)	97
(4), (5)	98
18	89, 98, 99
(1)	98
(6)	99
22	90, 91, 98, 99
Matrimonial Proceedings (Children) Act 1958	
s 13	122, 144, 151
Merchant Shipping (Oil Pollution) Act 1971	35
Military Service Act 1916	16
Mines (Working Facilities and Support) Act 1966	44
National Health Service (Scotland) Act 1947	117

xviii *Table of Statutes*

	PAGE
National Health Service (Scotland) Act 1972	53
National Insurance Act 1965	
s 22(1)	115
National Parks and Access to the Countryside Act 1949	48
Night Poaching Act 1828	51
Noise Abatement Act 1960	35
Offices, Shops and Railway Premises Act 1963	
s 53	54
Patents Act 1949	83
s 92	66
Patents Act 1977	83, 86
s 1	83
(2), (4), (5)	83
25	83
31	86
44	152
60(1), (2)	84
(5), (6)	85
61(1), (3)	85
63(1)	85
69	85
70	87
72	84
82	86
88	87
98(1)	85
Patents, Designs and Marks Act 1986	67
Sch 2	66
3	81
Performers' Protection Act 1963	16, 78
Performers' Protection Act 1972	16, 78
Pipe Lines Act 1962	45, 46
ss 1, 2, 4	46
s 28(5)(c)	46
69	46
Sch 2 para 9(1)	46
Prescription and Limitation (Scotland) Act 1973	
s 25	36
Prevention of Oil Pollution Act 1971	35
Protection of Birds Act 1954	51
Public Health (Scotland) Act 1897	35
s 16	35
26	53
171	35
Race Relations Act 1976	
s 71	161

	PAGE
Railway Clauses Consolidation (Scotland) Act 1845	45
Railway Regulation Act 1840	51
Railway Regulation Act 1868	51
Railway Regulation Act 1871	51
Recorded Delivery Act 1966	27
Registered Designs Act 1949	76, 81
s 1(2), (3)	81
2(1)	81
7(1)	81
9(1)	82
(2)	81, 82
25	82
45(2)	82
Representation of the People Act 1949	
s 63(1)(b), (c)	163
91	170
Rights of Entry (Gas and Electricity Boards) Act 1954	53
Rivers (Prevention of Pollution) (Scotland) Act 1951	32
Rivers (Prevention of Pollution) (Scotland) Act 1965	32
Road Traffic Act 1934	118
Salmon and Freshwater Fisheries (Scotland) Act 1951	51
Scotland Act 1978	164
Sheriff Court (Scotland) Act 1907	
s 27	154
Succession (Scotland) Act 1964	159
ss 26, 27	122
Supreme Court Act 1981	
s 31	116
Temperance (Scotland) Act 1913	16
Temperance (Scotland) Act 1920	118
Town and Country Planning (Scotland Act) 1972	2, 17, 194
s 84	195
(1)	117, 196
(3)	196
(5)	194
85(1)	196
(10)	23, 194, 195
87	2, 17, 196
166	196
Town and Country Planning (Scotland) Act 1977	
s 4	195
Trade Descriptions Act 1968	
s 12(1), (2)	66

Table of Statutes xix

	PAGE
Trade Marks Act 1938	62, 66, 67, 70
s 2	62, 67
4	67, 68
(1)	68
(2)	67
5	67, 68
6	67, 69, 70
68	70
(1), (2)	66
(2A), (2B)	70
Trade Marks (Amendment) Act 1984	66, 67, 70
s 1	70
(3)	70
(5)(a)	67
(b)	66, 70
(7)	70
Sch 1	70
para 2	67, 68
(3)	67
3	67, 68
4	70
25	66
Sch 2	70
para 3	70
Trade Union Act 1984	101, 108
s 10	103, 111
11	112
(11)	111

	PAGE
Trade Union and Labour Relations Act 1974	101, 111
s 13	103, 104, 107, 109
(1)	101, 103, 106
(a)	102, 103, 109, 111
(b)	102, 103, 109
(2)	104, 105
(4)	100, 102, 106
14	100-101, 102
(1), (2)	102
15	105-106, 110
16	112
17(1)	112
29(1)	106, 109
(a), (b)	106
Trade Union and Labour Relations (Amendment) Act 1976	101
s 3(2)	101, 102, 103, 106, 111
Trades Disputes Act 1906	100
s 3	100, 101
4	100, 102
Transport Act 1947	16
Trespass (Scotland) Act 1865	51
Vexations Actions (Scotland) Act 1898	20
Water (Scotland) Act 1946	113

List of Cases

	PAGE
A & D Bedrooms Ltd v Michael (1984) ..	129, 130, 131, 133, 179-180
AB v CD (1905)	133
Abel's Exors v Edmond and Edmond (1863)	125
Adam and Spowart v Alloa Police Commissioners (1874)	34
Adams v Secretary of State for Scotland and South-Eastern Regional Hospital Board (1958)	117
Advocate (Lord). *See* Lord Advocate	
Agma Chemical Co Ltd v Hart (1984)	181-182
Agnew v Lord Advocate (1873)	48
Aird v Tarbert School Board (1907)	124
Alaska Packers' Assocn v Crooks & Co (1901)	69
Alexander v Mackenzie (1847)	71
Alexander v Picker (1946)	19
Alexander & Sons v Southern Scotland Traffic Commissioners (1936)	118
Allen v Gold Reefs of West Africa Ltd (1900)	56
Allen & Leslie (International) Ltd v Wagley (1976)	136
Allison's (Electrical) Ltd v McCormick (1982)	26
Allsopp v Wheatcroft (1872)	130
Almeroth v Chivers & Sons Ltd (1948)	34
American Cyanamid Co v Ethicon Ltd (1975)	88, 142, 146, 173, 176, 187, 193-194
Amp Inc v Utilex Pty Ltd (1972) ...	82
Amstrad Consumer Electronics v British Phonographic Industry Ltd (1986)	72
Anderson v Aberdeen Agricultural Hall Co Ltd (1879)	29, 35

	PAGE
Anderson v Kirkintilloch Magistrates (1948)	16, 166
Anderson v Moncrieff (1966) ..	135, 152
Anderson v Stoddart (1923)	136
Anderson v Sutherland (James) (Peterhead) Ltd (1940)	148
Anderson v Wilson (1972)	18
Andrew (John H) & Co Ltd v Kuehnrich (1913)	68
Angus v National Coal Board (1955)	42, 44
Anisminic v Foreign Compensation Commission (1969)	115, 118
Annan v Leith Licensing Authority (1901)	4
Anthony v Rennie (1981)	129
Argyle (Duke of) v M'Arthur (1861)	13, 132
Argyllshire Weavers Ltd v Macaulay (A) (Tweeds) Ltd (1965)	64
Aristoc Ltd v Rysta Ltd (1945)	68
Armistead v Bowerman (1888)	49
Arneil v Paisley Town Council (1948)	1, 149
Arthur v Aird (1907)	12
Aspden v Seddon (1875)	42
Associated Provincial Picture Houses Ltd v Wednesbury Corpn (1947)	118, 161
Attwood v Lamont (1920)	130
Ayala & Co v Dowell (1893)	145
Ayr Magistrates v Secretary of State for Scotland (1965)	113
Bain v Assets Co (1905)	18
Baird v Kerr (1877)	8
Baird & Co v Monkland Iron and Steel Co (1862)	43, 143, 146
Baird and Scott v Thomson (1825)	52
Baker v Hedgecock (1889)	127
Ball v Metal Industries Ltd (1957)	57, 144

List of Cases

	PAGE
Ballachulish Slate Quarries Co Ltd v Grant (1903)	13, 126, 130, 144
Bank of Scotland v Stewart (1891) .	42
Bankier Distillery Co v Young's Collieries Ltd (1899)	4
Banks v Fife Redstone Quarry Co Ltd (1954)	187-188
Bargaddie Coal Co v Wark (1859) .	36
Barr v Baird & Co (1904)	42
Barrie (James) (Sand and Gravel) Ltd v Lanark DC (1979)	2, 17
Baschet v London Illustrated Standard Co (1900)	75
Bass, Ratcliff & Gretton Ltd v Laidlaw (1886)	63
Bass, Ratcliff & Gretton Ltd v Laidlaw (1908)	63
Bayer v Baird (1898)	62
Beattie & Son v Pratt (1880)	25
Begg v Jack (1874)	145
Bell v Bell (1983)	93, 94
Ben Nevis Distillery (Fort William) Ltd v North British Aluminium Co Ltd (1948)	33, 38, 39
Bennets v Bennet and Lucas (1903)	24
Bentley-Stevens v Jones (1974)	57
Bents Brewery Co Ltd v Hogan (1945)	133
Berlitz School of Languages Ltd v Duchene (1903)	126, 138
Bicket v Morris (1866)	37, 49
Bile Beans Manufacturing Co Ltd v Davidson (1906)	59, 63
Birmingham Vinegar Brewery Co Ltd v Powell (1897)	68
Blair v Hunter Finlay & Co (1870)	44
Bland v Yates (1914)	30
Blantyre (Lord) v Dunn (1845)	138
Bliersbach v MacEwan (1959)	121
Bloom v Schulman (1934)	86
Bluebell Apparel Ltd v Dickinson (1980)	128, 129, 144
Bollinger v Costa Brava Wine Co Ltd (1960)	60, 63, 64
Bolton v Stone (1951)	35
Bonthrone v Downie (1878)	49
Boord & Son v Thom & Cameron (1907)	67
Boord & Son Inc v Bagots, Hutton & Co Ltd (1916)	62
Borland v Lochwinnoch Golf Club (1986)	135, 153

	PAGE
Botanic Gardens Picture House Ltd v Adamson (1924)	35
Bowie, Petitioner (1967)	139
Bowie v Ailsa (Marquis of) (1887)	47
Bowring (UK) Ltd v Smith (1987)	129
Brady v Napier & Son (1944)	24
Breadalbane (Earl of) v Colquhoun's Trustees (1881)	47
Breadalbane (Marquis of) v M'Gregor (1848)	8
British Airports Authority v Ashton (1983)	105, 144
British Industrial Plastics Ltd v Ferguson (1940)	132
British Legal Life Assurance and Loan Co Ltd v Pearl Life Assurance Co Ltd (1887)	7
British Leyland Motor Corpn Ltd v Armstrong Patents Co Ltd (1986)	82
British Motor Trade Assocn v Gray (1951)	13, 131, 132, 144
British Phonographic Industry Ltd v Cohen, Cohen, Kelly, Cohen & Cohen Ltd (1983)	87, 148
British Road Services v Slater (1964)	34
British Thomson-Houston Co Ltd v Charlesworth Peebles & Co (1922)	84, 86
Brock v Forth Pilotage Authority (1947)	117
Brocket Estates v M'Phee (1949)	11
Broder v Saillard (1976)	30
Brown v Boyd (1841)	41
Brown v Brown (1985) ...	93, 94, 95, 144
Brown v Edinburgh Magistrates (1931)	17
Brown v Edinburgh University Court (1973)	146, 160
Brown v Kidston (1852)	140
Brown v Lee Constructions Ltd (1977)	41, 143, 182
Brown v Stewart (1898)	56
Browne v La Trinidad (1887)	57
Brown's Trustees v Hay (1898)	133, 145
Bryanston Finance Ltd v de Vries (No 2) (1976)	58
Buccleuch (Duke of) v Cowan & Sons (1886)	32
Buccleuch (Duke of) v Smith (1911)	52
Buchanan v Douglas (1853)	123

xxii List of Cases

	PAGE
Buchanan v Glasgow Corpn Water-Works Commissioners (1869) ...	23
Buchanan and Henderson & Dimmack v Andrew (1872) ..	42
Buckhaven and Methil Magistrates v Wemyss Coal Co Ltd (1932)	14, 48
Burke v Spicers Dress Designs (1936)	75
Burland v Earle (1902)	56
Burnet v Barclay (1955)	48
Burton's Trustees v Scottish Sports Council (1983)	2, 47, 184-185
Bute (Marquis of) v M'Kirdy & M'Millan Ltd (1937)	48
Caird v Sime (1887)	73
Cairncross v Lorimer (1860)	19
Calder v Adam (1870)	10
Calder Chemicals Ltd v Branton (1984)	136
Caledonian Ry Co v Baird & Co (1876)	30, 32, 49
Caledonian Ry Co v Cochran's Trustees (1897)	21
Caledonian Ry Co v Glasgow and South-Western Ry Co (1903) ...	4
Caledonian Ry Co v Henderson (1876)	45
Caledonian Ry Co v Sprot (1856)	42, 144
California Redwood Co v Merchant Banking Co of London (1886) ..	22
Calman v PCL Packaging (UK) (1982)	84
Cameron v Macdonnell (1822)	21
Cameron and Gunn v Ainslie (1848)	48
Campbell v Central Regional Council (1981)	176
Campbell v Leith Police Commissioners (1870)	116, 118
Campbell v Mackay (1959)	53, 138
Campbell v Muir (1908)	49
Campbell's Trustees v Sweeney (1911)	47
Canon KK's Application (1982)	84
Carlton (Edinburgh) Hotel Co Ltd v Lord Advocate (1921)	4
Carnegie v Kintone (Lord) and Gammell (1829)	10
Carnegie v Mactier (1836)	52
Carron v Ogilvie (1806)	47

	PAGE
CBS Inc v Ames Records & Tapes Ltd (1981)	72, 77
Cellular Clothing Co Ltd v Maxton & Murray (1899)	59, 61, 62, 63
Cellular Clothing Co Ltd v Schulberg (1952)	69, 151
Central Motors (St Andrews) Ltd v St Andrews Magistrates (1961)..	34
Central Regional Council v Clackmannan DC (1983) ..	2, 17, 117, 195, 195-196
Chalmers v Dixon (1876)	30
Chill Foods (Scotland) Ltd v Cool Foods Ltd (1977)	127, 131, 146, 180, 192-193
Christie Miller v Bain (1879)	137
Christison's Trustees v Callender-Brodie (1906)	159
Clark v Beattie (1909)	24
Clifton v Bury (Viscount) (1887)	183
Clippens Oil Co Ltd v Edinburgh and District Water Trustees (1897)	4, 38, 45, 137
Clippens Oil Co Ltd v Edinburgh and District Water Trustees (1903)	44
Clouston v Edinburgh and Glasgow Ry Co (1865)	58
Coca-Cola Co v Struthers (William) & Sons Ltd (1968)	68
Codex Corpn v Racal-Milgo Ltd (1983)	85
Colagiacomo v Colagiacomo (1983)	93, 94
Colquhoun v Montrose (Duke of) (1801)	47
Colquhoun v Paton (1859)	9, 10, 141
Colquhoun and Cameron v Mackenzie (1894)	3, 16
Colquhoun's Curator Bonis v Glen's Trustee (1920)	132, 144
Colville v Middleton (1817)	37
Commercial Plastics Ltd v Vincent (1964)	129, 130, 180
Conn v Renfrew Corpn (1906)	14
Cooper and Wood v North British Ry Co (1863)	29
Copland v Maxwell (1871)	50
Cormack v McIldowie's Exors (1972)	24, 159
Costa v Costa (1929)	136
Council of Civil Service Unions v Minister for the Civil Service (1984)	161

List of Cases xxiii

	PAGE
Cousins v International Brick Co Ltd (1931)	57, 144
Cowan v Kinnaird (Lord) (1865)	19
Cowan v Millar (1895)	63
Cowan & Sons v Buccleuch (Duke of) (1876)	8, 49
Cowan and Mackenzie v Law (1872)	12
Cowie v Cowie (1986)	96, 186
Cowie v Strathclyde Regional Council (1985)	51, 183
Cox v Edinburgh Tranways Co (1898)	56
Cramp (GA) & Sons Ltd v Smythson (Frank) Ltd (1944)	71
Cranleigh Precision Engineering Ltd v Bryant (1964)	133, 145
Cranston & Elliot Ltd v Dobson (1899)	10
Crawford v Paisley Magistrates (1870)	142
Crawford (Earl of) v Paton (1911)	132
Crawford's Trustees v Lennox (1896)	63
Crooke v Scots Pictorial Publishing Co Ltd (1906)	3, 145
Crookston v Lindsay, Crookston & Co Ltd (1922)	56, 57
Cruickshank v Irving (1854)	10
Crystalate Gramophone Record Manufacturing Co Ltd v British Crystalite Co Ltd (1934)	63
Cumming v Inverness Magistrates (1953)	17, 145
Cunningham v The Scotsman (1986)	22
Cutsforth v Mansfield Inns Ltd (1986)	161-162
Daniels v Daniels (1978)	55
Davey v Harrow Corpn (1957)	41
Dante v Assessor for Ayr (1922)	23
Davidson v Thomson (1890)	19
Davie v Stark (1876)	13
Daw v Eley (1867)	123
Deacons v Bridge (1984)	131
Deane v Lothian Regional Council (1986)	140, 143, 172
Dennistoun v Bell and Brown (1824)	47
Dewar (John) & Sons Ltd v Dewar (1900)	59
Dick v Fleshers of Stirling (1827)	136
Dickson v Dickie (Neil's Trustees) (1863)	10
Dixon v Caledonian and Glasgow and South-Western Ry Companies (1880)	44

	PAGE
Dobbie v Halbert (1863)	7
Dodd v Hilson (1874)	32
Donaghy v Rollo (1962)	14
Donald v Humphrey (1839)	33
Dorling v Honnor Marine Ltd (1965)	82
Dowling v Billington (1890)	86
Dowson & Mason Ltd v Potter (1986)	131, 133
DPP v Luft (1977)	163
Draper v Trist (1939)	61, 62
Drummond (Home). See Home Drummond.	
Dryburgh v Fife Coal Co Ltd (1905)	42
Dudgeon v Thomson (1877)	84
Duff v Wood (1858)	25
Dumbarton Steamboat Co Ltd v MacFarlane (1899)	127, 130
Dumbarton Water-Works Commissioners v Blantyre (1884)	24
Dumphries and Maxwelltown Water-Works Commissioners v M'Culloch (1874)	30, 32
Duncan Sandys (Lord) v House of Fraser plc (1985)	168
Dunlop Pneumatic Tyre Co Ltd v Dunlop Motor Co Ltd (1907)	59
Dunnachie v Young & Sons (1883)	63
Dunoon Picture House Co Ltd v Dunoon Corpn (1921)	13
Dupont Steels Ltd v Sirs (1980)	103, 104
Durham v Hood (1871)	43
Earl Car Sales (Edinburgh) Ltd v City of Edinburgh DC (1984)	2, 17, 195, 196
Eastes v Russ (1914)	130
Edgar v Board of Management of the City of Glasgow Friendly Soc (1914)	3
Edge (William) & Sons Ltd v Nicholls (William) & Sons Ltd (1911)	68
Edinburgh and District Water Trustees v Clippens Oil Co Ltd (1900)	42
Edinburgh DC v Parnell (1980)	118
Edwards v Halliwell (1950)	56, 57
Elderslie Estates v Gryfe Tannery Ltd (1959)	32, 38, 40
Ellice v Invergarry and Fort Augustus Ry Co (1913)	58

xxiv List of Cases

	PAGE
Empire Meat Co Ltd v Patrick (1939)	130
Erven Warnink BV v Townend (J) & Sons (Hull) Ltd (1979)	59, 60, 64
Esso Petroleum Co Ltd v Harper's Garage (Stourport) Ltd (1968) ..	128, 130, 131
Estmanco (Kilner House) Ltd v GLC (1982)	55, 144
Eutectic Welding Alloys Co Ltd v Whitting (1969)	135
Ewen v Turnbull's Trustees (1857) .	32
Ewing (Archibald Orr) & Co v Colquhoun's Trustees. *See* Orr Ewing (Archibald) & Co v Colquhoun's Trustees	
Exchange Telegraph Co Ltd v Giulianotti (1959)	131
Exchange Telegraph Co Ltd v White (1961)	147
Express Newspapers Ltd v MacShane (1980)	103, 104
Express Newspapers plc v Liverpool Daily Post and Echo plc (1985) .	73, 145, 168
Express Newspapers plc and Star v NGA (1985)	138
Faccenda Chicken Ltd v Fowler (1986)	131, 133, 134
Fairbairn v Scottish National Party (1980)	120, 141, 144, 170
Farquhar & Gill v Aberdeen Magistrates (1912)	12, 117
Farmer v Nelson (1885)	30
Fellowes v Fisher (1975)	130, 176
Fergusson v M'Culloch (1953) .	30, 31, 35, 36
Fergusson v Pollok (1901)	33, 34, 48
Fergusson-Buchanan v Dumbarton CC (1924)	137, 149
Fife v Orr (1895)	142
Fife CC v Ry Executive, Scottish Region (1951)	16
Flaxcell Ltd v Freedman (1981)	60, 63, 189-190
Fleet v Metropolitan Asylums Board, Darenth Smallpox Camp Case (1886)	30
Fleming v Gemmill (1908) .	11, 30, 32, 39, 49
Fleming v Hislop (1886)	33, 38, 39
Football League Ltd v Littlewood Pools Ltd (1959)	71

	PAGE
Forbes v Leys, Mason & Co (1824)..	12
Forster & Sons Ltd v Suggett (1918)	129
Forth Conservancy Board v Russell (Archibald) Ltd (1946)	44
Forth Yacht Marina Ltd v Forth Road Bridge Joint Board (1984)	137, 145, 146, 186
Foss v Harbottle (1843)	55, 56, 144
Francis, Day & Hunter v Feldman & Co (1914)	73
Fraser v Campbell (1895)	19
Fraser's Trustees v Cran (1877) .	30, 33
Fraser's Trustees v Cran (1879)	138
Free Church General Assembly v Rainy (1904)	141
Galbreath v Armour (1845)	9
Galt v Philip (1984)	105
Gauldie v Arbroath Magistrates (1936)	149
Gavin v Ayrshire CC (1950) .	2, 29, 32
Gay v Malloch (1959)	49
Geils v Thompson (1872)	51
General Radio Co v General Radio Co (Westminster) Ltd (1957)	63
George Hensher Ltd v Restawhile Upholstery (Lancs) Ltd. *See* Hensher (George) Ltd v Restawhile Upholstery (Lancs) Ltd	
George Packman & Sons v Young. *See* Packman (George) & Sons v Young	
Giblin v Lanarkshire CC Middle Ward District Committee (1972)	28, 144
Gibson v Bonnington Sugar Refining Co Ltd (1869)	49
Gibson & Reid v City of Glasgow Profiteering Act Committee (1920)	23
Gillespie v Lucas & Aird (1893) .	23, 37
Glasgow and South Western Ry Co v Boyd & Forrest (1918)	18, 24
Glasgow City and District Ry Co v Glasgow Coal Exchange Co Ltd (1885)	125
Glasgow, Yoker & Clydebank Ry Co v Lidgerwood (1895)	24
Glen v Caledonian Ry Co (1868)	143, 145
Glynn v Keele University (1971) ..	118
Glynn v Weston Feature Film Co (1916)	75

List of Cases xxv

Case	Page
Gold v Houldsworth (1870)	13, 132
Gould v M'Corquodale (1869)	9
Gouriet v Union of Post Office Workers (1978)	112
Graham v Hamilton (Duke of) (1868)	44
Graham v North British Bank (1849)	13
Grahame v Kircaldy Magistrates (1882)	18
Grahame v M'Kenzie (1810)	52
Grahame v Secretary of State for Scotland (1951)	18
Grand Hotel Co of Caledonia Springs v Wilson (1904)	63
Grant v Airdrie Magistrates (1939)	26
Grant v Henry (1894)	47
Grant (William) & Sons Ltd v Cadenhead (William) Ltd (1985)	145, 188-189
Gray (Lord) v Petrie (1848)	138
Great North of Scotland Ry Co v Mann (1892)	62, 63
Green v Lord Advocate (1918)	16, 23
Greenhalgh v Arderne Cinemas Ltd (1950)	56
Greenock Parochial Board v Coghill & Son (1878)	24
Greig v Insole (1978)	131
Gribben v Gribben (1976)	135
Grieve v Douglas-Home (1965)	117
Grieve v Kilmarnock Motor Co Ltd (1923)	145
Grosvenor Developments (Scotland) v Argyll Stores Ltd (1987)	147
Group 4 Total Security Ltd v Ferrier (1985)	130, 179, 180
Hadmor Productions Ltd v Hamilton (1982)	104, 106
Hagart v Fyfe (1870)	47, 145
Haig (John) & Co Ltd v Forth Blending Co Ltd (1954)	59, 61, 62
Haig (John) & Co Ltd v Haig (John DD) Ltd (1957)	63
Hallam v Gye & Co (1835)	20
Halsey v Esso Petroleum Co Ltd (1961)	33
Hamilton v Lanarkshire CC (1971)	118, 166
Hammersmith (London Borough of) v Magnum Automated Forecourts Ltd. See London Borough of Hammersmith v Magnum Automated Forecourts Ltd	
Hands v Perth CC (1959)	33, 39, 137
Harakas v Baltic Mercantile and Shipping Exchange Ltd (1982)	120, 141, 142, 169-170
Harms Inc and Chappell & Co v Martans Club (1927)	77
Harper v Secretary of State for the Home Department (1955)	114
Harpers Ltd v Barry, Henry & Co Ltd (1892)	73
Harris v Harris (A) Ltd (1936)	55, 56
Harrison v Southwark and Vauxhall Water Co (1891)	39
Harvey v Wardrop (1824)	43
Harvey (GA) & Co (London) Ltd v Secure Fittings Ltd (1966)	82
Harvie v Robertson (1903)	30
Hastie (John) & Co Ltd v Brown (1906)	84
Haughhead Coal Co v Gallocher (1903)	24
Hawker Siddely Dynamics Engineering v Real Time Developments Ltd (1983)	84
Hay v Leslie (1896)	33
Hay's Trustees v Young (1877)	1, 51
Hayman v Lord Advocate (1952)	115
Hecla Foundry Co v Walker, Hunter & Co (1889)	82
Henderson v Clippens Oil Co Ltd (1883)	84
Henderson v Maclellan (1874)	152, 153
Henderson & Son Ltd v Munro & Co (1905)	63, 120
Hensher (George) Ltd v Restawhile Upholstery (Lancs) Ltd (1974)	74, 75
Herbage v Pressdram Ltd (1984)	120
Herbert Morris Ltd v Saxelby. See Morris (Herbert) Ltd v Saxelby	
Heriot's Trust v Carter (1903)	3
Heritors of Bathgate v Russell (1908)	42
Highland Distilleries Co plc v Speymalt Whisky Distributors Ltd (1985)	18, 61, 189, 190-191
Hill v Dixon (1850)	36, 37
Hill v Wood (1863)	37, 42
Hislop v MacRitchie's Trustees (1880)	36
Hoare & Co v McAlpine (1923)	31
Holling v Yorkshire Traction Co (1948)	34
Holroyd v Edinburgh Magistrates (1921)	21

xxvi List of Cases

	PAGE
Home Drummond v M'Lachlan (1908)	154
Home Drummond v Thomson (1907)	136, 153
Hood v Traill (1884)	9
Hope v Bennewith (1904)	48
Houldsworth v Wishaw Burgh Commissioners of Police (1887)	19, 36
Howling's Trustees v Smith (1905)	58
Hoy v Hoy and Ramsay (1968)	121, 144
Hunter & Aikenhead v Aitken (1880)	49
Hutchison v Hutchison (1890)	8
Hutchison, Main & Co v Pattullo Bros (1888)	83
Incandescent Gas Light Co Ltd v M'Culloch (1897)	4, 85
Infabrics Ltd v Jaytex Ltd (1981)	75
Inglis v Shotts Iron Co (1881)	29, 144
Innes v Kircaldy Burgh (1963)	13, 17, 117, 145, 165
International Electric Co of New York Ltd v Commissioners of Customs and Excise (1962)	113
Inverurie Magistrates v Sorrie (1956)	1, 51, 52, 144
Ireland v Smith (1895)	30
Irvine v Robertson (1873)	145
Irving v Leadhills Mining Co (1856)	44
Jack v Begg (1875)	124
Jack v Waddell's Trustees (1918)	27
James Barrie (Sand and Gravel) Ltd v Lanark DC. See Barrie (James) (Sand and Gravel) Ltd v Lanark DC	
Jamieson & Co v Jamieson (1898)	62, 69
Jennings v Stephens (1936)	77
John Dewar & Sons Ltd v Dewar. See Dewar (John) & Sons Ltd v Dewar	
John Haig & Co Ltd. See Haig (John) & Co Ltd	
John Hastie & Co Ltd v Brown. See Hastie (John) & Co Ltd v Brown	
John Walker & Sons Ltd v Douglas McGibbon & Co Ltd. See Walker (John) & Sons Ltd v McGibbon (Douglas) & Co Ltd	
Johnson v Grant (1923)	135, 138

	PAGE
Johnston v Constable (1841)	31, 34
Johnston v Orr Ewing (1882)	62, 68
Johnston v Thomson (1877)	15
Johnston v White (1877)	47
Johnstone v Johnstone (1967)	122, 144
Jolly v Brown (1828)	11
Keeney v Strathclyde Regional Council (1986)	3
Kelson v Imperial Tobacco Co (of Great Britain and Ireland) Ltd (1957)	53
Kelso School Board v Hunter (1874)	1
Kennedy v Fort-William Police Commissioners (1877)	125
Kewly v Andrew (1843)	26
Kinloch v Robertson (1756)	31
Kinnell & Co Ltd v Ballantyne & Sons (1910)	59, 64, 65
Kinnes and Kinnes v Adam & Sons (1882)	24, 25, 26
Kirkintilloch Kirk-Session v Kirkintilloch Burgh School Board (1911)	13
Kirkwood's Trustees v Leith and Bremner (1888)	29
Kores Manufacturing Co Ltd v Kolok Manufacturing Co Ltd (1958)	131
Ladbroke (Football) Ltd v William Hill (Football) Ltd (1964)	73
Laing v Muirhead (1822)	33
Lamond v Glasgow Corpn (1968)	35
Lang Bros v Goldwell Ltd (1982)	60, 64
Langlands v Manson (1962)	4
Laws v Florinplace Ltd (1981)	34, 187
LB Plastics Ltd v Swish Products Ltd (1979)	74
Leitch & Co Ltd v Leyden (1931)	12
Leith-Buchanan v Hogg (1931)	10, 47
Leng (Sir WC) & Co Ltd v Andrews (1909)	130
Leonard v Lindsay & Benzie (1886)	41
Leslie v Young & Sons (1893)	73
Lever Bros Port Sunlight Ltd v Sunniwite Products Ltd (1949)	68
Levin v Farmers Supply Assocn of Scotland (1973)	134, 185
Licences Insurance Corpn and Guarantee Fund v Shearer (1907)	24

List of Cases xxvii

	PAGE
Lindsay v Wemyss and March (Earl of) (1872)	15
Liston v Galloway (1835)	10
Littlewoods Organisation Ltd v Harris (1978)	129
Liverpool Corpn v Coghill & Son Ltd (1918)	36
London Borough of Hammersmith v Magnum Automated Forecourts Ltd (1978)	17, 145, 166-167
London Ferro-Concrete Co Ltd v Justicz (1951)	69
London, Midland and Scottish Ry Co v M'donald (1924)	9, 10
London University Press Ltd v University Tutorial Press Ltd. *See* University of London Press Ltd v University Tutorial Press Ltd	
Lord Advocate v Arnold (1951)	20
Lord Advocate v Cooney (1984)	20
Lord Advocate v Raynes, Lupton & Co (1859)	48
Lord Advocate v Rizza (1962)	20
Lord Advocate v Sharp (1879)	48
Lowson v Reid (1861)	26
Luxmore v Red Deer Commission (1979)	19
Lyle & Scott Ltd v British Investment Trust Ltd (1957)	57
Macallan-Glenlivet plc v Speymalt Whisky Distributors Ltd (1983)	61, 62, 189, 191-192
Macartney v Gilchrist (1831)	15
M'Bean v Young (1859)	42
McCafferty v McCafferty (1986)	94, 95
M'Carroll v M'Kinstery (1926)	18
McCombe v Read (1955)	41, 52
MacCormick v Lord Advocate (1953)	14
McDaid v Clydebank DC (1984)	2, 17, 23, 194-195
Macdonald v Blythswood (Lord) (1914)	124
M'Donald v Dempster (1871)	11
M'Douall v Lord Advocate (1875)	48
Macdougall v Gardiner (1875)	56, 144
M'Ewen v Steedman and M'Alister (1912)	11, 30, 31, 40
M'Ewen v Steedman and M'Alister (1913)	40
Macfie v Scottish Rights of Way and Recreation Soc (1884)	19, 144

	PAGE
M'Gavin v M'Intyre Bros (1890)	30, 32
Macgregor v Balfour (1899)	37
M'Gregor v M'Laughlin (1905)	20
M'Gregor v National and Local Government Officers Assocn (1979)	177-178
M'Intosh v Scott (1859)	41
M'Intyre Bros v M'Gavin (1890)	36, 49
M'Intyre's Trustees v Cupar-Fife Magistrates (1867)	47, 49
Mackay v Greenhill (1858)	33
Mackay v Mackay (1914)	71
M'Kean v Davidson (1823)	47
McKenna v McKenna (1984)	96, 136, 153
M'Kenzie v British Linen Co (1881)	18
Mackenzie v Imlay's Trustees (1912)	13
M'Kerron v Gordon (1876)	10
MacKillop v Mactaggart (1939)	24
M'Kinnon v Hamilton (1866)	26
Mackay v Macdonald (1928)	135, 138
Macleod v Davidson (1886)	51, 52, 53
M'Leod v St Andrews Magistrates (1924)	35
M'Neil v Rolled Steel Forge Co (1930)	71
M'Neill v M'Murchy, Ralston & Co (1841)	24, 26
Macrae & Dick Ltd v Philip (1982)	131
MacRobbie v M'Lellan's Trustees (1891)	23, 24
McTaggart v Dalry Co-operative Soc Ltd (1980)	26
M'Vicar v Kerr (1857)	26
Maguire v M'Neil Ltd (1922)	29, 30, 31
Malloch v Aberdeen Corpn (1974)	117
Mann v Goldstein (1968)	58
Manson v Forrest (1887)	34, 35, 40
Marchetti v Marchetti (1901)	8
Marina Shipping Ltd v Laughton (1982)	110
Marine Associates Ltd v City of Aberdeen Corpn (1978)	2, 17
Marshall v Sidebotham (1900)	69
Marshall (Thomas) (Exports) v Guine (1978)	133
Martin v Nisbet (1893)	120
Mason v Provident Clothing & Supply Co Ltd (1913)	127, 130
Mather v Mather (1986)	95
Matheson v Fraser (1911)	153
Mavor v Campbell (1948)	13

xxviii *List of Cases*

	PAGE
Maxwell v Glasgow and South-Western Ry Co (1866)	10
Meade v London Borough of Haringey (1977)	173-174
Meek v Lothian Regional Council (1980)	119, 143, 165
Meek v Lothian Regional Council (1983)	119, 143, 163
Meikle v Meikle (1895)	129
Melrose-Drover Ltd v Heddle (1901)	62
Menzies v Breadalbane (Marquis of) (1901)	49
Menzies v Macdonald (1864)	137
Menzies v MacDonald (1870)	4
Merchant Adventurers Ltd v Grew (M) & Co Ltd (1971)	74, 75
Mercury Communications Ltd v Scott-Garner (1984)	107
Merricks v Heathcot-Amory (1955)..	114
Merry & Cuninghame Ltd v Alexander (1926)	23
Methven Simpson Ltd v Jones (1910)	126
Metropolitan Asylum District Managers v Hill (1881)	33, 37
Mid and East Calder Gas-Light Co v Oakbank Oil Co Ltd (1891)	44, 45
Midlothian CC v National Coal Board (1960)	44
Midlothian CC v Oakbank Oil Co Ltd (1904)	36
Miller v Hunter (1865)	125
Miller v Mac Fisheries Ltd (1922)	18
Miller v Stewart (1835)	26
Milligan v Broadway Cinema Productions Ltd (1923)	79
Miln v Mudie (1828)	183
Milne v Leslie (1888)	15
Milton v Glen-Moray Glenlivet Distillery Co Ltd (1898)	44
Montgomerie v Donald (James A) & Co (1884)	63
Montgomerie & Co v Young Bros (1903)	8
Montgomery and Marshall v Watson (1861)	50
Morris (Herbert) Ltd v Saxelby (1916)	131
Morris Motors v Lilley (trading as G & L Motors) (1959)	132
Moss's Empires Ltd v Assessor for Glasgow (1917)	21

	PAGE
Muirhead v Glasgow Highland Soc (1864)	19, 37
Mulvein v Murray (1908)	127, 130, 182
Murchland v Nicholson (1893)	84
Murdoch v Murdoch (1973)	2
Murray v Dumbarton CC (1935)	118, 174
Mushets Ltd v Mackenzie Bros (1899)	132
Mutter v Fyfe (1848)	33
National Assocn of School Teachers v Scottish Joint Negotiating Committee for Teaching Staff (1987)	171-172
National Cash Register Co Ltd v Kinnear (1948)	149
Neill's Trustees v Dixon (William) Ltd (1880)	42
Neilson v Househill Coal & Iron Co (1842)	83
Neville v Neville (1921)	153
News Group Newspapers Ltd v Soc of Graphical and Allied Trades 1982 (1986)	109
News International v Soc of Graphical and Allied Trades 1982 (1986)	110, 144
News International v Transport and General Workers Union (1986)	110, 111
Nicol v Blott (1986)	41, 183
Nicol (D and J) v Dundee Harbour Trustees (1915)	9, 12, 117
Nordenfelt v Nordenfelt (Maxim) Gun and Ammunition Co Ltd (1894)	13, 128, 130
Norfar v Aberdeenshire Education Authority (1923)	16
North British Ry Co v Moore (1891)	36
North British Ry Co v Perth Magistrates (1885)	47
North British Ry Co v Turners Ltd (1904)	44
NWL Ltd v Woods (1979)	88, 104, 146
Office Cleaning Services Ltd v Westminster Window and General Cleaners Ltd (1946)	193
Ogston v Aberdeen District Tramways Co (1896)	33
Oliver's Trustees v Walker (WG) & Sons (Edinburgh) Ltd (1948)	56

	PAGE		PAGE
Ormiston v Redpath, Brown & Co (1866)	21	Portobello Magistrates v Edinburgh Magistrates (1882)	32
Orr Ewing (Archibald) & Co v Colquhoun's Trustees (1877)	40, 47, 49, 144	Pratt v Maclean (1927)	130
		Premier Cycle Co Ltd v Premier Tube Co Ltd (1896)	63
Overseas League v Taylor (1951)	135	Price's Patent Candle Co Ltd v Ogston & Tennant Ltd (1909)	68
Packman (George) & Sons v Young (1976)	145, 182	Prince v Secretary of State for Scotland (1985)	114, 165-166
Paperchase Products Ltd v Ridlington (1980)	62	Proctor v Bennis (1887)	86
Parish v Judd (1960)	34		
Parker v Lord Advocate (1904)	48	Quin & Axtens Ltd v Salmon (1909)	57
Partington v National and Local Government Officers' Assocn (1981)	119		
Pasickniak v Dojacek (1928)	75	R v Governor of Pentonville Prison, ex parte Herbage (1986)	116
Paterson v Paterson (R) & Sons Ltd (1917)	57		
		R v Poplar BC (No 2) (1922)	8
Paterson v Robertson (1944)	51	R v Tronah Mines Ltd (1952)	163
Paton v Trustees of BPAS (1978)	122	Ramsay and Alloa Coal Co v Blair (1876)	44
Pattison v Fitzgerald (1823)	8, 135		
Pavlides v Jensen (1956)	56	Rander v Pattar (1985)	129, 144, 145, 181
PCUK v Diamond Shamrock Industrial Chemicals (1981)	84		
Pease v Pease (1967)	120, 144	Rank Film Distributors Ltd v Video Information Centre (1981)	79
Performing Right Soc v Harlequin Record Shops (1979)	77	Rankin v M'Lachlan (1864)	15, 140
Performing Right Soc v Hawthorn's Hotel (Bournemouth) Ltd (1933)	77	Rankine v Logie Den Land Co Ltd (1902)	19
Performing Right Soc v Mitchell and Booker (Palais de Danse) (1924)	7	RCA Corpn v Pollard (1982)	78
		Reddaway & Co v Banham & Co Ltd (1896)	64
Performing Right Soc v Rangers FC Supporters Club, Greenock (1974)	77	Reed Stenhouse (UK) Ltd v Brodie (1986)	130, 180
		Remington Typewriter Co v Sim (1915)	130
Peter Pan Manufacturing Corpn v Corsets Silhouette Ltd (1963)	134	Rennie (JA and DS) v Scottish Milk Records Assocn (1985)	117, 162-163
Phestos Shipping Co Ltd v Kurmiawan (1983)	104		
Philip v Pennell (1907)	73	Rentokil Ltd v Hampton (1982)	127, 130, 177
Phonographic Performance Ltd v McKenzie (1982)	77, 145, 167-168		
		Rentokil Ltd v Kramer (1986)	130, 131, 180-181
Phonographic Performance Ltd v Pontins Ltd (1967)	77	Rhind v Kemp & Co (1893)	21
Plasticisers v Stewart (1973)	86	Richmond (Duke of) v Lossiemouth Burgh (1905)	32
Plessey Co plc v Wilson (1983)	104, 105, 106		
		Riddel and Raeside v Clydesdale Horse Soc (1885)	22, 145
Plowman (GW) & Son Ltd v Ash (1964)	181	Rigby & Beardmore v Downie (1872)	19, 32, 36
Pollock v Garrett (1957)	57, 144		
Pollock v Goodwin's Trustees (1898)	21	Robertson, Petitioner (1911)	8
Pollok School Co Ltd v Glasgow Town Clerk (1946)	118	Robertson v Lord Advocate (1950)	113
		Robertson v Salmon (1868)	42

xxx *List of Cases*

	PAGE
Robertson v Stewarts and Livingston (1872)	30, 32, 33, 39
Robertson v Thomas (1887)	29
Robertson v Thorburn (1927)	21
Robertson v Wright (1885)	53
Rodger v Herbertson (1909)	126
Rodger (Builders) Ltd v Fawdry (1950)	182
Rolled Steel Products (Holdings) Ltd v British Steel Corpn (1985)	55, 58
Rollingson v Kerr (1958)	34
Rolls Razor Ltd v Rolls (Lighters) Ltd (1949)	68
Rookes v Barnard (1944)	109
Ross v Powrie & Pitcaithley (1891)	49
Royal Baking Powder Co v Wright, Crossley & Co (1899)	69
Royal Warrant Holders' Assocn v Deane & Beal Ltd (1912)	66
Royal Warrant Holders' Assocn v Lipman (1933)	66
Royal Warrant Holders' Assocn v Robb (1935)	66
Roxburgh v Seven Seas Engineering Ltd (1980)	134
Russell v Bute (Marquess of) (1882)	42
Rysta Ltd, Application (1943)	68
St Andrews Ladies' Golf Club v Denham (1887)	10, 11
St Stephen Shipping Co Ltd v Guinane (1984)	110
Saltman Engineering Co Ltd v Campbell Engineering Co Ltd (1963)	131, 133
Sandys (Lord Duncan) v House of Fraser plc. *See* Duncan Sandys (Lord) v House of Fraser plc	
Sangster v Burness (1857)	26
Schroeder (A) Music Publishing Co Ltd v Macaulay (1974)	128
Scotsman Publications Ltd v John Edwards (Advertising Services) Ltd (1980)	74
Scotsman Publications Ltd v Soc of Graphical and Allied Trades 1982 (1986)	112
Scott v Dundee Magistrates (1886)	48
Scott v M'Dowall (1857)	16
Scott v Napier (Lord) (1869)	11
Scott v Scott (1881)	30, 32

	PAGE
Scottish Farmers' Dairy Co (Glasgow) Ltd v M'Ghee (1933)	129, 130, 178, 181
Scottish Milk Marketing Board v Drybrough & Co Ltd (1985)	62, 190
Scottish Milk Marketing Board v Paris (1935)	142, 146
Scottish Union and National Insurance Co v Scottish National Insurance Co Ltd (1909)	65
Scottish Vacuum Cleaner Co Ltd v Provincial Cinematograph Theatres Ltd (1915)	85, 86
Seafield (Countess Dowager) v Kemp (1899)	49
Seaspray SS Co Ltd v Tennant (1908)	26
Secretary of State for Employment v Associated Soc of Locomotive Engineers and Firemen (No 2) (1972)	111
Shaw v Applegate (1978)	37
Shawsrigg Fireclay and Enamelling Co Ltd v Larkhall Collieries Ltd (1903)	43
Shell UK Ltd v Lostock Garage Ltd (1977)	128
Shepherd v Menzies (1900)	53
Shiell v Mossman (1871)	24
Shinwell v National Sailors' and Firemen's Union of Great Britain and Ireland (1913)	120
Shotts Iron Co v Inglis (1882)	33, 38
Shuttleworth v Cox Bros & Co (Maidenhead) Ltd (1927)	56
Silly Wizard Ltd v Shaughnessy (1983)	78
Singer Machine Manufacturers v Wilson (1877)	62
Singer Manufacturing Co v Kimball & Morton (1873)	59, 61, 69
Sirdar Rubber Co Ltd and Maclulich v Wallington, Weston & Co (1907)	84
Skinner & Co v Perry (1893)	87
Slater v M'Lellan (1924)	13, 14, 28, 33, 47, 185
Smith v Grigg (1924)	194
Smith v Inner London Education Authority (1978)	146, 172-173
Smith v Lerwick Harbour Trustees (1903)	48

	PAGE
Smith v Smith (1983)	93, 94
Smith (CR) (Glaziers) (Dunfermline) Ltd v McKeag (1986)	175
Soc of Accountants in Edinburgh v Corpn of Accountants Ltd (1893)	65
Soc of Accountants in Edinburgh v Corpn of Accountants Ltd (1903)	65
Solihull Metropolitan BC v National Union of Teachers (1985)	112
SOS Bureau Ltd v Payne (1982)	129, 131
Southern Bowling Club Ltd v Ross (1902)	54, 145
Spencer v Kennedy (1926)	57
Spider's Web v Marchant (1961)	30
Square Grip Reinforcement Co Ltd v Macdonald (1966)	102, 144
Square Meals Frozen Foods Ltd v Dunstable Corpn (1974)	17
Stafford BC v Elkenford Ltd (1977)	18, 167
Stark's Trustees v Duncan (1906)	136, 138
Stearn v Prentice Bros Ltd (1919)	30
Steel v Gourock Police Commissioners (1871)	30
Steers v Rogers (1893)	83
Steiner v Breslin (1979)	130, 178-179
Stenor Ltd v Whitesides (Clitheroe) Ltd (1948)	82
Steuart v Stephen (1877)	11, 51
Stevenson v Hawick Magistrates (1871)	34
Stewart v Stewart (1899)	129
Stewart and Briggs v Bell's Trustee (1883)	84
Stewart and M'Millan v Roach (1950)	54
Stirling CC v Falkirk Magistrates (1912)	12, 117
Stornoway Magistrates v Macdonald (1971)	17
Strathkelvin DC v Secretary of State for the Environment (1987)	116
Summerlee Iron Co Ltd v Lindsay (1907)	9
Symington v Wilsons and Union Tube Co Ltd (1904)	3
Taff Vale Ry Co v Amalgamated Soc of Ry Servants (1901)	8, 100, 102
Tasker v Tasker (1952)	188
Tattersall v Tattersall (1983)	96, 144
Taylor v Campbell (1926)	129, 130
Taylor & Foulstone v National Union of Mineworkers (Yorkshire Area) (1984)	111
Tennant & Co v Thomson (1870)	146
Terrapin Ltd v Builders Supply Co (Hayes) (1960)	185
Thomas v National Union of Mineworkers (South Wales Area) (1985)	33, 108, 109, 144
Thomas v Williams (1880)	69
Thomas Marshall (Exports) v Guinie See Marshall (Thomas) (Exports) v Guinie	
Thomson & Co v Dailly (1897)	63
Thomson-Schwab v Costaki (1956)	34
Thompson v Barke (J) & Co (Caterers) Ltd (1975)	55
Thurlow v Tait (1893)	10
Trainer v Renfrewshire Upper District Committee (1907)	147
Trapp v Aberdeenshire CC (1960)	118, 174-175
Trotter v Farnie (1832)	29
Underhill v Ministry of Food (1950)	113
University of London Press Ltd v University Tutorial Press Ltd (1916)	71
Van Berkel v Simpson (RD) Ltd (1907)	84
Vettese v Vettese (1951)	13
Vokes (CG) Ltd v Evans & Marble Arch Motor Supplies Ltd (1931)	62
Waddell v BBC (1973)	171
Wakefield v Renfrew Commissioners of Supply (1878)	117
Walker v Junor (1903)	138
Walker, Hunter & Co v Falkirk Iron Co (1887)	82
Walker (John) & Sons Ltd v McGibbon (Douglas) & Co Ltd (1972)	64
Wallace-James v Montgomerie & Co Ltd (1899)	3
Ward v Ward (1983)	93, 94
Ware v Garston Haulage Co Ltd (1944)	34

xxxii List of Cases

Case	Page
Warnink (Erven) BV v Townend (J) & Sons (Hull) Ltd. *See* Erven Warnink BV v Townend (J) & Sons (Hull) Ltd	
Warrand v Watson (1905)	1, 52
Warrand v Watson (1906)	1
Watney v Menzies (1898)	16
Watson v Merrilees (1848)	26
Watt v Jamieson (1954)	28, 29, 34, 38, 39, 144
Watt v Lord Advocate (1979)	115, 116
Webster v Lord Advocate (1984)	2, 31
Webster v Lord Advocate (1985)	2, 31
Welsbach Incandescent Gas Light Co Ltd v M'Mann (1901)	138
Wemyss v Ardrossan Harbour Co (1893)	2, 24
Westminster Corpn v London & North Western Ry Co (1905)	117
Wheeler v Leicester City Council (1985)	160-161
White v Dixon (1881)	145
White v Dixon (William) Ltd (1883)	42, 144
Whitwham v Westminster Brymbo Coal & Coke Co (1896)	41
William Grant & Sons Ltd v William Cadenhead Ltd. *See* Grant (William) & Sons Ltd v Cadenhead (William) Ltd	
Williams & Son v Fairbairn (1899)	13, 129, 130, 136
Williamson v Meikle (1909)	64, 65
Wills' Trustees v Cairngorm Canoeing and Sailing School (1976)	47, 185
Wilson v Bank of Scotland (1987)	25
Wilson v Bartholomew & Co (1860)	21
Wilson v Brown and Gibson (1859)	42
Wilson v Gibb and Brattesani (1903)	30
Wilson v Gilbert (1863)	149
Wilson v Gilchrist (1900)	123, 137
Wilson v Glasgow and South Western Ry Co (1850)	57
Wilson v Independent Broadcasting Authority (1979)	23, 117, 143, 164
Wilson v Mackie (1875)	25
Wilson v Shepherd (1913)	3, 12, 145
Wilson v Waddell (1876)	43
Wilsons v Brydone (1877)	34
Winans v Macrae (1885)	52, 53
Withers (Thomas) & Sons Ltd v Withers (Samuel) & Co Ltd (1926)	69
Wolfe v Richardson (1927)	1
Wolthekker v Northern Agricultural Co (1862)	20, 24, 26
Wood v Boosey (1868)	71
Woolley & Son v Morrison (1904)	59
Wright v Kennedy (1946)	35
Wright v Thomson (1974)	188
Wyatt v Kreglinger & Fernau (1933)	130
Wylie and Lockhead v McElroy & Sons (1873)	19
Wyllie v Fisher (1907)	7
Ygnis SA v McFarlane Bros (Heat) Ltd (1969)	84
Young & Co v Bankier Distillery Co (1893)	44, 49
Young and Neilson v Rosenthal & Co (1884)	86
Zetland (Earl of) v Tennent's Trustees (1873)	49

Table of Statutory Instruments

	PAGE
Act of Sederunt (Civil Jurisdiction of the Sheriff Court) 1986 (1986/1946) S 146)	152
Act of Sederunt (Consistorial Causes) 1984 (SI 1984/255)	152
para 3(15)	15
Act of Sederunt (Ordinary Cause Rules) (Sheriff Court) 1983 (1983/747 (S66))	152
r 3	152
4	152
7	153
rr 33 to 78	153
r 78(3)	154
rr 79 to 84	153
r 90(3)	154
91	154
Act of Sederunt (Amendment of Ordinary Cause Rules) 1986 (1986/1230) (S 102)	152
Act of Sederunt (Patent Rules) 1978 (SI 1978/955)	85
Act of Sederunt (Rules of Court Amendment No 11) (Consistorial Actions) 1976 (SI 1976/1994)	122
Act of Sederunt (Rules of Court Amendment No 2) (Judicial Review) 1985 (SI 1985/500)	4, 116

	PAGE
Design Rules 1949 (SI 1949/2368) r 26	81
Patent Rules 1978 (SI 1978/216)	83
Rules of Court 1965	
para 79	147
90	148, 151
paras 90A, 91 to 93, 95, 95A, 96, 107	148
para 170c	122, 151
188D(9)	96
(15)	95
paras 192, 234, 235	147
para 236	147
(a)	147, 148
(b)-(e)	149
238(a), (d)	149
(e), (f)	150
paras 240, 241, 244	150
para 245(a)	150
(b)	151
paras 246, 247	151
para 255(1), (2)	152
260B	4
Form No 28	147
Appendix	
Form A	152

Chapter 1
Nature of the remedy

General principles

Interdict is a remedy granted by the court either against a wrong in course of being done or against an apprehended violation of a party's rights. It will only be granted upon evidence of a wrong or on grounds of reasonable apprehension that such a violation is intended. Thus in a case of interdict against trespass it must be shown that there has been actual trespass or an explicit threat to trespass. The mere allegation by a party that he has the right to enter upon land belonging to another is not enough.[1]

It must be shown to the satisfaction of the court that there is a substantial question to try but the court will rarely dismiss a petition for interdict at a preliminary stage as, for example, in the course of a hearing on interim interdict. The court must not treat applications, before they have been continued for trial, as if they were adjusted records and test the relevancy of the cause on that basis. It will only be where the court is satisfied, from such pleadings as are before them, that there cannot be any substantial question between the parties, that it will take the somewhat drastic step of dismissing the petition at a preliminary stage.[2]

The process of interdict is by its nature *quasi* criminal. If the party interdicted fails in any particular to observe the interdict he is liable to summary punishment by way of admonition, fine or imprisonment and may be found liable in expenses. Decree of interdict will be granted only for cogent reasons and in the exercise of proper judicial discretion. The party seeking interdict may be allowed to amend his crave but if interdict cannot be granted in accordance with the original or amended crave it cannot be granted at all.[3] The interdict sought must be precise in its nature and wording and so framed that the party against whom it

---

1 *Hay's Trustees v Young* (1877) 4 R 398 at 401 per Lord Ormidale; *Warrand v Watson* (1905) 8 F 253 and (1906) 8 F 1098; approved in *Inverurie Magistrates v Sorrie* 1956 SC 175.
2 *Wolfe v Richardson* 1927 SC 305 at 309; followed in *Arneil v Paisley Town Council* 1948 SLT (Notes) 46.
3 *Kelso School Board v Hunter* (1874) 2 R 228 at 232 per Lord Deas.

1

is granted may understand what are his rights and what are the restrictions placed upon him.[4] In the words of the Lord President (Emslie) in *Murdoch v Murdoch*,[5] 'Where interdict is granted by the Court, the terms of the interdict must be no wider than are necessary to curb the illegal actings complained of and so precise and clear that the person interdicted is left in no doubt what he is forbidden to do.'

Scope of the preventative process

Interdict is a preventative process and it may competently be invoked in suitable circumstances to restrain the violation of rights not yet committed but only reasonably apprehended. In the case of some inherently objectionable works, however, it is competent to apply for interdict against the construction of the works *ab ante* and without waiting for the inevitable nuisance to occur[6]. The interdict may however be limited in scope to allow steps being taken to obviate the nuisance;[7] but it has been held incompetent to challenge by interdict the validity of an anticipated notice under the Town and Country Planning Act (Scotland) 1972.[8] In *Marine Associates Ltd v City of Aberdeen Corporation*[9] however, interim interdict was granted against operating a stop notice under s 87 of the Town and Country Planning (Scotland) Act 1972 but the remedy was refused in *Central Regional Council v Clackmannan District Council* [10] and likewise in *Earl Car Sales (Edinburgh) Ltd v City of Edinburgh District Council*.[11] But where an enforcement notice was defective and no other remedy remained to the aggrieved party, the jurisdiction of the Court of Session to restrain the notice by interdict was sustained.[12]

Negative interdict

A negative interdict is incompetent. It is in form an order upon a party *not* to refrain from doing something and is, in other words, an order for specific implement. Such an order cannot be obtained by way of an action of interdict. In *Wemyss v Ardrossan Harbour Co*[13] Lord MacLaren pointed out: 'the substance of it is that we are asked to interdict the arbiter from not hearing the Pursuer's witness and to grant a negative

4 *Burton's Trs v Scottish Sports Council* 1983 SLT 418 at 419.
5 1973 SLT (Notes) 13.
6 *Gavin v Ayrshire County Council* 1950 SC 197 at 207 per Lord President Cooper. See also *Webster v Lord Advocate* 1984 SLT 13 and 1985 SLT 361.
7 Ibid.
8 *Barrie (James) (Sand and Gravel) Ltd v Lanark District Council* 1979 SLT 14.
9 1978 SLT (Notes) 41.
10 1983 SLT 666.
11 1984 SLT 8.
12 *McDaid v Clydebank District Council* 1984 SLT 162.
13 (1893) 20 R 500 at 505.

interdict. That has never been done and I presume your Lordships would not now wish to create such a precedent'.

Despite these restrictions upon their competency, actions of interdict have in recent years increased substantially in number, particularly in the fields of matrimonial relations, restrictive covenants and industrial disputes. The complexities which have always attended actions of interdict between husband and wife have been greatly exacerbated by the Matrimonial Homes (Family Protection) (Scotland) Act 1981 as amended by the Law Reform (Miscellaneous Provisions) (Scotland) Act 1985. The mass of legislation enacted in the past decade affecting the operations of trade unions and relations between employer and employee has created an entirely new body of law in which the remedy of interdict figures prominently.[14]

Completed and continuing wrongs

Where a wrong has already been accomplished and completed but there are averments of intention to continue the wrong, interdict is appropriate.[15] It will not be granted against repetition of a completed act in the absence of any threat of repetition.[16] There are exceptions however where a wrong complained of is protracted and only partially completed, as where a building is externally completed but internally unfinished,[17] or where a a wrong continues by way of encroachment or trespass.[18] Where there are actings consequent upon some wrong already completed interdict may in certain circumstances be sought to prevent the consequential happenings. Thus interdict was granted against a company from making a contract which was *ultra vires* and holding a meeting for that purpose although these events had passed. But in that case the contract was a continuing one.[19]

As to the doubtful competency of an action of interdict to enforce a positive obligation see *Keeney v Strathclyde Regional Council*.[20]

Personal nature of interdict

The remedy is purely personal and directed against the person named

---

14 See p 100 below.
15 *Wilson v Shepherd* 1913 SC 300 at 306 per Lord Salveson.
16 *Crooke v Scots Pictorial Publishing Co Ltd* (1906) 13 SLT 232.
17 *Heriot's Trust v Carter* (1903) 10 SLT 514.
18 *Colquhoun and Cameron v Mackenzie* (1894) 22 R 23 at 25; *Wallace-James v Montgomerie & Co* (1899) 2 F 107 at 114.
19 *Symington v Wilsons and Union Tube Co* (1904) 11 SLT 589; but contrast *Edgar v Glasgow Friendly Society* (1914) 2 SLT 408 (where the consequential proceedings were harmless and interdict refused).
20 1986 SLT 490.

4 *Nature of the remedy*

in the action as the party who has violated or threatened the pursuer's rights. Thus the existing owner of a property cannot be interdicted in respect of a nuisance committed by a previous owner.[1] But the position may be different where an interdict is directed against the tenant under a lease. In such circumstances it may be enforceable against his successor as assignee of the lease.[2]

Judicial review of statutory functions

Under the Court of Session Act 1868 s 89, where the respondent in an application has, before or after the institution thereof, done any act which the court might have prevented by interdict, the court may in the interdict proceedings ordain the respondent to perform any act which may be necessary for reinstating the complainer in his possessory rights and for granting specific relief against the illegal act complained of.[3]

By s 91 of the same Act the Court of Session may order specific performance of any statutory duty under such conditions as seem proper. Such an order may be made against any public official or public body upon whom the duty is laid, either expressly or by implication. The process is commonly called the supervisory jurisdiction of the Court.[4] The procedure which has now been greatly expedited, is by way of an application for judicial review as laid down by Act of Sederunt.[5] The powers of the Court in such an application include the making of orders for reduction, declarator, suspension, interdict and implement.

Where the party in default is a local authority recourse may also be had to the Local Government (Scotland) Act 1973 s 211 which supplements but does not restrict s 91 of the Court of Session Act 1868.

---

1 *Bankier Distillery Co v Young's Collieries Ltd* (1899) 2 F 89.
2 *Menzies v MacDonald* (1870) 8 SLR 81.
3 *Incandescent Gas Light Co v M'Culloch* (1897) 5 SLT 190; *Clippens Oil Co v Edinburgh and District Water Trustees* (1897) 25 R 370; *Caledonian Railway Co v G S W Railway Co* (1903) 11 SLT 510.
4 *Annan v Leith Licensing Authority* (1901) 9 SLT 63; *Carlton (Edinburgh) Hotel Co v Lord Advocate* 1921 SC 237; *Langlands v Manson* 1962 SC 493.
5 Rules of Court, para 260B as inserted by Act of Sederunt (Rules of Court Amendment No 2) (Judicial Review) 1985. See p 114 below further as to judicial review.

Chapter 2
Jurisdiction

Under Civil Jurisdiction and Judgments Act 1982

The Court of Session and the Sheriff Courts (except in cases involving judicial review) have jurisdiction to try actions of interdict provided the defender is, or can be made, subject to their jurisdiction under the Civil Jurisdiction and Judgments Act 1982.[1]

The rules in regard to jurisdiction over defenders domiciled in Scotland are contained in Sch 8 to the Act. Rule 1 provides that persons shall be sued in the courts for the place where they are domiciled; but by r 2(10) special and alternative provisions are made for actions of interdict. In terms of that rule the defender may be sued in the courts of the place where it is alleged that the wrong is likely to be committed. The pursuer has thus the choice of pursuing his action in the Sheriff Court of the place where the defender is domiciled in Scotland or in the Sheriff Court of the place in Scotland where the alleged wrong is likely to be committed, or in the Court of Session.

Where the defender is domiciled in England and Wales or Northern Ireland, he is nevertheless subject to the jurisdiction of the Scottish courts, if what is sought to be prevented is a threatened wrong, which would amount to a delict or quasi-delict, likely to occur in Scotland (or in the case of Sheriff Court Proceedings, in the Sheriffdom) (Sch 4; art 5(3)). If what is complained of is a threatened breach of contract, the Scottish courts have jurisdiction to grant interdict, if Scotland is the place of performance of the obligation which the defender is threatening to breach (Sch 4, art 5(1)).

Where the defender is domiciled outside the United Kingdom but within another EEC member state, it appears that the Scottish courts have no jurisdiction to interdict merely because a threatened wrong, which would amount to a delict or quasi-delict, is likely to occur in Scotland: Sch 1, art 5(3) confers jurisdiction in delict or quasi-delict only on the courts of the place where a harmful event has already occurred (subject to what is said below as to protective measures). But

---

[1] 1982 c 27.

if what is complained of is a threatened breach of contractual obligation, the Scottish courts would have jurisdiction to interdict it if Scotland were the place of performance of the obligation which the defender is threatening to breach (Sch 1, art 5(1)).

Where the defender is domiciled both outside the United Kingdom and outside the EEC, the Scottish courts have jurisdiction in exactly the same circumstances as where the defender is domiciled in Scotland, i.e. Sch 8, r 2(10) applies.

Domicile as the basis of jurisdiction

Domicile for the purpose of the Act has now a statutory meaning differing widely from its long established meaning in Scots law. Section 41(2), (3) and (4) provide that an individual is domiciled in the United Kingdom if, and only if, (a) he is resident in the United Kingdom, and (b) the nature and circumstances of his residence indicate that he has 'a substantial connection' with the United Kingdom. Section 41(6) however qualifies the requirement under (b) by providing that, where a defender has been resident in the United Kingdom, or in a particular part thereof, for a period of three months or more, then unless the contrary be shown, he is presumed to have a substantial connection with the United Kingdom and with that part.

In the case of any company, partnership or unincorporated body, what s 42(1) of the Act describes as its 'seat' is declared to be its domicile. Section 42(3) provides that such a company, partnership or body has its 'seat' in the United Kingdom if, and only if (a) it was incorporated under the law of a part of the United Kingdom and has its registered office or some other official address therein, or if (b) its central management and control is exercised in the United Kingdom. The company, partnership or body is held to have its 'seat' in a particular part of the United Kingdom (e.g. Scotland) if and only if it has its seat in the United Kingdom and (a) it has its registered office or some other official address in that part, or (b) its central management and control is exercised in that part, or (c) it has a place of business in that part.

The company, partnership or body is held to have its seat in a particular place in the United Kingdom (e.g. Edinburgh) if and only if it has its seat in the part of the United Kingdom in which that place is situated and (a) it has its registered office or some other official address in that place, or (b) its central management and control is exercised in that place, or (c) it has a place of business in that place.

Interdict as a protective measure

Section 27(1) of the Act deals with certain protective measures (including the granting of interim interdict) which the Court of Session is authorised to put into effect where proceedings have been commenced, or, in the case of interim interdict, are to be commenced, in any of the member states of the European Community, or in England, Wales or Northern Ireland. In determining whether proceedings have been commenced in any of the said countries, it is not necessary to show that any document has been served upon or notice given to the defender. This protective power vested in the Court of Session applies by virtue of s 24(2) of the Act to cases where (a) the subject of the proceedings in the member state or in England, Wales or Northern Ireland includes a question as to the jurisdiction of these courts, and (b) to any proceedings in such courts which involve a reference to the European Court. The power of the Court of Session to order inspection of documents etc. under s 1 of the Administration of Justice (Scotland) Act 1972 is extended to include cases specified in s 27(1) of the 1982 Act.

Principals and agents as defenders

Acts comprising threatened wrongs by an agent may be restrained by action of interdict against the agent alone,[2] and if the principal has directed or authorised the perpetration or threatened perpetration of wrongful acts, he may also be called as a defender. In *Wyllie v Fisher*[3] (which involved interdict against a poinding creditor and the Sheriff Officer instructed by him), it was shown that the officer called as co-defender had given no indication of an intention to remove or sell the poinded goods and it was held that there could be no presumption he would do so. In these circumstances the court granted him *absolvitor* with expenses.

Employer and employee

Similar principles apply in the case of wrongful acts perpetrated or threatened by employees. In such cases interdict is competent against the employee and, if the employer has authorised or directed the acts, or having been informed of the acts, allows them to continue, he also may be sued for interdict.[4] The rule of interdict against the employer, where the act is committed by the employee, can operate harshly. In *Performing Right Society v Mitchell*[5] interdict was granted against owners of a dance hall for breach of music copyright by a band under contract to a lessee despite the band having been given written instructions not

---

2 *Dobbie v Halbert* (1863) 1 M 532.
3 1907 SC 686.
4 *British Legal Life Assurance and Loan Co v Pearl Life Assurance Co* (1887) 14 R 818.
5 [1924] KB 762.

to breach the copyright. But compare the position in *Montgomerie & Co v Young Bros*,[6] where the employer failed to use all available means of stopping the wrongful acts.

Collective liability

Where a number of persons unite in committing acts which lead or may lead to a collective injury, interdict may be obtained against all those involved, whether or not they are proved to be individually responsible.[7] But where other persons are involved in activities peripheral to the alleged injury, interdict may be refused. Thus where a number of persons illegally removed sea wrack from the foreshore and another individual bought the sea wrack and carted it away, interdict was granted against those who removed the sea wrack from the foreshore but was refused against the carter who bought it.[8] In England it has been held that interdict may be granted against a body of respondents in general and collective terms and against their 'servants, agents and others' acting by their authority.[9] Interdict may be craved against anyone acting on behalf of a named defender.[10] Occasionally the words 'and others' or 'and all others' have been included in the interdict granted but what, if any, value this may have for the pursuer is doubtful.[11]

Interdict against corporate bodies

Where the order for interdict is directed against a corporate body, it may be enforced against the individual members thereof. In such cases however knowledge of the interdict must be brought home to the individual members, failing which these individuals may be exempt from penal consequences following upon any breach of the interdict.[12]

---

6 (1903) 11 SLT 600.
7 *Cowan & Sons v Duke of Buccleuch* (1876) 4 R (HL) 14 and *Breadalbane (Marquis of) v M'Gregor* (1848) 7 Bell App 43.
8 *Baird v Kerr* (1877) 14 SLR 434.
9 *Taff Vale Railway v Amalgamated Society of Railway Servants* [1901] AC 426.
10 *Hutchison v Hutchison* (1890) 18 R 237; *Marchetti v Marchetti* 1901) 3 F 888; *Robertson, Petitioner* 1911 SC 1319.
11 *Pattison v Fitzgerald* (1823) 2 S 536.
12 *R v Poplar Borough Council (No 2)* [1922] 1 KB 95.

Chapter 3
Title to sue

Interrelation of title and interest

In order to sue an action of interdict the pursuer must aver some legal relationship which confers upon him a right which the defender has either infringed or denied.[1] The questions of title to sue and interest to maintain the action are closely related and are often intermingled.[2] In some cases the nature of the action itself implies an interest to maintain. Thus a proprietor of land whose property is encroached upon has not only a right to sue but, by implication, a direct interest to prevent the encroachment.[3] To this extent his interest is presumed. By contrast, when a party endeavours by interdict to enforce a negative servitude placed upon his neighbour, the pursuer must aver and show a material interest in the enforcement of the servitude, the latter in itself not being a right of property. Averment of a contingent injury alone will not suffice to establish interest. Similar considerations will apply when the interdict sought is to enforce a feuing restriction placed upon a neighbour.[4]

Heritable and possessory titles

a Proprietors of heritage

The proprietor of a heritable property has a general right to resist damage to or encroachment upon his property. In *Calquhoun v Paton*[5] Lord Cowan set out the principle thus:

> To justify the interposition of the court in granting an interdict the party applying for it must show a legal title to the subjects of which his use and

---

1 *D & J Nicol v Dundee Harbour Trustees* 1915 SC (HL) 7 at 12 and 13 per Lord Dunedin.
2 *Summerlee Iron Co v Lindsay* 1907 SC 1161 at 1165.
3 *Galbreath v Armour* (1845) 4 Bell App 374.
4 *Gould v M'Corquodale* 1869) 8 M 165 at 172; *Hood v Traill* (1884) 12 R 362.
5 *Colquhoun v Paton* (1859) 21 D 996 at 1001 per Lord Cowan; *LMS Railway Co v M'donald* 1924 SC 835 at 840 per Lord President Clyde.

10   *Title to sue*

enjoyment and right of possession are alleged to be unlawfully interfered with; and further he must show either that there has been plain invasion of his property by a party having no right or title whatever in or to the subject or its use; or, against a competing title, he must show that he has had possession (by virtue of his title) for at least seven years prior to the attempt to innovate upon it'.

While the production of some title is an essential requirement, any lawful title which *ex facie* applies to the subjects and is coupled with possession will suffice.[6] An unrecorded personal title may be enough; or a lease.[7] A liferenter or a bond holder in possession may resist encroachment by interdict. The production of a completed feudal title in unnecessary, at least in the case of alleged encroachment.[8] A notarial instrument standing alone however has been held insufficient without further proof.[9] The description in a title must *ex facie* fit with the lands alleged to have been encroached upon.[10] If the subjects encroached upon are not named in the complainer's title an action of interdict cannot be maintained unless coupled with a declarator of ownership.[11]

The possession relied upon in support of the title must be legal and not wrongful and not be attributable to force, illegality or permission.[12] In the face of a competing title from a defender, the pursuer must aver at least seven year's possession.[13] The title produced must fit with the possession averred and will not avail the pursuer if it excludes or conflicts with the possession maintained. As regards servitudes, the only title necessary to enforce them is a title to the dominant tenement.[14]

As to the possessory right of protection, in the words of Lord Balgray in *Liston v Galloway*,[15] 'There is no rule of our law more salutary in itself or better established than that which declares that a party who has enjoyed peaceable possession of a right for seven years is entitled to be protected in it against the summary inversion of the state of possession'.

b Landlord and tenant

The lease of premises does not of itself deprive the landlord of his title

  6 *Colquhoun v Paton* (1859) 21 D 996 at 1002 per Lord Cowan; *LMS Railway Co v M'donald* 1924 SC 835 at 840.
  7 *Rankine on Land Ownership* (4th edn) p 10; *St Andrews Ladies Golf Club v Denham* (1887) 14 R 686.
  8 *Cranston & Elliot v Dobson* (1899) 2 F 271.
  9 *Leith-Buchanan v Hogg* 1931 SC 204 at 214.
 10 *Dickson v Dickie and Ors (Neil's Trs)* (1863) 1 M 1157.
 11 *Carnegie v Lord Kintore and Gammell* (1829) 8 S 251; *Cruickshank v Irving* (1854) 17 D 286; but see *Thurlow v Tait* (1893) 1 SLT 62.
 12 *McKerrow v Gordon* (1876) 3 R 429 at 433; *Liston v Galloway* (1835) 14 S 97.
 13 *Calquohoun v Paton (above); Maxwell v G S W Railway* (1866) 4 M 447 at 455.
 14 *Calder v Adam* (1870) 8 M 645; *M'Kerron v Gordon (above)*.
 15 (1835) 14 S 97.

to sue an action of interdict in respect of any material injury or serious nuisance affecting the subjects let and which might, by the operation of prescription or otherwise, become unchallengeable.[16] He may pursue an action to prevent the establishment of a right of way but not a minor trespass to take a shortcut over land, where no right of way was asserted.[17] But where the permission or acquiescence of the tenant would render legal an act of trespass, interdict may be refused unless landlord and tenant join in the action.[18] As regards casual or temporary nuisance where subjects have been let, 'the law of Scotland allows a proprietor to apply for interdict in respect of operations of a third party complained of by the tenant and which are reasonably calculated to lower the letting value of the tenement'.[19]

The tenant, by virtue of his lease, may sue an action of interdict without the consent of his landlord where there is encroachment or trespass upon or injury to the subjects let.[20] Given the necessary period of possession, the tenant under a long lease may acquire a possessory right of access over adjoining land occupied by a tenant of the same landlord.[1] Where a tenant raises an action of interdict to protect the subjects let but fails to give notice to the landlord, so that he may intervene if he thinks it necessary, the tenant's warrandice against the landlord may be prejudiced.

The trespass, operation or encroachment must be of a continuing nature and not an isolated incident. In *Brocket Estates v M'Phee and Others*[2] a landlord sought to interdict efforts by his tenant to establish a smallholding on the tenanted land. The wrong was regarded as a continuing one and the landlord's title to sue upheld.

c Joint proprietors

Joint ownership or *pro indiviso* ownership carries a title to sue an action of interdict. Each proprietor has a title to vindicate or protect his own individual interest. Thus, for example, in a freshwater loch each of the riparian proprietors may sue to prevent trespass or encroachment upon the loch or pollution of its waters.[3] Where several parties have rights in common or are possessed of a common interest in a subject, they may sue together in one action to protect their respective interests. But two

---

16 Burn Murdoch on Interdict para 47.
17 *Stewart v Stephen* (1877) 4 R 873. *Jolly v Brown* (1828) 6 S 872.
18 Ibid.
19 *M'Ewen v Steedman & M'Alister* 1912 SC 156 at 163.
20 *Fleming v Gemmill* 1908 SC 340 at 348; *St Andrews Ladies Golf Club v Denham* (1887) 14 R 686.
1 *M'Donald v Dempster* (1871) 10 M 94.
2 1949 SLT (Notes) 35.
3 *Scott v Lord Napier* (1869) 7 M (HL) 35 at 50.

proprietors of separate lands cannot obtain a joint interdict against trespass on their estates.[4]

Servitudes

Servitude of right of way, access, passage and support and of air and prospect, are conventional real rights and not rights of property. The degree to which they may be enforced or prevented from being abused must necessarily depend upon the nature of the servitude and the terms in which it is imposed. In order to sue an action of interdict based upon a servitude the pursuer must aver a patrimonial interest to enforce or restrain the servitude and in the consequence of so doing. In this sense, patrimonial interest means that the pursuer must be a party to some legal relationship which gives him a right which the defender is alleged either to have infringed or denied.[5]

Title as regards corporeal moveables

A person entitled to possession of corporeal moveables may by interdict prevent another from removing them or wrongfully using them or interfering with his possession or right therein.[6] An owner who is dispossessed of his moveables may interdict another from using or disposing of them. But in *Leitch & Co v Leyden*[7] where a grocer filled customers' empty bottles from a soda fountain, some of which belonged to aerated water manufacturers who had retained a right of property in their bottles, interdict against the grocer was refused on the ground of no title to sue and it was said no duty to examine the bottles was owed in the absence of a contractual relationship between the grocer and the manufacturers.

Title arising from patrimonial interest

Apart from proprietors of heritage who have a patrimonial interest by virtue of their title to vindicate invasion of their property or its environment (such as to prevent obstruction of the road *ex adverso* of their property), other classes of persons may have special types of patrimonial interest. Thus a ratepayer may interdict *qua* ratepayer the levying of an illegal rate upon him.[8] Water trustees have been interdicted from levying assessments to meet parliamentary expenses.[9]

4 *Arthur v Aird* 1907 SC 1170 at 1174; see also *Forbes v Leys, Mason & Co.* (1824) 2 S 603.
5 *D & J Nicol v Dundee Harbour Trustees* 1915 SC (HL) 7.
6 *Wilson v Shepherd* 1913 SC 300.
7 1931 SC (HL) 1.
8 *Stirling County Council v Falkirk Magistrates* 1912 SC 1281; *Farquhar & Gill v Aberdeen Magistrates* 1912 SC 1294.
9 *Cowan and Mackenzie v Law* (1872) 10 M 578; *Farquhar & Gill v Aberdeen Magistrates (above)*.

In *Dunoon Picture House Co Ltd v Corpn Dunoon*[10] a trading picture house company obtained interdict *qua* ratepayers against competitive trading by a local authority *ultra vires* of their powers. Where a ratepayer sought declarator and interdict of a resolution reducing rents by 25 per cent, alleged to be *male fides* and null and void, the action was held not barred by failure to aver *ultra vires* of the local authority.[11] If a defender uses a public road, in such a way as to interfere with the use of the road by other members of the public he may be restrained by interdict.[12]

Title and interest arising under contract

Interdict is an appropriate remedy where a party to a contract undertakes to refrain from a particular course of action but thereafter does what he should not have done. Conditions in restraint of trade, if they are not void as being unreasonable or contrary to the public interest, may be enforced by interdict, provided that the pursuer has an interest to enforce the condition.[13] An undertaking by a landlord in a lease not to use an adjoining property in a competing business has been held enforceable by interdict.[14] In partnership contracts one partner has title to sue an action of interdict against other partners in order to restrain breaches of the partnership agreement.[15] Interdict may be sought against one partner without the necessity of calling the firm.[16] Similarly, a title to sue lies with a superior to prevent breach of conditions in a feu charter, as also in the granter of a disposition[17] and a landlord against his tenant as respect conditions in the lease or perversion or conversion of the subjects.[18]

Interdict may be obtained in order to defeat efforts to induce a party to breach his contract. Where purchasers of motor cars were required to covenant not to resell within a specified period and a dealer knowingly induced the purchaser to sell within the said period, interdict was granted.[19]

A miner who shortly before he ceased to be a member of a trade union raised an action to restrain the union from parting with certain

---

10 (1921) 2 SLT 197.
11 *Innes v Kirkcaldy Burgh* 1963 SLT 325.
12 *Slater v M'Lellan* 1924 SC 854 at 858.
13 *Nordenfelt v Maxim Nordenfelt Guns and Ammunition Co* [1894] AC 535; *Williams & Son v Fairbairn* (1899) 1 F 944; *Ballachulish Slate Quarries Co v Grant* (1903) 5 F 1105; *Vettese v Vettesse* 1951 SLT (Notes) 61; *British Motor Trade Assocn v Gray* 1951 SC 586. See p 127.
14 *Davie v Stark* (1876) 3 R 1114 at 1121; but see *Mackenzie v Imlay's Trustees* 1912 SC 685.
15 *Graham v North British Bank* (1849) 11 D 1165.
16 *Mavor v Campbell* 1948 SLT (Notes) 66.
17 *Kirkintilloch Kirk-Session v Kirkintilloch Burgh School Board* 1911 SC 1127.
18 *Gold v Houldsworth* (1870) 8 M 1006; *Duke of Argyll v M'Arthur* (1861) 23 D 1236.
19 *British Motor Trade Asscn v Gray* 1951 SC 586.

funds was held to have a title and interest to sue at the time of raising the action.[20]

Title and interest of members of the public: actio popularis

An action of interdict is competent at the instance of any member of the public whose exercise of a public right has been interfered with. It is a universal principle applying to the exercise of public rights by individual members of the public that they must so regulate and, if necessary, restrict their individual participation in the public right as to make it consistent with equal participation by every other member of the public.[1] Thus, any person claiming to use a public right of way is entitled to sue *actio popularis* in order to vindicate or protect that right. His material interest consists in his averment of his use of the right of way.

By contrast, a private individual has no title to vindicate or protect a general public right. In *MacCormick v Lord Advocate*[2] where a member of the public sought to interdict the use of the numeral 'Second' in the designation of Her Majesty Queen Elizabeth, it was held *inter alia* that the point at issue was outwith the scope of *actio popularis*. Again an individual ratepayer has been held to have no title to challenge alleged maladministration of the common goods funds of a burgh, the right to do so being reserved to the Crown.[3] Similarly, in *Buckhaven and Methil Magistrates v Wemyss Coal Co Ltd*,[4] magistrates seeking to interdict dumping of rubbish on the foreshore (which was prohibited by statute, preserving the rights of the Crown) were held to have no title to sue without the consent of the Crown, in whom the right to the foreshore was vested.

---

20 *Donaghy v Rollo* 1962 SLT (Notes) 95.
1 *Slater v M'Lellan* 1924 SC 854 at 858 per Lord President Clyde.
2 1953 SC 396.
3 *Conn v Renfrew Corpn* (1906) 8 F 905.
4 1932 SC 201.

Chapter 4
Exclusion of the remedy

Where other common law remedies are available

Where some alternative legal process is available to remedy an alleged wrong, interdict will in many cases be excluded. The correct remedy may be a common law process or an appeal under statutory provisions. An action of interdict raised in connection with a matter already the subject of legal proceedings has been held incompetent. Thus in *Milne v Leslie*[1] an application to interdict an unqualified person from future appearance in the Small Debt Court was held incompetent, the appropriate procedure being to obtain an order debarring the person only if and when he appeared. In *Lindsay v Wemyss and March (Earl of)*[2] where, in a sequestration for rent, goods had been attached and the pursuer sought to have them withdrawn from sale and to interdict the defender from selling or disposing of them, it was held the pursuer's remedy lay in appearance in the sequestration to claim the goods and interdict was refused. In *Macartney v Gilchrist*,[3] where the pursuer having an unconstituted claim as creditor against the defender sought by interdict to prevent the defender selling his horses by auction, the application was held incompetent. Interdict cannot be used as a replacement for arrestment, or indeed any other form of competent diligence.

In *Johnston v Thomson*[4] where a landlord sought to interdict a tenant in possession from entering to cultivate the land and from interfering with the landlord's cultivation, interdict was held to be incompetent since removal or ejection was the appropriate process. Suspension and interdict against cultivation is competent only where the tenant is not in possession of the land. A clause of irritancy in a lease cannot be enforced by interdict, the appropriate remedy being an action of removing.[5] It is otherwise when a tenant under a lease subject to

---

1 (1888) 15 R 460.
2 (1872) 10 M 708.
3 (1831) 9 S 646.
4 (1877) 4 R 868.
5 *Rankin v M'Lachlan & Ors* (1864) 3 M 128.

irritancy is not in possession: thus in *Colquhoun and Cameron v Mackenzie*,[6] where a crofter whom the landlord had declined to accept as a legatee under the Crofters Holdings (Scotland) Act 1886 was held not to have been in possession and interdict against his entering or possessing was granted. Where several *pro indiviso* proprietors held a servitude of pasture and dispute arose as to excessive pasturage by one, interdict was refused on the ground that an action of division was available and appropriate.[7]

In criminal proceedings

On the other hand, where a criminal prosecution in respect of a wrong is competent, an action for interdict against the alleged wrongdoer may also be available. For example, although heather burning is an offence under a penal statute, interdict against any offender has been held competent.[8] The unauthorised use of the Royal Arms may be the subject of interdict and may also be prosecuted as an offence, but it is otherwise under the Performing Rights Acts.[9]

Interdicts excluded by statutory remedies

Where Parliament has provided a statutory remedy for an alleged wrong, interdict will, unless in most exceptional circumstances, be excluded. The language of the statute must show that the statutory remedy by way of appeal or otherwise has been substituted for the common law jurisdiction of the court.[10] In *Green v Lord Advocate*[11] the pursuer sought suspension and interdict of a calling-up notice under the Military Service Act 1916. The court held the action to be incompetent since the remedy made available by the Act was that the pursuer should state his objections before the Sheriff, if and when summary criminal proceedings were brought against him. Where objection was taken to the proposed form of a poll under the Temperance (Scotland) Act 1913, and interdict of the poll was sought, this was refused on the ground that the Act provided for an action of reduction of the poll *ex post facto*[12] and in *Fife County Council v Railway Executive*,[13] where the Executive sought to close a railway line and the local authority petitioned for interdict on the ground of breach of statutory duty, this was held incompetent since the Transport Act 1947

---

6 (1894) 22 R 23.
7 *Scott v M'Dowall* (1857) 19 D 769.
8 *Watney v Menzies* (1898) 6 SLT 189.
9 See p 80 below.
10 *Norfor v Aberdeenshire Education Authority* 1923 SC 881 at 888.
11 1918 SC 667.
12 *Anderson v Kirkintilloch Magistrates* 1948 SC 27.
13 1951 SC 499.

had committed all such questions to the jurisdiction of the Transport Tribunal. In *Cumming v Inverness Magistrates* [14] a local authority resolved to erect a bus shelter on a public pavement. Adjoining proprietors objected and sought a common law interdict. This was refused on the ground that the proper remedy for the pursuers was an appeal to the Sheriff under s 339 of the Burgh Police (Scotland) Act 1892. The decision in *Cumming* was followed in *Stornoway Magistrates v MacDonald*.[15] But as to the right of complaint to the Secretary of State under s 356 of the Local Government (Scotland) Act 1947 see *Innes v Kirkcaldy Burgh* .[16] Interdict, as a means of preventing *a priori* the granting of a licence by the magistrates for the showing of films on Sundays, was held incompetent in *Brown v Edinburgh Magistrates*.[17]

Interdict under the Town and Country Planning Act (Scotland) 1972

The validity of an anticipated enforcement notice under the Town and Country Planning Acts cannot be challenged by interdict[18]. Interim interdict was however granted against operating a stop notice under s 87 of the Town and County Planning (Scotland) Act 1972, in *Marine Associates v City of Aberdeen Corpn*[19] where the enforcement notice was under appeal and enforcement of a stop notice would have brought the complainer's whole operation to a halt; but was refused in *Central Regional Council v Clackmannan District Council*[20] and also in *Earl Car Sales (Edinburgh) Ltd v City of Edinburgh District Council*.[1]

Where an enforcement notice under the 1972 Act was defective through no fault of his own and no other remedy remained to the aggrieved party, the inherent jurisdiction of the Court of Session to restrain the notice was upheld.[2] A similar inherent jurisdiction in the High Court in England was upheld in *London Borough of Hammersmith v Magnum Automated Forecourts Ltd*,[3] where, pending issue of judgment in an appeal to the magistrates under the Control of Pollution Act 1974, the defendant continued to flout the statutory provisions. Although the statutory remedy of appeal had not been exhausted, the defendant continued to act in plain breach of the law and the court held he must

14 1953 SC 1.
15 1971 SLT 154.
16 1963 SLT 325.
17 1931 SLT 456.
18 *Barrie (James) (Sand & Gravel) v Lanark District Council* 1979 SLT 14; approving *Square Meals Frozen Foods Ltd v Dunstable Corp* [1974] 1 WLR 59.
19 1978 SLT (Notes) 41.
20 1983 SLT 666.
1 1984 SLT 8.
2 *McDaid v Clydebank District Council* 1984 SLT 162.
3 [1978] 1 All ER 401, CA.

Mora and taciturnity

Silence or taciturnity, in the face of intrusion upon the legal rights of a party which might be the subject of interdict, will not of itself bar the bringing of such an action. But if the potential complainer remains silent for any lengthy period and the intruder is induced to act in reliance upon the failure to object, a plea of mora and taciturnity may bar an action of interdict. Mere delay however for any period short of the prescriptive period, and in the absence of words or actions inferring non-objection or acquiescence in the status quo, will not bar the action.[5] As to delay in raising proceedings as a ground for refusal of interim interdict see *Highland Distilleries Co v Speymalt Whisky Distributors*.[6]

Res judicata

A preliminary plea of *res judicata* in an action of interdict will be upheld as in other forms of action if the real matter in issue is the same as that already decided by decree *in foro* of a competent court, in an action between the same parties or parties having identical interests.[7] For a full discussion of the competency of a plea of *res judicata* in an action of interdict, see *Glasgow and South Western Railway Company v Boyd and Forrest*.[8] A plea of *res judicata* may be rebutted by averments of *res noviter* and the tendering of new evidence of which the party was unaware and could not have discovered by reasonable diligence. Where a pursuer sought merely to repeat the case previously presented, fortified by a recently discovered writing, a plea of *res judicata* was sustained[9] on the ground that his averments failed to establish that the exercise of reasonable diligence on his part could not have secured production of the writing in the first action. An offer to produce witnesses who might have given evidence at the first trial but have only subsequently been discovered has been held insufficient to found the plea of *res noviter*[10] but the discovery of a document believed to have been lost will amount to *res noviter* provided it is shown that the party tendering it had not been negligent.[11]

4 [1977] 2 All ER 519, CA.
5 *M'Kenzie v British Linen Co* (1881) 8 R (HL) 8; *Bain v Assets Co* (1905) 7 F (HL) 104 at 108.
6 1985 SLT 85 at 89.
7 *Grahame v Kirkcaldy Magistrates* (1882) 9 R (HL) 91.
8 1918 SC (HL) 14. Followed in *Grahame v Secretary of State for Scotland* 1951 SLT 312 and *Anderson & Ors v Wilson & Anr* 1972 SLT 170.
9 *McCarroll v M'Kinstery* 1926 SC (HL) 1.
10 *Miller v Mac Fisheries Ltd* 1922 SC 157.
11 Fn 9 above.

In *Luxmoore v Red Deer Commission*[12] an action of interdict in which parties reached an extra-judicial settlement and sought *absolvitor* in order to make the case *res judicata* between them, the court, of consent upon joint minute, pronounced decree refusing the prayer of the petition, this being a more appropriate course. It was stated such a decree would be as much *res judicata* as *absolvitor*.

Where a member of the public has petitioned for declarator of right of way the decision will be *res judicata* in any subsequent action for declarator and for interdict raised by or defended by any other member of the public or by a local authority or by a Rights of Way Society.[13]

Acquiescence

The plea of acquiescence is not infrequently advanced as a defence in an action of interdict, particularly in cases involving the invasion of heritable rights, but there must be some evidence of consent to surrender any legal right.[14] The use of property which has no justification in title must, in the absence of prescriptive right, be ascribed to tolerance. To be successful the defender must show that, by some unjustifiable, patent and irremediable act, he intruded upon the legal right of the pursuer without objection by him, by either words or conduct. Mere silence is not enough.[15] The action must have been taken with the knowledge of the pursuer. The limits within which the plea of acquiescence may be taken are not easy to define. In *Cowan v Lord Kinnaird*[16] where a defender carried out extensive operations on a river to enable him to draw off water, all at considerable expense and with the knowledge of the pursuer, and without objection by him, a plea of acquiescence was held irrelevant. The plea is commonly met in actions of declarator of nuisance and interdict[17] and in actions of interdict in respect of interference with servitude rights.[18]

Immunity of the Crown

The court has no jurisdiction to grant interdict against the Crown or against any of its officers where the result would be to grant relief against the Crown. Instead the court is authorised to make an order declaring the rights of parties.[19]

12 1979 SLT (Notes) 53.
13 *MacFie v Scottish Rights of Way Society* (1884) 11 R 1094; *Alexander v Picken* 1946 SLT 91.
14 *Davidson v Thomson* (1890) 17 R 287; but see *Fraser v Campbell* (1895) 22 R 558; *Rankine v Logie Den Land Co* (1902) 4 F 1074.
15 *Cairncross v Lorimer* (1860) 3 Macq 827, HL; *Wylie and Lochhead v McElroy & Sons* (1873) 1 R 41.
16 (1865) 4 M 236.
17 *Rigby & Beardmore v Downie* (1872) 10 M 568; *Houldsworth v Wishaw Burgh Comrs of Police* (1887) 14 R 920; see further as to acquiescence in nuisance p 36 below.
18 *Muirhead v Glasgow Highland Society* (1864) 2 M 420.
19 Crown Proceedings Act 1947 s 21(a) applied to Scotland by s 43(a).

Chapter 5
Interdict against legal proceedings and wrongful use of diligence

1 AGAINST LEGAL PROCEEDINGS

General principles

A person cannot in general be prevented, whether by interdict or otherwise, from commencing civil proceedings or taking any proper steps preparatory thereto, or from lodging information with the police or Procurator Fiscal which may lead to a criminal prosecution. An exception arises under the Vexatious Actions (Scotland) Act 1898 under which any litigant who has 'habitually or persistently instituted vexatious legal proceedings without any reasonable ground' may be debarred from raising further proceedings, unless with the consent of the Lord Advocate. Whether a person is a vexatious litigant depends not only on the number of actions raised but on how he conducts himself in the legal process, in the taking of a number of hopeless appeals, and generally the extent of his abuse of the process.[1]

There may be grounds for an action of interdict and possibly damages where civil proceedings are raised maliciously or out of spite. The *dicta* in *Hallam v Gye & Co*,[2] *M'Gregor v M'Laughlin*[3] and *Wolthekker v Northern Agricultural Company*[4] indicate that where there are clear and distinct averments of malice and *mala fides* on the part of the pursuer in such civil proceedings, interdict may be granted against him at the instance of the defender in these proceedings.

Abuse of process

Where an action properly raised is persisted in, after the cause of the action has disappeared, there arises an abuse of process. Thus where the case is pursued in the knowledge that the debt sued for has been paid, interdict against taking of decree of enforcement thereof may be

---

1 *Lord Advocate v Arnold* 1951 SC 256; *Lord Advocate v Rizza* 1962 SLT (Notes) 8. *Lord Advocate v Cooney* 1984 SLT 434.
2 (1835) 14 S 199.
3 (1905) 8 F 70 at 76.
4 (1862) 1 M 211 at 213.

obtained.⁵ Where a tender for the amount sued for has been lodged or a cheque delivered including the expenses of process, the taking of decree may be restrained.⁶

Where a cheque is tendered in full settlement of a claim together with the expenses of process, decree may not be taken unless and until the cheque has been dishonoured. In *Robertson v Thorburn*⁷ where proceedings in a summary removing, based on half yearly tenancy, were found to be fundamentally null from the outset, suspension of decree was granted. Where in the Sheriff Court a judgment is unappealable or leave to appeal is refused, suspension and interdict may be sought to preserve the status quo and to sist diligence *ad interim*.⁸ And in any appeal the respondent holding the decree appealed against may be restrained by interdict from enforcing it, pending the decision on the appeal.⁹

Court of Session's power to control inferior courts and adminstrative bodies

In the exercise of its wide jurisdiction to regulate the proceedings of inferior courts, the Court of Session may control their actions at any stage. In *Moss's Empires Ltd v Assessor for Glasgow*¹⁰ where an entry in the valuation roll had been increased in amount without service of the statutory notice, Lord Shaw expressed the principle thus: 'It is within the jurisdiction of the Court of Session to keep inferior jurisdicatories and administrative bodies right in the sense of compelling them to obey those conditions without the fulfilment of which they have no power whatsoever.' The jurisdiction may be exercised by reduction of decree of an inferior court or in appropriate circumstances by interdict of proceedings in progress.

In the field of ordinary litigation, a complainer who has himself initiated proceedings, or an application to a body such as a local authority, requesting them to exercise an administrative function, cannot obtain interdict against the defender or against the local authority simply to suspend an anticipated adverse decision.¹¹

Interdict against publication of proceedings

Interdict is not competent to prevent publication of proceedings held in

---

5 *Ormiston v Redpath, Brown & Co* (1866) 4 M 488; *Rhind v Kemp & Co* (1893) 21 R 275.
6 *Pollock v Goodwin's Trustees* (1898) 25 R 1051 at 1055.
7 1927 SLT 562.
8 *Caledonian Rly Co v Cochran's Trustees* (1897) 24 R 855; *Wilson v Bartholomew & Co* (1860) 22 D 1410.
9 *Cameron v Macdonnell* (1822) 2 S 103.
10 1917 SC (HL) 1 at 11.
11 *Holroyd v Edinburgh Magistrates* 1921 SLT 259.

open court whether British or foreign. In *Riddel and Raeside v Clydesdale Horse Society*[12] where the pursuers sought to prevent publication of evidence to be taken before a commissioner authorised by the Circuit Court of Illinois at the request of the Lord Advocate, the Lord President (Inglis) stated the rule thus: 'If this is a fair and accurate report of proceedings in a Court of competent jurisdiction reported for a legitimate purpose, I do not see it is possible to entertain an application for interdict.' The more complex question of whether the contents of a document not read out in open court may be published in the press report of proceedings in the case was dealt with in *Cunningham v The Scotsman*.[13] Holding that a press report of proceedings in a claim for damages for defamation, which contained extracts from the summons not read out in open court, might be entitled to qualified privilege, Lord Clyde said:

> The test in my view is not what is actually read out – although all that is read out is published – but what is, in the presentation of the case, intended to be published and so put in the same position as if it had been read out. If it is referred to and founded on before the Court with a view to advancing the submission, it is to be taken as published.

Restraint of proceedings in foreign courts

Proceedings in a foreign court may in special circumstances be restrained by interdict in Scotland where the subject matter is already *sub-judicata* in a Scottish court. In *California Redwood Co v Merchant Banking Co of London*[14] the defenders who had lodged claims in the liquidation of a Scottish company on which no deliverance had been made raised proceedings in the New York State Supreme Court to recover money alleged to be involved in their claim against the liquidator. On a petition by the liquidator seeking to restrain further proceedings by the defenders in the New York Supreme Court, the Court of Session granted interdict. Where proceedings have been commenced, or are about to be commenced, in any of the member states of the European Community or in England, Wales, or Northern Ireland, interdict may be initiated by the Court of Session as a protective measure under s 27(1) of the Civil Jurisdiction and Judgments Acts 1982.

Restraint of statutory bodies

The court cannot interdict the doing of anything done in lawful implement of statutory authority, nor anything done under powers of

---

12 (1885) 12 R 976 at 983.
13 (1986) Scotsman 28 November.
14 (1886) 13 R 1202.

statute, if it is done within the terms of the authority granted.[15] But it may interdict actings authorised by statute if done without taking all reasonable precautions to avoid harm[16] or if implement of the statute is alleged to have been carried out in a biased way.[17]

Where the aggrieved party has open to him an alternative remedy such as appeal under statute against a statutory body's decision, interdict will be refused.[18] The proceedings of statutory bodies set up to deal with specific complaints by members of the public may be subject to interdict where they purport to entertain complaints not falling within the statute under which they operate.[19]

Where the whole statutory procedure laid down for a particular purpose, as for example following a poll of ratepayers in an application for extension of burgh boundaries, had been exhausted and no other remedy remained, interdict was held competent. The effect was to halt further proceedings in the extension pending the initiation of new proceedings. Similarly, where a planning authority served enforcement notices on an occupier of premises but failed to serve notice on the owner who had no knowledge of the notices, and the occupier failed to appeal to the Secretary of State within the statutory time limit, interdict was granted prohibiting the planning authority from proceeding upon the notices. The court held that in such circumstances the appellate jurisdiction of the Court of Session was not excluded, notwithstanding s 85(10) of the Town and Country Planning (Scotland) Act 1972, which declared that, except by appeal to the Secretary of State, an enforcement notice should not be questioned in any proceedings.[20]

Decree taken in breach of contract

An agreement to delay or refrain from taking decree, if breached, may be actionable simply as a breach of contract.[1]

Arbitration

Interdict may competently be sought to stay arbitration proceedings by a plea of *res judicata* where the subject matter of the arbitration has already been decided by a competent court, in an action involving the

---

15 *Buchanan v Glasgow Corpn Water-works Commissioners* (1869) 7 M 853.
16 *Gillespie v Lucas and Aird* (1893) 20 R 1035.
17 *Wilson v IBA* 1979 SLT 279.
18 *Green v Lord Advocate* 1918 SC 667; *Dante v Assessor for Ayr* 1922 SC 109.
19 *Gibson & Reid v City of Glasgow Profiteering Act Committee* (1920) 2 SLT 84.
20 *Merry & Cuninghame Ltd v Alexander* 1926 SLT 424. See also *McDaid v Clydebank District Council* 1984 SLT 162.
 1 *MacRobbie v M'Lellan's Trs* (1891) 18 R 470 at 475 per Lord MacLaren.

same parties and the same objective and grounds of claim.[2] But it is not to be assumed that arbiters will exercise their jurisdiction or act otherwise than they should. The court will not lightly interfere with the action of an arbiter properly appointed and acting *ex facie* within his powers.[3] In arbitration proceedings where the arbiter has exceeded, or is about to exceed, his jurisdiction or fails to exercise it, matters are frequently allowed to run their course to final decree, when an action of reduction can be raised.[4] If however it is clear that proceedings in course are outwith the terms of the referral to the arbiter, the proceedings may be halted by interdict.[5] Interdict may also be granted where the party seeking the arbitration has clearly mistaken his remedy.[6] Where a proprietor sought to interdict the executors of an agricultural tenant from insisting on the appointment of an arbiter to fix compensation for disturbance, on the ground that the deceased's tenant's interest had not passed to his executors and the arbiter had no jurisdiction, it was held that, although interdict was a competent procedure, the question of jurisdiction could more conveniently be dealt with in the arbitration proceedings.[7]

2 INTERDICT AGAINST WRONGFUL USE OF DILIGENCE

General principles

As a general rule interdict or suspension and interdict may be sought against the execution of diligence if it is in process or threatened without probable cause or where there have been irregularities in procedure leading up to the diligence,[8] or if it is used unjustifiably[9] or maliciously and without probable cause.[10] In *MacRobbie v M'Lellan's Trustees*[11] approved in *Clark v Beattie*[11] (action for damages) it was made clear that if diligence has followed upon a decree which is bad, not

---

2 *Glasgow & South Western Railway Co v Boyd & Forrest* 1918 SC (HL) 14.
3 *Licences Insurance Corpn and Guarantee Fund v Shearer* 1907 SC 10 at 15 per Lord Kyllachy; *Bennet v Bennets and Lucus* (1903) 5 F 376.
4 *Glasgow, Yoker & Clydebank Railway Co v Lidgerwood* (1895) 23 R 195 at 198 per Lord MacLaren.
5 *Wemyss v Ardrossan Harbour Co* (1893) 20 R 500 at 504 per Lord President; *Dumbarton Water-Works Commissioners v Blantyre* (1884) 12 R 115.
6 *Greenock Parochial Board v Coghill* (1878) 5 R 732.
7 *Cormack v McIldowie's Executors* 1972 SLT (Notes) 40 at 41 per Lord Keith.
8 *Shiell v Mossman* (1871) 10 M 58; *MacKillop v Mactaggart* 1939 SLT 65; *Brady v Napier* 1944 SC 18.
9 *Haughead Coal Co v Gallocher* (1903) 11 SLT 156; *Wolthekker v Northern Agricultural Co* (1862) 1 M 211; *Kinnes v Adam* (1882) 9 R 698.
10 Ibid.
11 (1891) 18 R 470, 1909 SC 299. See also *M'Neill v M'Murchy, Ralston & Co* (1841) 3D 554.

merely wrong upon the merits (as in reversal on appeal), but because of some intrinsic fault which makes it no decree at all, then there has been wrongful use of diligence. No averment of malice is then necessary.

Inhibition and arrestment

Inhibition or arrestment may be the subject of interdict if it is proved to be wrongful in respect of faulty procedure or if shown to be injurious or oppressive.[12] The mere threat of inhibition or arrestment may ground an action of interdict.[13]

Wrongful use of sequestration

Where a petition for sequestration is presented in good faith by a creditor no liability is incurred even though the petition is refused unless malice or want of probable cause is shown.[14] If however the debt upon which the notour bankruptcy is based is fictitious or the petitioner is not truly a creditor, the proceedings may be restrained without averment of malice[15] or want of probable cause.

In *Wilson v Bank of Scotland*[16] the respondents had executed a charge for payment upon a bond by the petitioner. After the *induciae* on the charge had expired the respondents sought to sequestrate the petitioner. Thereupon the petitioner brought an action of interdict seeking to halt the progress of the sequestration. The court held that, since the *induciae* had expired without any suspension of the charge, notour bankruptcy had been established and that an application for interdict came too late.

Interdict in liquidation proceedings

The position is similar in a petition for liquidation of a company. If the petition is presented in good faith and upon a debt truly existing, then, in order to restrain proceedings or recover damages for wrongous use of the proceedings, there must be averment of malice and want of probable cause.[17] At any time after presentation of a winding up petition and before a winding up order has been made, where any action is pending against the company, any creditor or contributor of the company may apply to the courts to stay the proceedings by interdict.[16]

---

12 *Beattie & Son v Pratt* (1880) 7 R 1171 at 1173 per Lord Ormidale; *Wilson v Mackie* (1875) 3 R 18.
13 Ibid and see *Duff v Wood* (1858) 20 D 1231.
14 *Kinnes and Kinnes v Adam & Sons* (1882) 9 R 698.
15 *Kinnes* ibid at 702 per Lord President Inglis.
16 1987 SLT 117.

Diligence sought periculo petentis

Diligence which has been regularly executed and follows upon a valid decree in the ordinary course of legal proceedings merely amounts to the use by the pursuer of a legal remedy to which he is entitled and cannot be restrained unless malice is averred.[18] The situation is different where the pursuer seeks a type of diligence or remedy founded upon *ex parte* statements, as for example arrestment upon a summary warrant for recovery of rates or a warrant *meditatione fugae* or an interim interdict. In such cases the diligence or remedy is granted *periculo petentis*. If the *ex parte* statements are shown to be unfounded in fact the diligence or remedy may be restrained by interdict.[19] No averment of malice is required in such circumstances.

Suspension and interdict of poinding

Where a charge upon a decree has been irregularly executed but no poinding has followed, the operation of the charge may be halted by simple suspension.[20] If however an irregular charge has been followed by a regular poinding or a regular charge has been followed by an irregular poinding, an action of suspension and interdict is required.[1] Examples of the grounds for such actions are: delay in reporting the poinding;[2] omitting to fix the place and date of sale;[3] incorrect or lack of specification of the debt;[4] insufficient notice or inadequate publication of the date of sale.[5] If the value of the goods poinded greatly exceeds the amount of the debt and expenses, the poinding may be restrained.[6] Where a decree for payment by instalments was obtained and the pursuers executed a charge after the date of the first instalment but before the date for the second instalment and thereafter poinded for the whole amount of the debts, an action of interdict by the debtor restraining the judicial sale was successful.[7] And in *Allison's (Electricals) v McCormick*[8] (an application for warrant to sell poinded goods) where

---

17 *Seaspray S S Co v Tennant* (1908) 15 SLT 874.
18 *Grant v Airdrie Magistrates* 1939 SC 738 at 758.
19 *Wolthekker v Northern Agricultural Co* (1862) 1 M 211 at 213; *Kinnes and Kinnes v Adam* (1882) 9 R 698.
20 *Lowson v Reid* (1861) 23 D 1089 at 1094; *Watson v Merrilees* (1848) 10 D 370. See also generally as to suspension of diligence, *Stewart on Diligence* p 754.
1 *Stewart on Diligence* p 758.
2 *Miller v Stewart* (1835) 13 S 483.
3 *McVicar v Kerr* (1857) 19 D 948; *Kewly v Andrew* (1843) 5 D 860.
4 *Sangster v Burness* (1857) 20 D 355.
5 *M'Neil v M'Murchy, Ralston & Co* (1841) 3 D 554.
6 *McKinnon v Hamilton* (1866) 4 M 852.
7 *McTaggart v Dalry Coop Society* 1980 SLT (Sh Ct) 142.
8 1982 SLT (Sh Ct) 93.

there was no firm averment that the goods had been offered back to the debtor or his agent this was held fatal to the application.

Failure to comply with the procedures laid down in the Debtors (Scotland) Act 1838 and the Execution of Diligence (Scotland) Act 1926, as amended by the Recorded Delivery Act 1966 has been held to justify interdict proceedings. The Law Reform (Diligence) (Scotland) Act 1973 limits the items of domestic furnishing which may be poinded. The items in question may be varied by Order of the Secretary of State. Where an exempted article is poinded the debtor may, without prejudice to any other remedy (including interdict), appeal to the Sheriff who may release the article from poinding. The Sheriff may grant interdict against the sale of poinded goods notwithstanding that he granted the warrant for sale.[9]

---

9 *Jack v Waddell's Trustees* 1918 SC 73.

Chapter 6
Interdict against nuisance, encroachment upon heritable property, water rights and the foreshore

1 AGAINST NUISANCE

Nature and categories of nuisance liable to interdict

Nuisance has been described as 'whatever obstructs the public means of commerce and intercourse, whether in highways or navigable rivers; whatever is noxious or unsafe, or renders life uncomfortable to the public generally, or to the neighbourhood; whatever is intolerable or offensive to individuals in their dwellinghouses, or inconsistent with the comfort of life.'[1] Nuisance is a wrong of strict liability and it is unnecessary to prove intention to injure or negligence on the part of the person against whom the complaint is laid. In some cases liability for personal injury arising out of nuisance has been established without proof of negligence.[2] Further consideration of such cases is however outwith the scope of the present work.

There are three categories of nuisance, namely, common law nuisance; nuisance declared by statute[3]; and conventional nuisance, where the wrong arises from contravention of or failure to fulfil the terms of an agreement between the complainer and the alleged wrongdoer.

Common law nuisance

Common law nuisance is an infringement by a neighbour or third party of the natural rights of enjoyment and use of land by the owner or occupier thereof or by the general public. Any conduct which causes serious disturbance or substantial inconvenience to a neighbour or material damage to his property constitutes a nuisance at common law.[4] To be actionable by way of interdict the nuisance must be repeated or continuing and not an isolated act and must cause material inconvenience, harm or discomfort. Whether particular conduct

---

1 *Bell's Principles* para 974.
2 *Giblin v Lanarkshire County Council* 1927 SLT 563.
3 *Slater v M'Lellan* 1924 SC 854 at 858.
4 *Bell's Principles* above; *Burn Murdoch on Interdict* para 219; *Watt v Jamieson* 1954 SC 56.

amounts to a nuisance is a question of degree and circumstance and of the nature of the neighbourhood wherein it occurs.[5] Where a locality has been long appropriated to the kind of operation from which the nuisance is alleged to arise, the conduct said to create the nuisance may be less objectionable. In *Inglis v Shotts Iron Co*,[6] Lord Justice Clerk Moncrieff laid down the general principle thus:

> The general rule is that everyone is bound so to use his property as not to injure his neighbour. It is equally certain that this rule must suffer modification according to the varied considerations of social life. Things which are forbidden in a crowded urban community may be permitted in the country. What is prohibited in enclosed land may be tolerated in the country. Vicinity or proximity may make that a nuisance which may cease to be so at a distance; and the habit and practice of a neighbourhood has some weight in cases of this kind. Nor, in extreme cases, do I doubt that the comparative interests at stake may be taken into view.

Anticipated nuisance

When the subject of an application for interdict is an anticipated nuisance the general rule must be formulated with greater precision. There are certain operations which are defined by law as nuisance because the law holds they cannot be carried on without constituting a nuisance.[7] In the case of such inherently objectionable works it is competent to apply for interdict against the construction *ab ante* and without waiting for the inevitable nuisance to materialise.[8] Even in cases of this notorious description, the interdict, if granted, may be limited in scope so as to admit of care and contrivance to obviate the nuisance.[9] But where the subject of complaint does not fall within this extreme category but consists of works which, when completed and brought into use, may or may not at some future time create a nuisance, it by no means follows that their construction can be interdicted out of hand. In such cases apprehension will not normally be equated with realisation unless it is made to appear that the creation of a nuisance is in a practical sense a necessary and virtually inevitable consequence of the construction of the proposed works or the performance of a projected operation.[10] The matter was summarised

---

5 *Watt v Jamieson* 1954 SC 56.
6 (1881) 8 R 1006 at 1021. See also *Cooper & Wood v N B Railway Co* (1863) 1 M 499; *Anderson v Aberdeen Agricultural Hall Co* (1879) 6 R 901; *Robertson v Thomas* (1887) 14 R 822; *Maguire v M'Neill* 1922 SC 174 (steam hammers).
7 *Kirkwood's Trustees v Leith and Bremner* (1888) 16 R 255.
8 *Gavin v Ayrshire County Council* 1950 SC 197 at 207 per Lord President Cooper.
9 *Trotter v Farnie* (1832) 10 S 423.
10 *Gavin v Ayrshire County Council* above at 207.

thus by Lord President Inglis in *Steel v Gourock Police Commissioners*,[11] 'If it could be demonstrated or if it were relevantly stated that the operations of the Commissioners would *necessarily* have the effect of causing a nuisance there might be a question for our consideration.'

A common law nuisance may arise from the keeping of noisy or smelly animals,[12] or animals which pollute the water supply;[13] or by the causing of excessive noise,[14] or from heat and fumes,[15] or vibration,[16] or smells,[17] or sewage,[18] or infectious germs,[19] or pollution of running water by sewage due to improper use of drains by tenants,[20] or pollution of canals[1] or dry ditches.[2]

Nuisance by animals

Interdict may be granted against causing or permitting a substantial increase in the number of animals normally found on the land but which, due to multiplication, cause damage, loss or injury to the property or person of a neighbour. Thus interdict has been granted to prevent damage by depredation of game and of foxes, rabbits, rats and mice[3] and from dumping excessive quantities of manure and rubbish and so attracting rats.[4] The keeping of normally unobjectionable domesticated animals or other animals in captivity may in certain circumstances amount to a nuisance. Thus nuisance may be caused by dogs making an excessive noise[5] and similarly by horses in their stables.[6] Nuisance may also arise from keeping of pigeons, rabbits and other birds and animals if they are permitted to destroy a neighbour's crops.

Nuisance by noise and vibration

At common law nuisance may arise from the use of plant and

11 (1871) 10 M 954.
12 *Ireland v Smith* (1895) 3 SLT 180; *Spider's Web v Marchant* 1961 CLY 6359 (noisy dogs).
13 *Dumfries Water-Works Commissioners v M'Cullock* (1874) 1 R 975 (sheep dipping).
14 *Ferguson v M'Culloch* 1953 SLT (Sh Ct) 113 (operating a sawmill).
15 *Wilson v Gibb and Brattesani* (1903) 10 SLT 293.
16 *M'Ewen v Steedman & M'Alister* 1912 SC 156; *Maguire v M'Neil* 1922 SC 174.
17 *Robertson v Stewarts and Livingston* (1872) 11 M 189; *Chalmers v Dixon* (1876) 3 R 461; *Harvie v Robertson* (1903) 5 F 338.
18 *Fraser's Trustees v Cran* (1877) 4 R 794.
19 *Fleet v Metropolitan Asylums Board* (1886) 2 TLR 361, CA.
20 *Robertson v Stewarts and Livingston* (1872) 11 M 189; *Caledonian Railway Company v Baird* (1876) 3 R 839; *M'Gavin v M'Intyre Bros* (1890) 17 R 818; *Fleming v Gemmill* 1908 SC 340.
1 *Caledonian Railway Company v Baird* (above).
2 *Scott v Scott* (1881) 8 R 851.
3 *Farrer v Nelson* (1885) 15 QBD 258.
4 *Stearn v Prentice Bros* [1919] 1 KB 394, but see *Bland v Yates* (1914) 58 Sol Jo 612.
5 *Spider's Web v Marchant* 1961 CLY 6359.
6 *Brodier v Saillard* 1976 2 Ch 692.

machinery which by reason of its operation causes excessive noise or vibration. Much will depend on the degree of noise, continuous or intermittent, upon the circumstances of use, and the nature of the environment. Interdict has been granted against the use of a printing press in circumstances which created excessive noise and vibration[7] and against the operation of a smithy on an upper floor[8] and in respect of the working of a sawmill[9] which was held to be a nuisance and contravened conditions in a feu charter under which the complainer had a *jus quaesitum tertio* to enforce the conditions. But the operation of a steam hammer in an industrial area has been held unobjectionable. In the leading case of *Maguire v M'Neill Ltd*[10] forgemasters carrying on business in a district where industries were mainly of the heavy metal type and steam hammers were in common use installed a number of heavy drop hammers of a kind not previously known in the district. Neighbouring proprietors sought interdict to prevent the use of the drop hammers which were alleged to have caused a nuisance by noise and vibration, damage to buildings and interference with the comfortable enjoyment of a neighbouring church and presbytery, a school and business premises. After proof, it was held that the complainers had failed to prove structural damage due to the drop hammers and had failed to establish such material interference with the occupation of their premises as, having regard to the character of the locality, amounted to a nuisance. In *Webster v Lord Advocate* however the noise caused by construction of staging for the Edinburgh Military Tattoo was ordered to be restrained within defined limits.[11]

Certain nuisances arising from excessive noise are specifically permitted by statute. Thus the Civil Aviation Act 1949 ss 40 and 41 as amended by the Civil Aviation Act 1982 Sch 1, para 13 absolve aircraft operators from liability for noise of their aircraft in flight, and provide that no action for nuisance will lie in respect of noise or vibration caused by aircraft on aerodromes.

Nuisance by pollution of water

At common law, a proprietor of land may not pollute water which flows through his land in a non-navigable river so as to render it unfit for use. Any downstream proprietor may restrain an upper proprietor from so

7 *Johnston v Constable* (1841) 3 D 1263.
8 *Kinloch v Robertson* 1756 Mor 1137.
9 *Fergusson v M'Culloch* 1953 SLT (Sh Ct) 113.
10 1922 SC 174 and see *Hoare & Co v McAlpine* [1923] 1 Ch 167.
11 1984 SLT 13 appealed and terms of interdict modified 1985 SLT 361. See also as to vibration *Hoare & Co v McAlpine* [1923] 1 Ch 167; *M'Ewan v Steedman and M'Alister* 1912 SC 156.

doing. In *Duke of Richmond v Lossiemouth Burgh*[12] the discharge of sewage into the sea, to the prejudice of salmon fishings, was restrained by interdict. But where objection was taken to the proposed construction of a sewage scheme, with outflow into a stream from which cattle drank, and an anticipated nuisance was averred it was held that the averments fell short of showing that the defender's operations would necessarily create a common law nuisance.[13] The cause or original source of the pollution is immaterial.[14] A plea that all reasonable steps have been taken to remedy the pollution has been held irrelevant. A proprietor may not introduce into a stream as it flows through his land any impurity or artificial matter such as refuse from a dye works and it must be permitted to flow through the land in the same state as it was before.[15] The pollution, to be actionable, must cause material injury and the size of the stream may be relevant as also the quality of the water before pollution. It is not necessary that the pollution should cause injury to health. Thus in *Dumfries and Maxwelltown Water-Works Commissioners v M'Culloch*[16] sheep, after being dipped, were washed in a loch from which the Town drew its water supply. It was held that there had been pollution, although this was not proved to be deleterious to health. In *Fleming v Gemmill*[17] where pollution of a stream occurred by the respondent's tenants improperly discharging sewage into drains designed to receive only waste water, the landlord was held liable on the ground that misuse of the drains by his tenants could have reasonably been anticipated. A right to pollute water in a loch or stream in a particular manner, and to a certain extent, may be acquired by prescription. Where that occurs the primary use of the water (e.g. for drinking) may be taken away, leaving only a right to a secondary purpose.[18] In such event the proprietor who has acquired the right by prescription may not increase the level of pollution nor introduce a new kind of pollution if, by so doing, he destroys the lower proprietor's secondary purpose.[19]

The penal provisions of the Rivers (Prevention of Pollution) (Scotland) Acts 1951 and 1965, in respect of the pollution offences

---

12 (1905) 12 SLT 166.
13 *Gavin v Ayrshire County Council* 1950 SC 197.
14 *Scott v Scott* (1881) 8 R 851; *Dodd v Hilson* (1874) 1 R 527.
15 *Elderslie Estates v Gryfe Tannery Ltd* 1959 SLT (Notes) 71; *Duke of Buccleuch v Cowan* (1866) 5 M 214; *Rigby & Beardmore v Downie* (1872) 10 M 568; *Robertson v Stewarts and Livingston* (1878) 11 M 189; *Caledonian Railway Company v Baird & Company* (1876) 3 R 839; *M'Gavin v M'Intyre Bros* (1890) 17 R 818; *Fleming v Gemmill* 1908 SC 340.
16 (1874) 1 R 975.
17 See fn 15 above.
18 *Duke of Buccleuch v Cowan* (above) but see *Portobello v Edinburgh Magistrates* (1882) 10 R 130.
19 *Ewen v Turnbull's Trustees* (1857) 19 D 513.

created by these statutes, do not deprive an aggrieved party of the civil remedy of interdict.

Pollution of the air

Interdict may be granted to any occupier of land against those who allow an unreasonable amount of impurities to escape into the atmosphere and so cause perceptible unpleasantness or injury to health or property.[20] The cases in which this ground of action has been established are numerous and include a wide variety of nuisance elements such as sewage,[1] smoke,[2] chemical fumes,[3] heat and infectious germs[4] but not the establishment of a hospital for infectious diseases, even in a populous urban area. As with nuisance by noise and vibration, the factors to be considered include the distance of the complainer's property from the source of the alleged pollution, the locality and nature of the environment and the degree of inconvenience, unpleasantness or injury occasioned. A special factor may be the direction of the prevailing wind. The question of whether the operation of special types of industrial works, for example a brick kiln, may constitute a common law nuisance depends upon the location and local circumstances.[5]

Nuisance arising from misuse of the highway and foreshore

Where a person by his use of the highway on foot or with animals or in a vehicle creates a nuisance, interdict may be granted in favour of the occupiers fronting the highway.[6] The use of the public highway in a manner which interferes with the public right to use it or with the free movement of workers proceeding to and from their place of work may be actionable.[7] Similarly where an adjacent occupier by his act or neglect interferes with the public use of the highway, an action will lie

---

20 *Robertson v Stewarts and Livingston* (1872) 11 M 189.
1 *Hands v Perth County Council* (1959) 75 Sh Ct Rep 173; *Mackay v Greenhill* (1858) 20 D 1251.
2 *Laing v Muirhead* (1822) 2 S 73.
3 *Fraser's Trustees v Cran* (1877) 4 R 794; *Shotts Iron Company v Inglis* (1882) 9 R (HL) 78; *Fleming v Hislop* (1886) 13 R (HL) 43; *Ben Nevis Distillery (Fort William) v North British Aluminium Company* 1948 SC 592; *Halsey v Esso Petroleum Company* [1961] 2 All ER 145.
4 *Mutter v Fyfe* (1848) 11 D 303; *Metropolitan Asylum District Managers v Hill* (1881) 6 App Cas 193.
5 *Donald v Humphrey* (1839) 1 D 1184; for an extensive citation of such cases see *Burn Murdoch on Interdict* para 230 (Note 29).
6 *Slater v A & J M'Lellan* 1924 SC 854 (garden and house damaged by fire on vehicle); *Ogston v Aberdeen District Tramways Co* (1896) | 24 R (HL) 8 (horses injured by salt placed on roadway); but see *Fergusson v Pollok* (1901) 3 F 1140 (no appreciable risk from a rifle range); *Hay v Leslie* (1896) 4 SLT 124 (traction engine blowing off steam).
7 See *Thomas v NUM (South Wales Area)* [1985] 2 All ER 1; *Fergusson v Pollok* (above).

at the instance of a road user. Thus where an occupier fronting the highway allowed clouds of steam to be emitted over the highway and caused danger to passing traffic interdict was granted;[8] as also where smoke was allowed to blow across a public road[9] and where a branch of a tree projected across the road.[10] But in *Central Motors (St Andrews) Ltd v St Andrews Magistrates*[11] where a Lammas Fair was held under authority of a Royal Charter granted in 1620 and had been enlarged by prescriptive use to an extent that traffic congestion was caused in the streets of a burgh, interdict was refused.

Slates left in the gutter and an unlighted vehicle left in the roadway (if it constitutes a dangerous obstruction) have been held to constitute nuisance where they caused danger to road users.[12]

Members of the public have the right to use the foreshore for recreation and for access and interference with that right may be actionable.[13]

Miscellaneous common law nuisances

Numerous other activities by proprietors, occupiers of land and others may constitute a nuisance when they create discomfort, inconvenience or danger to a material extent. Creating discomfort by excessive heat from a boiler flue;[14] allowing sulphur-impregnated fumes from a gas water heater to escape into a vent in a mutual gable;[15] constructing a mill lade immediately adjacent to a public green;[16] keeping a brothel;[17] the construction of a urinal by a local authority;[18] storing offensive materials[19] have all been held to be common law nuisances and have been restrained by interdict. Likewise the opening of a sex shop, described by the court as a business repugnant to the sensibilities of ordinary men and women, has been restrained.[20]

---

8 *Holling v Yorkshire Traction Company* [1948] 2 All ER 662.
9 *Rollingson v Kerr & Ors* 1958 CLY 2427.
10 *BRS v Slater* [1964] 1 All ER 816 but the defender must be shown to have been aware of nuisance.
11 1961 SLT 290.
12 *Almeroth v Chivers & Sons*[1948] 1 All ER 53; *Parish v Judd* [1960] 3 All ER 33; *Ware v Garston Haulage Co* [1944] KB 30.
13 *Ferguson v Pollock* (above); see also p 48 below.
14 *Wilsons v Brydone* (1877) 14 SLR 667; *Johnston v Constable* (1841) 3 D 1263.
15 *Watt v Jamieson* 1954 SC 56.
16 *Stevenson v Hawick Magistrates* (1871) 9 M 753.
17 *Thomson-Schwab v Costaki* [1956] 1 All ER 652; *Bell's Principles* s 974.
18 *Adam and Spowart v Alloa Police Commissioners* (1874) 2 R 143.
19 *Manson v Forrest* (1887) 14 R 802.
20 *Laws v Florinplace Ltd* [1981] 1 All ER 659.

Nuisance arising from playing of games

The playing of lawful games, while creating a duty of care on the part of the players for the safety of members of the public, may also, on the gound of nuisance, give rise to an action of interdict against the managing body of a club or other organisation. But when balls were occasionally hit out of a cricket ground and one passed over a seven foot fence and struck the plaintiff 100 yards away, the action was dismissed on the ground the risk was small and the chance of injury remote.[1] Where golf balls were driven outside the golf links and on to adjoining footpaths and lanes where pedestrians were struck and injured, the owners of the links were found liable in damages.[2]

Statutory nuisance

Various statutes declare certain kinds of conduct and operations to be, when proved, statutory nuisances. Thus under the Public Health (Scotland) Act 1897, where a nuisance, as defined by s 16, is found to exist, the local authority may by a civil process require the owner or occupier of premises to remedy the situation or may itself remove the cause of the nuisance. The Act specifically reserves (s 171) the common law remedies available to an aggrieved person and an action of interdict at the instance of that person would therefore be competent. Where a local authority obtains an order for removal of a nuisance under the Act, appeal will lie only to the Court of Session.[3] Examples of nuisances declared by statute are also to be found in the Noise Abatement Act 1960, the Merchant Shipping (Oil Pollution) Act 1971, the Prevention of Oil Pollution Act 1971, the Deposit of Poisonous Waste Act 1972, the Control of Pollution Act 1974, the Coal Mines Refuse Act 1952 and the Clean Air Acts 1956 and 1968.

Conventional nuisance

Where, in a contract, restrictions are imposed against the use of premises in such a way as to create a nuisance, failure to comply with the restrictions imposed may be restrained by interdict.[4] The nuisance may be one defined and established by the terms of the contract and in that event need not necessarily be a nuisance at common law.[5] If not so defined by the contract, it must be shown that the act prohibited would

---

1 *Bolton v Stone* [1951] AC 850.
2 *M'Leod v St Andrews Magistrates* 1924 SC 960; see also *Lamond v Corporation of Glasgow* 1968 SLT 291.
3 *Wright v Kennedy* 1946 JC 142.
4 *Bell's Principles* s 974; *Manson v Forrest* (1887) 14 R 802; but see *Botanic Gardens Picture House v Adamson* 1924 SC 549; *Fergusson v M'Culloch* 1953 SLT (Sh Ct) 113.
5 *Anderson v Aberdeen Agricultural Hall Company* (1879) 6 R 901 at 904.

be a nuisance at common law.[6] In the case of feuing restrictions and conditions questions may arise as to whether a third party seeking to interdict a breach of the restrictions or conditions and not having a *jus quaesitum tertio* may sue an action of interdict.[7]

2 DEFENCES TO INTERDICT AGAINST NUISANCE

Prescription

The right to object to a nuisance may be cut off by the operation of the negative prescription where the nuisance has continued without interruption for, and no objection has been made within, the negative prescriptive period of 20 years.[8] In such circumstances, operations constituting nuisance may be continued but only to the extent that they existed at the expiry of the prescriptive period. Any extension of the nuisance, or introduction of a fresh nuisance stemming from the same source, will nullify the prescriptive right.[9] Thus in *M'Intyre Bros v M'Gavin*[10] factory owners, who had acquired a prescriptive right to take pure water from a stream at a particular place and in a particular way and thereafter restore it to the stream in a polluted form, were held not entitled to take the water at any other place or in any other way, if the effect would be to increase the pollution of the stream. The negative prescription cannot run from a date prior to that on which the nuisance becomes apparent or could reasonably have been ascertained.[11]

Acquiescence[12]

Where the nuisance has existed for a time shorter than the negative prescription period of 20 years, objection and any action of interdict may still be barred if the complainer has unequivocally acquiesced in the continuation of the nuisance. There must however be some act by the complainer expressly or clearly implying acceptance of the nuisance. In *Houldsworth v Wishaw Burgh Comrs of Police*,[13] a case involving discharge of sewage on to the complainer's land, where the

---

6 *Fergusson v M'Culloch* 1953 SLT (Sh Ct) 113.
7 *Hislop v M'Ritchie's Trustees* (1880) 8 R (HL) 95; *N B Railway Company v Moore* (1891) 18 R 1021.
8 *Rigby & Beardmore v Downie* (1872) 10 M 568 at 573; *Midlothian County Council v Oakbank Oil Company* (1904) 6 F 387 at 397; Prescription and Limitation (Scotland) Act 1973 s 25.
9 *Rigby & Beardmore v Downie* above.
10 (1890) 20 R (HL) 49 at 52 per Lord Watson.
11 *Liverpool Corporation v Coghill & Son* [1918] 1 Ch 307.
12 See further as to Acquiescence at p 19 above.
13 (1887) 14 R 920; *Bargaddie Coal Co v Wark* (1859) 3 MacQ 467, HL; *Hill v Dixon* (1850) 12 D 808.

discharge had been greatly increased; and in *Hill v Dixson*[14] where a railway line was laid across a highway, it was held that there had been no acquiescence. Acquiescence may bar objection to nuisance where the complainer, having knowledge of the contravention of his rights, allows the other party to execute works which it would be impossible or at least difficult to undo.[15] A singular successor may be barred from objecting to works consented to by his predecessor as in *Muirhead v Glasgow Highland Society*.[16] Where there had been consent to operations and an agreement entered into, works in excess of the agreement were objected to and a plea of acquiescence by the complainer was repelled.[17] The plea of acquiescence to the nuisance is more likely to be applicable where the thing acquiesced in is visible and obvious.[18]

Licence and statutory authority

Where a statute grants certain powers, authority to do those acts, indispensible to the exercise of these powers, is likewise granted by implication.[19]

> When Parliament has given express powers to construct certain buildings or works according to plans and specifications upon a particular site and for a specific purpose, the use of these works or buildings in the manner contemplated and sanctioned by the Act, cannot, except in so far as negligent, be restrained by injunction, although such use may constitute a nuisance at common law.[20]

But the statutory powers may be exercised only for the purpose for which they were granted and must be executed by the authorised body or public or local authority with proper skill and diligence. In *Gillespie v Lucas and Aird* where, under statutory powers, blasting operations were undertaken for the construction of a railway, interdict was granted to prevent blasting on a scale likely to cause damage to a neighbouring cottage occupied by the complainer.[1]

The granting of a planning permission for the particular use of premises does not imply a right to create a nuisance in the operation of such use or in the implementation of the planning permission. Similarly

---

14 Fn 13 above.
15 *Shaw v Applegate* [1978] 1 All ER 123.
16 *Muirhead v Glasgow Highland Society* (1864) 2 M 420; *Bicket v Morris* (1866) 4 M (HL) 44 at 47 per Lord Chancellor; *Macgregor v Balfour* (1899) 2 F 345 at 352; *Colville v Middleton* 29 May 1817 FC and *Muirhead v Glasgow Highland Society* above at 427 per Lord Deas.
17 *Hill v Wood* (1863) 1 M 360.
18 Fn 16 above.
19 *Maxwell on the Interpretation of Statutes* (12th edn).
20 *Metropolitan Asylum District Managers v Hill* (1881) 6 App Cas 193 at 211 per Lord Watson.
1 (1893) 20 R 1035.

the granting of a licence by a local authority for the sale of excisable liquor, or for the conduct of a betting office, or the operating of gaming machines, under the Licensing (Scotland) Act 1976 and the Betting, Gaming and Lotteries Act 1963, carries no licence to create a nuisance greater than that necessary and incidental to the use for the purpose licensed.[2]

Coming to the nuisance

It is now settled that there is no obligation to tolerate a nuisance where an adjacent proprietor has commenced the nuisance prior to the complainer acquiring his property. The plea, which found support in earlier Scots cases, is now of little consequence. In *Fleming v Heslop*,[3] Lord Halsbury disposed of the matter thus, 'It is clear that whether the man went to the nuisance or the nuisance came to the man, the rights are the same.'

Public interest

Where the effect of interdict would be to create great and immediate public inconvenience, the court has power to make a declaratory finding that a nuisance exists but to suspend the imposition of interdict pending the carrying out of remedial measures. A proof of the complainer's averments, before answer, will frequently be required before suspension or interdict is considered. Similar considerations may apply where interdict would materially affect the production of a major or vital product.[4] But a mere allegation of loss to the respondent will not suffice to defeat or suspend a petition for interdict.[5] In considering the question of public interest and the importance thereof, the court is exercising an equitable jurisdiction. It must have careful regard to the effect which interdict would have upon the legitimate interests of the respondent and also upon the general public. The cases fall into two categories, namely either (a) those where the interdict would be attended by consequences to the respondent as injurious, or more so, than the wrong complained of by the petitioners, or (b) where the interdict would cause great and immediate public inconvenience.[6] Whether this general rule falls to be applied in any given case is a matter for consideration after the facts have been ascertained and after a declaratory finding that a nuisance exists. Unless both these

2 *Walker on Delict* (2nd edn) p 971.
3 (1886) 13 R (HL) 43 at 49.
4 *Ben Nevis Distillery (Fort William) v North British Aluminium Co* 1948 SC 592.
5 *Shotts Iron Co v Inglis* (1882) 9 R (HL) 78 at 89; *Watt v Jamieson* 1954 SC 56.
6 *Clippens Oil Co v Edinburgh and District Water Trustees* (1897) 25 R 370 at 383 per Lord MacLaren; affirmed in *Ben Nevis Distillery (Fort William) v North British Aluminium Co* above; but see *Elderslie Estates v Gryfe Tannery Ltd* 1959 SLT (Notes) 71.

conditions are satisfied the question of exercising this special jurisdiction does not properly arise (per Lord President Cooper in *Ben Nevis Distillery (Fort William) Ltd v North British Aluminium Co Ltd*).[7] It is not possible *ab ante* to predict merely from an examination of averments whether a proper case for the exercise of that special jurisdiction will eventually be made.

Normal and familiar use of property

Generally speaking, a plea that a respondent, in creating a nuisance, is merely making normal and familiar use of his property, is irrelevant. The balance in such cases has to be held between the freedom of a proprietor to use his property as he pleases, and the duty on one proprietor not to inflict material loss or inconvenience on adjoining proprietors. In every case the answer must depend upon fact and degree.[8] If the acts complained of arise from actings necessary in the common and ordinary use of lands and houses, a complainer may have no redress by way of interdict.[9] Actings which, if continued or prolonged, might be actionable as a nuisance, may be done with impunity if they are merely occasional or temporary and incidental to the normal use of the property.[10] Repairs to property, reconstruction and partial demolition will not be actionable, provided they are carried out with reasonable skill and reasonable precautions are taken to minimise the disturbance of neighbours.[11]

Possibility of remedial measures

Where the court is satisfied that remedial measures to mitigate or nullify the nuisance are possible, the defender may be given the opportunity to execute the necessary works at the sight of the court. The matter may be referred to a man of skill for opinion upon the proposed remedial measures. The grant of interim interdict may sometimes be suspended pending assessment of the results of the remedial measures by the man of skill. In some cases the court may make a declaratory finding that a nuisance exists and postpone the grant of interdict.[12] In *Fleming v Gemmill*[13] where drains had been improperly installed by a proprietor, a nuisance was declared to exist but interdict was deferred to allow submission of a scheme to obviate

---

7 Ibid.
8 *Watt v Jamieson* 1954 SC 56 at 58 per Lord President Cooper.
9 *Fleming v Hislop* (1886) 13 R (HL) 43 at 49; *Robertson v Stewarts and Livingston* (1872) 11 M 189.
10 *Walker on Delict* (2nd edn) p 973.
11 *Harrison v Southwark and Vauxhall Water Co* [1891] 2 Ch 409.
12 *Hands v Perth County Council* (1959) 75 Sh Ct Rep 173.
13 1908 SC 340.

pollution from the drains. And in *M'Ewen v Steedman & M'Alister*[14] where a gas engine caused vibration and the defenders effected remedial measures, the court remitted to a man of skill to report on the efficacy of the measures.

Judicial undertakings to modify nuisance

Occasionally simple undertakings to modify buildings or works from which nuisance is anticipated may be accepted by the court. In *Manson v Forrest*[15] where the defender, who proposed to erect a byre for cows in an urban area, had given an undertaking as to the nature of the construction, the management of the cows and preparation of food, interdict was refused but the terms of the undertaking were incorporated in to the interlocutor so that the conduct of affairs could be monitored.

In *Elderslie Estates v Gryfe Tannery Ltd* a plea that all resonable steps had been taken to remedy pollution but these had proved largely ineffective was held irrelevant.[16]

3 INTERDICT AGAINST ENCROACHMENT UPON HERITABLE PROPERTY AND RIGHTS OF SUPPORT

The nature of encroachment

Encroachment differs from trespass in that, while the latter represents an intrusion of a temporary nature, the former amounts to some permanent deprivation of a person's free and legal use of his property. Encroachment is defined by *Hume*[17] as consisting in 'the permanent usurpation by another of some portion of a man's land which deprives him of the free use of it for the future'.

Where encroachment occurs this in itself may be sufficient in Scotland to justify action, and averment of existing loss or damage to the pursuer is unnecessary, provided there remains the possibility of such loss or damage occurring in the future. The principle was expressed by Lord Blackburn in *Orr Ewing (Archibald & Co) v Colquhoun's Trustees*[18] thus:

> The Court of Session in its equitable exercise of its jurisdiction would not order the removal of the erection if convinced that the damage was only nominal but where there is injury to the proprietory rights in running

14 1912 SC 156 and 1913 SC 761.
15 (1887) 14 R 802.
16 1959 SLT (Notes) 71.
17 Lectures III 202.
18 (1887) 4 R (HL) 116 at 126.

streams, the present injury producing no damage, may hereafter produce much. Where the intrusion is a present sensible injury to the proprietory right of the owner of the other part of the *alveus* or of the opposite bank of a running stream he may have it removed if it is impossible to predicate that it may not produce serious damage in future, though the complaining party is not yet in a position to quantify the present damage.

If unlawful encroachment is threatened or, having been completed, continues despite protest, an action of interdict is competent. The major forms of encroachment are by mining and quarrying; by the withdrawal of support for a neighbour's land or buildings, unless authorised by contrast; by abstraction of water and interference with the flow of rivers and streams; and by actings which restrict another's enjoyment of a servitude right.

Miscellaneous encroachments

Apart from major encroachments of the foregoing nature, numerous other *ex facie* minor activities have been held to be encroachments and may be restrained by interdict. Thus a proprietor may not construct or add to a building on his land so that part of the building projects over his neighbour's property;[19] tree roots must not be allowed to penetrate beneath a neighbour's property;[20] nor must rubbish be dumped on a neighbour's property;[1] and soil from subsidence must not be allowed to flow on to the neighbour's land. In the absence of a servitude right of support, shoring timbers may not be allowed to rest on a neighbour's property. Constructing a vent through an upper storey and attaching a flue to an outside gable have been held actionable, as also the erection of a sign over a common entrance or to a neighbour's property; the swinging of the jib of a tower crane over the pursuer's property;[2] and occupying land included in a neighbour's title but not in the occupier's.[3]

Encroachment on burial grounds

In the case of burial grounds, whether public grounds owned and operated by local authorities or by commercial undertakings, or churchyard burial grounds vested in the Kirk Sessions, the owners of lairs may by interdict prevent encroachment upon their lairs but not

---

19 *M'Intosh v Scott* (1859) 21 D 363; *Leonard v Lindsay & Benzie* (1886) 13 R 958; *Rankine on Land Ownership* (4th edn) p 134.
20 *McCombe v Read* [1955] 2 QB 429; *Davey v Harrow Corpn* [1957] 2 All ER 305, *Rankine* p 633.
1 *Whitwham v Westminster Brymbo Coal & Coke Co* [1896] 1 Ch 894.
2 *Brown v Lee Constructions Ltd* 1977 SLT (Notes) 61.
3 *Nicol v Blott* 1986 SLT 677.

the simple enclosure of lairs by kerbstone or railing.[4] The alternation of the burial ground by the owners acting *ultra vires* may be prevented[5] and in the carrying out of necessary works and maintenance violation of the graves must be avoided.[6] Building over or above privately owned lairs may be restrained.[7] For a full discourse on rights in burial grounds see *Burn-Murdoch on Interdict*,[8] the Burial Grounds (Scotland) Act 1855 and the Local Government (Scotland) Act 1973.

Right of support

Where there are no buildings erected on his land, the landowner has generally an absolute right to support of his land at its natural level.[9] But in *Edinburgh and District Water Trustees v Clippens Oil Co Ltd*[10] the opinion was expressed that the proprietor of heath land had no such absolute right.

Mining operations

Where the owner of minerals lying beneath the surface (being the superior) mines them under reserved powers in a feu disposition, and there is threatened damage to the surface buildings belonging to the vassal by loss of support, the mining operations cannot be restrained by interdict.[11] Apart from cases governed by contract, however, it matters not whether there has been negligence in the execution of the mining operations. If support is withdrawn and subsidence or a real threat of subsidence occurs, the right of support has been encroached upon.[12]

Different considerations apply (a) where, having disposed of or leased the minerals, the surface owner subsequently erects buildings over the workings and (b) where he dispones or leases the minerals, and buildings have already been erected over the site of the workings. In the former case the mineral operator is liable only for such damage as could reasonably have been in the contemplation of parties.[13] In the

---

4 *M'Bean v Young* (1859) 21 D 314; *Heritors of Bathgate v Russell* (1908) 16 SLT 210 and 646.
5 *Russell v Marquess of Bute* (1882) 10 R 302.
6 *Robertson v Salmon* (1868) 5 SLR 405.
7 *Wilson v Brown & Gibson*(1859) 21 D 1060; *Hill v Wood* (1863) 1 M 360.
8 Para 241 ff.
9 *Caledonian Railway Co v Sprot* (1856) 2 Macq 449, HL; *White v Dixon* (1883) 10 R (HL) 45 at 46. See also for a different view in special circumstances *Bank of Scotland v Stewart* (1891) 18 R 957.
10 (1900) 3 F 156 at 175.
11 *Buchanan and Henderson & Dimmack v Andrew* (1872) 11 M (HL) 13.
12 *Neill's Trustees v Dixon* (1880) 7 R 741 at 746 per Lord Ormidale; see also *Barr v Baird & Co* (1904) 6 F 524; distinguishing *White v Dixon* above and *Aspden v Seddon* (1875) 10 Ch App 394; and *Dryburgh v Fife Coal Co* (1905) 7 F 1083.
13 *Angus v NCB* 1955 SC 175.

latter case, in the absence of express provision in a contract, the surface owner has no natural right of support and his remedy will depend upon the existence or otherwise of a positive servitude granted expressly or by implication, or upon the doctrine of mutual forbearance as in common property. The doctrine of mutual forbearance has been expressed thus:

> In every case where the landed or surface estate is separated from the underground or mineral estate, the parties must always be, unless otherwise provided by express stipulation, subject to mutual forbearance. The owner of the upper or landed estate must not so use it as to entirely prohibit or destroy the use of the underground or mineral estate to the owner thereof. And neither ought the latter carry on his workings so as to render useless the right of the owner of the surface. This is a mutual obligation necessarily resulting from the division of the two estates and must be governed very much by the principles which are applicable to the enjoyment of common property.[14]

Numerous wrongs, apart from actual withdrawal of support, may arise from mining operations and questions may arise with the owner of the surface land or with the owners or tenants of the minerals beneath or with the owner or tenants of adjoining lands.

Thus, where one mine owner carried out subterranean blasting operations of extraordinary power close to the boundary between two mines and an inrush of water threatened dislocation of the mineral strata, interdict was granted.[15] Where separate grants of two adjacent workings of coal and fireclay were made and neither could be worked without interference with the other, interdict was granted against the tenant of the later lease.[16] Interdict has been granted in several cases involving the rights of mineral owners whose seams require 'working to the dip' and those whose seams involve what is known as 'working to the rise'. For a full discussion of these problems, most of which concern the disposal of accumulated water, both surface and subterranean, see the undernoted cases.[17]

Other problems which arise from the presence of water in mineral workings include the natural flow or artificial abstraction of water into mines and the discharging of surface water, both on the surface and underground. With the development of modern methods of mining such occurrences are less frequent. The principles which apply are

---

14 *Rankine on Land Ownership* (4th edn) p 495.
15 *Durham v Hood* (1871) 9 M 474.
16 *Shawsrigg Fireclay and Enamelling Co v Larkhall Collieries* (1903) 5 F 1131.
17 *Baird v Monkland Iron and Steel Co* (1862) 24 D 1418; *Harvey v Wardrop* (1824) 3 S 322; *Wilson v Waddell* (1876) 4 R (HL) 29.

explained in *Blair v Hunter Finlay & Co*,[18] *Irving v Leadhills Mining Co*,[19] *Milton v Glen-Moray Glenlivet Distillery Co Ltd*[20] and *Young & Co v Bankier Distillery Co*.[1]

The rights of mine operators to carry minerals from one mine to another by means of underground roads have been restrained by interdict where interference with surface or strata was apprehended.[2]

Under the Mines (Working Facilities and Support) Act 1966, where it is expedient in the national interest that specified minerals be worked but it is not reasonably possible to secure agreement between the parties concerned, the Court of Session may make an order permitting the working and establishing ancillary rights, including specific power to let down the surface, if necessary, for the exploitation of the minerals.

The Coal Industry Nationalisation Act 1946 s 48(1) provides that liabilities to which, apart from that section, colliery concerns would be subject for breaches of right of support, being breaches arising from acts or omissions done or occurring in the course of colliery activities, shall, in any case, where the course of action in respect of the breach of the right of support occurred on or after the primary vesting date, be enforceable against the National Coal Board as if the acts or omissions in question has been those of the Board and not those of the colliery concerns. The 'right of support' being an incidence of property applies only to the surface property and not to personal claims.[3]

Apart from the questions of restraint by interdict, a landowner whose property is damaged by subsidence caused by mineral workings has statutory claims for compensation under the Mines (Working Facilities and Support) Act 1966, the Coal Mining (Subsidence) Act 1950 s 1 and the Coal Mining (Subsidence) Act 1957. Special considerations apply in respect of damage, actual or apprehended, and on the question of interdict where the surface has been particularly heavily loaded as for example by railways[4], reservoirs, tanks,[5] water, gas[6] and sewage pipes[7] and similar constructions.[8]

In the case of railways, the majority of which are constructed under

---

18 (1870) 9 M 204.
19 (1856) 18 D 833.
20 (1898) 1 F 135 (sinking of well for distillery).
1 (1893) 20 R (HL) 76·
2 *Ramsay and Alloa Coal Co v Blair* (1876) 3 R (HL) 41; *Graham v Duke of Hamilton* (1868) 6 M 965.
3 *Angus v National Coal Board* 1955 SC 175 at 181.
4 *Dixon v Caledonian and Glasgow and South Western Ry Companies* (1880) 7 R (HL)116; *NB Railway Co v Turnets Ltd* (1904) 6 F 900.
5 *Clippens Oil Co v Edinburgh & District Water Trustees* (1903) 6 F (HL) 7.
6 *Mid & East Calder Gas-Light Co v Oakbank Oil Co* (1891) 18 R 788.
7 *Midlothian County Council v NCB* (1960) SC 308.
8 *Forth Conservancy Board v Russell 1946 SN 85 (support of sea wall)*.

the Railway Clauses Consolidation (Scotland) Act 1845 and special Acts incorporating the clauses of the 1845 Act, minerals under land acquired by a railway company are excepted from acquisition, unless specifically and separately purchased. A railway company may by notice exercise a statutory right to purchase the minerals on payment of compensation. If the company fails to exercise this right it cannot, at a later date, by interdict prevent the working of the minerals under the line or other land acquired.[9]

Rights not extinguished by prescription or acquiescence

While the natural right of support and the positive servitude of support may be lost by express contractual renunciation, they cannot be extinguished by the operation of the negative prescription or acquiescence. Although such pleas may involve certain elements in claims for damages, the right to restrain operations by interdict will remain in consequence of the continuing presence of the legal rights.[10]

Support of pipe lines

Where the right to lay pipe lines on or beneath land is acquired by voluntary conveyance or statutory authority, the pipe operator has an implied right to have them reasonably supported.[11]

But where gas pipes were laid over land and the pipe operators did not acquire the property on the land, it was held the operator could not restrain the ordinary working of minerals beneath the surface, even though this might cause subsidence and damage to the gas pipes. In *Clippens Oil Co Ltd v Edinburgh and District Water Trustees*[12] where the water authority attempted illegally to lay water pipes outwith the statutory limits of deviation they were restrained by interdict notwithstanding the pipes were only laid *pendente lite*.

Operations under the Pipe Lines Act 1962

In the case of crosscountry pipe lines (being those in excess of 10 miles) and certain local pipe lines, excluding gas, electricity and atomic energy and railway undertakers, the law in regard to the maintenance thereof, and the rights of parties arising from their operation, is now largely codified in the Pipe Lines Act 1962. It is unlawful for works to be executed on any land for the purpose of constructing any crosscountry pipe line to which the Act applies, except under a Pipe Line

---

9 *Caledonian Railway Co v Henderson* (1876) 4 R 140.
10 *Rankine on Land Ownership* (4th edn) p 505.
11 *Mid & East Calder Gas-Light Co v Oakbank Oil Co* (1891) 18 R 788.
12 (1897) 25 R 370.

Construction Authorisation granted by the Secretary of State for Energy, and within the limits of deviation laid down in the authorisation.[13] Works undertaken with local pipe lines (being less than 10 miles in length) to which the Act applies, require prior notice to and approval by the Secretary of State.[14] Where pipe line works have been unlawfully executed the operator may by notice be required to remove them. Entry upon land for the purpose of removal, either by the operator or by the Secretary of State, is illegal unless there has been prior consultation with the owner or lessee of the land.[15] Failing such consultation, entry could be restrained by interdict.

Where a compulsory purchase order has been made for the acquisition of land for a pipe line construction, a person aggrieved may apply to the Court of Session questioning the validity of the Order and seeking restraint on the operation and the court may make an interim order suspending the compulsory purchase order, pending final determination of the action.[16]

Where a building is erected within 10 feet of a buried pipe line to which the 1962 Act applies, without the consent of the Secretary of State, the party erecting it may be required, by notice from the Secretary of State, to demolish the building. If he fails to do so, the Secretary of State may enter upon the land and demolish the building. Any questions arising from these provisions are to be decided by the Sheriff.[17]

Where a person formulates proposals for pipe line works, to which the Act applies, the Secretary of State, in considering the same, is required to take into account a wide variety of matters relating to amenity conservation, protection of historic buildings, possibility of pollution of water and the restoration of agricultural land.

Nothing in the Pipe Lines Act 1962 or any compulsory rights order made thereunder will exonerate a person from any action for nuisance[18] by way of interdict or otherwise.

Support of adjacent buildings

Where two buildings are separated by a common gable, each property is subject to a servitude right of support in favour of the other property. Neither proprietor may demolish or interfere with the gable in a manner which would deprive the adjoining building of its support

---

13 Pipe Lines Act 1962 (c 58) s 1.
14 Ibid s 2.
15 Ibid s 4.
16 Ibid Sch 2, para 9(1).
17 Ibid s 28(5)(c), s 69.
18 Ibid.

from the common gable[19] and operations reasonably apprehended to cause loss of support may be restrained by interdict.

Similarly, in the case of property consisting of two or more flats the proprietors have a common interest in the roof, gables and walls. A lower proprietor may be prevented from carrying out operations on walls or gables external or internal but only where these operations would have the effect of endangering the support of the upper flats.[20] Reasonable apprehension of damage by an upper proprietor is enough to warrant action.[1]

4 INTERDICT AGAINST ENCROACHMENT UPON WATER RIGHTS AND THE FORESHORE

Navigable rivers

Navigable rivers are vested in the Crown, subject to the public right of navigation and transport of goods upstream, so far as practicable, and not merely within the tidal reaches.[2] Interference with the public right of navigation in public rivers may be restrained by interdict[3] at the instance of any member of the public whose right has been encroached upon.[4] In so far as it restricts the public right of navigation, the construction of buildings in the *alveus* of a river may be prevented[5] and similarly with bridges which obstruct the passage of the river.[6]

In the upper reaches beyond the tidal limit, the banks of the river belong to the riparian proprietors and thus use by the public for trout fishing may be prevented by interdict.[7] When use by custom of a tow path was established interdict was refused but the existence of a tow path does not of itself entitle the public to fish for trout therefrom.

Boats may be moored at the banks only where this is incidental to the right of navigation and the attachment of rafts and pleasure boats may be restrained.[8] In *Burton's Trustees v Scottish Sports Council*[9] where it was

19 *Bell's Principles* p 1001.
20 *Dennistoun v Bell and Brown* (1824) 2 S 784; *Brown v Boyd* (1841) 3 D 1205.
1 *M'Kean v Davidson* (1823) 2 S 480; *Johnston v White* (1877) 4 R 721 at 724 per Lord Shand.
2 *Colquhoun v Duke of Montrose* (1801) 4 Pat 221; *Bowie v Marquis of Ailsa* (1887) 14 R 649 at 667.
3 *Orr Ewing & Co v Colquhoun's Trustees* (1877) 4 R (HL) 116.
4 *Slater v M'Lellan* 1924 SC 854.
5 *Earl of Breadalbane v Colquhoun's Trustees* (1881) 18 SLR 607; cf *N B Railway Company v Perth Magistrates* (1885) 13 R (HL) 37; *Orr Ewing & Co v Colquhoun's Trustees* (above).
6 *M'Intyre's Trustees v Cupar-Fife Magistrates* (1867) 5 M 780; cf *Hagart v Fyfe* (1870) 9 M 127.
7 *Carron v Ogilvie* (1806) 5 Pat 61; *Grant v Henry* (1894) 21 R 358.
8 *Campbell's Trustees v Sweeney* 1911 SC 1319; cf *Leith-Buchanan v Hogg* 1931 SC 204.
9 1983 SLT 418. See also *Wills' Trustees v Cairngorm Canoeing and Sailing School* 1976 SC (HL) 30.

alleged that canoeing activities were injurious to fishings, interim interdict was refused pending a possible proof.

Rights in the foreshore

The foreshore, being all land between high and low water marks, is vested in the Crown in trust for the public use. The rights of the Crown may however be alienated by grant to a subject.[10] The position of land held in Udal Tenure is discussed in *Smith v Lerwick Harbour Trustees*.[11] Right to the foreshore may also be acquired by prescriptive possession following on a Crown grant of lands adjoining the foreshore. The public may use the foreshore for navigation[12] and for recreation.[13] This may include the shooting of wildfowl, but the creation of a nature reserve under the National Parks and Access to the Countryside Act 1949 and bye laws made thereunder may limit this and other public rights in the foreshore.[14] The public also have a right to white fishing and to use the foreshore for this purpose and to take shellfish.[15]

The rights of the public to navigation are not affected where the Crown alienates the foreshore and the public right of recreation may also be preserved where it has been enjoyed by prescriptive custom.[16]

Salmon fishings, mussel and oyster beds are part of the Crown property[17] and may also be alienated. These rights are personal to the Crown and are not held in trust for the public.[18] The Crown by virtue of its ownership of salmon fishing from the foreshore has also a right of access to these fishings through land adjoining the foreshore.[19] In *Buckhaven and Methil Magistrates v Wemyss Coal Co*[20] the title of the Lord Advocate to protect by interdict the rights of the public was suggested *obiter*. Individual members of the public have no title to sue actions of interdict relating to rights held by the Crown except those relating to the public rights of recreation and of navigation.[1]

---

10 *Agnew v Lord Advocate* (1873) 11 M 309.
11 (1903) 5 F 680.
12 *Agnew* above.
13 *Scott v Dundee Magistrates* (1883) 14 R 191; *Fergusson v Pollok* (1901) 3 F 1140; *Hope v Bennewith* (1904) 6 F 1004 and *Marquis of Bute v M'Kirdy and M'Millan* 1937 SC 93 (where the authorities are extensively reviewed).
14 *Burnet v Barclay* **1955 JC 34.**
15 *M'Douall v Lord Advocate* (1875) 2 R (HL) 49.
16 *Scott v Dundee Magistrates* above.
17 See fn 11 above.
18 *Parker v Lord Advocate* (1904) 6 F (HL) 37.
19 *Lord Advocate v Sharp* (1879) 6 R 108.
20 1932 SC 201 per Lord Sands.
1 *Cameron and Gunn v Ainslie* (1848) 10 D 446; *Lord Advocate v Raynes, Lupton & Co* (1859) 21 D 717.

Non-navigable rivers

Where a river is non-navigable and non-tidal the bed or *alveus* and the banks are the property of the proprietors of the land adjacent. If the river forms the boundary between two or more lands, each proprietor owns the bank *ex adverso* his property and the *alveus* up to the *medium filum*. Any operations by either proprietor upon the bed of the river, even within his own portion, will be actionable by interdict[2] if the operations interfere with the normal flow of the river or there is real apprehension of injury to the banks or any fishing or other rights in the river.[3]

All proprietors having lands fronting the river have a common interest in the water.[4] Any proprietor may abstract water *ex adverso* his lands for ordinary domestic purposes[5] but he may not, except by statutory authority or prescriptive right, impound the water for storage;[6] nor may he abstract water for irrigation or for commercial purposes if the reasonable flow for lower proprietors is thereby reduced or altered in quality.

> A riparian proprietor is entitled to the water of his stream in its natural flow without sensible diminution or increase and without sensible alteration in its character or quality. Any invasion of this right causing actual damage, or calculated to found a claim which may ripen into an adverse right entitles the party injured to the intervention of the court.[7]

The proprietor of salmon fishing in the river may fish from his own bank but if he owns only one bank he may fish only to the *medium filum* unless he has acquired a prescriptive right to fish beyond the *medium filum* or from banks not *ex adverso* of his lands[8] and he may be prevented from interfering with the *alveus*.[9]

A proprietor may not by his operations change the quality of the water which flows to the lower proprietors. Pollution of water which renders it unfit for primary domestic uses or for any special use in which a lower proprietor has been in the habit of employing it, may be prevented by interdict.[10]

---

2 *M'Intyre's Trustees v Cupar-Fife Magistrates* (1867) 5 M 780; *Gibson v Bonnington Sugar Refining Co* (1869) 7 M 394; *Menzies v Marquis of Breadalbane* (1901) 4 F 55.
3 *Bickett v Morris* (1866) 4 M (HL); *Orr Ewing v Colquhoun's Trustees* (1877) 4 R 344; *M'Intyre Bros v M'Gavin* (1890) 20 R (HL) 49; *Ross v Powrie & Pitcaithly* (1891) 19 R 314 at 321; *Gay v Malloch* 1959 SC 110.
4 *Bickett v Morris* above.
5 *Bonthrone v Downie* (1878) 6 R 324; *Cowan v Duke of Buccleuch* (1876) 4 R (HL) 14.
6 *Hunter & Aikenhead v Aitken* (1880) 7 R 510.
7 *Young & Co Bankier Distillery Co* (1893) 20 R (HL) 76 at 78 per Lord Macnaughton.
8 *Earl of Zetland v Tennent's Trustees* (1873) 11 M 469; *Campbell v Muir* 1908 SC 387.
9 *Gay v Malloch* above.
10 *Caledonian Railway Co v Baird & Co* (1876) 3 R 839; *Countess of Seafield v Kemp* (1899) 1 F 402; *Fleming v Gemmill* 1908 SC 340; cf *Armistead v Bowerman* (1888) 15 R 814.

As regards trout fishing, which is a pertenent of the land fronting a loch or river, a right of access to the banks in favour of the public does not confer a right to fish for trout.[11] An agricultural lease, in the absence of express permission, confers no right upon the agricultural tenant to fish for trout in a river or pond.[12]

Right of access to water and streams in the countryside

Where an access agreement or order has been made in respect of an area of land, including streams and lochs therein, designated as 'countryside' for the purpose of the Countryside (Scotland) Act 1967, any person entering thereon for the purpose of open air recreation without causing damage, is not to be deemed a trespasser and will not be subject to interdict or similar exclusion proceedings.[13]

---

11 *Montgomery and Marshall v Watson* (1861) 23 D 635.
12 *Copland v Maxwell* (1871) 9 M (HL) 1.
13 Countryside (Scotland) Act 1967 s 11.

Chapter 7
Interdict against trespass

The nature of trespass

Temporary intrusion into land or property without the permission of the owner or occupier and without legal right constitutes trespass.[1] Except in the exercise of a public duty or some public franchise or private right, no one is entitled, without the permission of the proprietor, to enter his land or house on foot, on horseback or in a vehicle or to swim or use a boat on his private loch or river.[2] Certain cases of trespass involve breach of statutory provisions as, for example, offences against the Trespass (Scotland) Act 1865,[3] the Railway Regulation Acts 1840, 1868 and 1871, the Night Poaching Act 1828, the Protection of Birds Act 1954, and the Salmon and Freshwater Fisheries (Scotland) Act 1951, and may be dealt with by criminal proceedings. Such proceedings under these Acts do not however preclude a civil action by way of interdict or otherwise by the owner or occupier against the trespasser. But it is otherwise in respect of offences under the Game (Scotland) Act 1832 s 16 of which bars civil actions where criminal proceedings are taken for the same trespass.

Competency of interdict

Interdict against trespass based upon one single incident is competent only where there are reasonable grounds for apprehending that the trespass will be repeated.[4] The action is competent where the trespasser maintains a legal right to enter upon the land[5] but not so if he makes no such claim or having made such a claim withdraws it from the record, causes no damage and acts in good faith.[6] If there is no damage caused or reasonably apprehended as a result of the trespass or

---

1 *Geils v Thompson* (1872) 10 M 327; *Cowie v Strathclyde Regional Council* 1985 SLT 333.
2 *Rankine on Land Ownership* (4th edn) p 139.
3 *Paterson v Robertson* 1944 JC 166.
4 *Hay's Trustees v Young* (1877) 4 R 398; *Steuart v Stephen* (1877) 4 R 873; but see *Macleod v Davidson* (1886) 14 R 92.
5 *Inverurie Magistrates v Sorrie* 1956 SC 175; *Steuart v Stephen* above.
6 *Hay's Trustees v Young* above; *Macleod v Davidson* above.

51

the trespass is trivial, interdict may be refused.[7] In *Inverurie Magistrates v Sorrie*[8] the proprietors of a golf course brought an action of interdict to prevent the respondent from exercising racehorses on their land. He denied exercising the horses in the manner complained of but asserted a legal right to do so if he wished. The petitioners failed to prove the exercising of the horses and the respondent failed to prove that he had a legal right to do so. Interdict was refused on the ground that no intention to trespass could be inferred from the mere assertion of a claim of right to carry out a particular action. But in *Macleod v Davidson*[9] where a right of pasture had been exercised and a legal right thereto asserted, and then withdrawn but the averments remained on record in the process, interdict was granted.

Claims for damages

A claim for damages may be combined with a crave for interdict against trespass where it can be shown that the owner or occupier has suffered loss as, for example, where crops have been damaged[10] or fences or gates destroyed or where the owner or occupier has been assulted or even merely insulted.[11]

Examples of trespass

In addition to the simple trespass on land by pedestrians or by driving or leaving vehicles on land, interdict may be invoked to prevent a wide variety of wrongs of the nature of trespass, occasioned, or seriously apprehended. Examples are of interdict against trespassing to fish but it must be shown that the respondent has either been seen fishing or has asserted a right to do so;[12] shooting without permission;[13] and fixing stake nets for white fishings which captured large quantities of salmon although there was no evidence of fish having been actually killed by any individual respondent.[14]

A proprietor may be restrained from allowing the roots of trees growing on his land to spread beneath his neighbour's land and so cause damage.[15] And it has been held actionable as a trespass in

---

7 *Winans v Macrae* (1885) 12 R 1051.
8 1956 SC 175. See also *Warrand v Watson* (1905) 8F 253.
9 (1886) 14 R 92.
10 *Baird and Scott v Thomson* (1825) 3 S 448.
11 *Grahame v M'Kenzie* 1810 Hume 641.
12 *Warrand v Watson* (1905) 8 F 253.
13 *Carnegie v Mactier and Ors* (1836) 14 S 1079.
14 *Duke of Buccleuch v Smith* 1911 SC 409.
15 *McCombe v Read* [1955] 2 All ER 458.

England to affix a projecting sign in the air space above a neighbour's building.[16] In Scotland this would be more akin to encroachment.

Trespass by animals

Trespass may arise where animals are allowed to stray on to, or are deliberately pastured on, land belonging to another.[17] In the case of straying animals, interdict was refused in *Robertson v Wright*[18] on the ground that a complainer must satisfy the court that the respondent had failed to take reasonable precautions to prevent the animals straying and this had not been proved. And in *Winans v Macrae*[19] where the trespass consisted of inadvertently allowing a pet lamb to pasture on a private forest road, the trespass was regarded as trivial and interdict was refused.

Trespass in execution of statutory authority

Where a person requires to enter upon the land or premises of another in furtherance of his public duty under statute or regulation, trespass, provided it causes no damage beyond that necessary for the execution of the duty, and that person is acting within his authority, is justified and cannot be prevented by interdict. In *Shepherd v Menzies*[20] a police constable and an inspector of the Scottish Society for the Prevention of Cruelty to Animals entered the complainer's farm to investigate reports of cruelty to a horse, which proved well founded. The complainer sought interdict against the Directors of the Society and the inspector. The court refused interdict, holding that the inspector was entitled to enter the farm if he had reasonable cause to believe that the Cruelty to Animals (Scotland) Act 1850 was being violated.

The number and variety of officials now authorised by statute to enter upon private property has increased greatly in recent years. In order to identify the exact extent of their powers of entry, with or without a warrant, reference must be made to the relevant statutes. Examples are to be found in the Health and Safety at Work Act 1974 s 19; Rights of Entry (Gas and Electricity Boards) Act 1954 as amended by the Gas Act 1972; Public Health (Scotland) Act 1897 s 26; Health Services and Public Health Act 1968, as amended by the National Health Service (Scotland) Act 1972; Docks and Harbours Act 1966 s 32; Agriculture (Safety and Welfare Provisions) Act 1956 s 10;

---

16 *Kelsen v Imperial Tobacco Co* [1957] 2 QB 334.
17 *Macleod v Davidson* (1886) 14 R 92.
18 (1885) 13 R 174. See *Campbell v Mackay* 1959 SLT (Sh Ct) 34 as to proof of breach of interdict against trespass by sheep.
19 (1885) 12 R 1051.
20 (1900) 2 F 443.

Civic Government (Scotland) Act 1982 ss 5, 60 and 99 and the Offices, Shops and Railway Premises Act 1962 s 53. In all these and similar cases, the right of the official to enter upon the property derives and can only derive from the specific authority bestowed upon him by the statute in question, or order made thereunder. If that authority is exceeded or if, having lawfully entered, he acts in a manner which is *ultra vires* in terms of the statute, he may be restrained by interdict if there is reasonable apprehension of repetition of the acts complained of.

In cases involving the activities of police officers, the need for fulfilment of the public interest figures largely. Where police officers acting on information received, that two men had stolen goods, obtained a warrant to search their houses, although neither man had been apprehended or charged, a court of seven judges held that neither the granting nor the execution of the warrant was illegal.[1] And in *Southern Bowling Club v Ross*[2] the court refused interdict where two police officers sought to enter club premises in disguise for the purpose of detecting offences.

Trepass in air space

Trespass in the air space by aircraft flying over a person's property is authorised by the Civil Aviation Act 1982 subject to regulations as to height, weather and other factors. Section 76 excludes any action of interdict in respect of trespass arising by reason only of the flight of aircraft over any property.

Rights under access agreements

Under the Countryside (Scotland) Act 1967, access agreements may be made between planning authorities, the Countryside Commission and landowners establishing the rights of members of the public to enter upon prescribed lands for open air exercise. Under s 11 of the Act, so long as he causes no damage, a member of the public entering such lands for the aforesaid purpose, is not a trespasser and cannot be restrained by interdict.

---

1 *Stewart and M'Millan v Roach* 1950 SC 318.
2 (1902) 4 F 405.

Chapter 8
Interdict of company proceedings

Rights of majority and minority shareholders

The right of a minority shareholder to restrain the internal operations of a limited company by interdict is subject to the rule in *Foss v Harbottle*[1] and is restricted to cases where the company, acting through its directors, proposes to carry out an act which is illegal in itself under the common law or by statute, or which is *ultra vires* of the company under its memorandum and articles of association, or where a resolution requires a specially qualified majority but is passed only by a simple majority. Such cases may extend beyond fraud at common law and include an abuse or misuse of power by a majority acting either as directors or shareholders. For a discussion of the exceptions arising under the rule in *Foss v Harbottle* see *Estmanco (Kilner House) Ltd v GLC*.[2] A majority shareholder, as opposed to a director, owes no fiduciary duty to the company, and when voting may consider his own interest, provided he genuinely believes that his actions are in the best interest of the company, but there must be some limit to the power of the majority to pass resolutions, which they believe to be in the best interest of the company, and yet remain immune from interference by the courts. It may be in the best interest of the company to deprive the minority of some of their rights or property, but this does not give the majority an unrestricted right to do this where these are circumstances amounting to a 'fraud on the minority' (per Sir Robert Megarry VC in *Estmanco (Kilner House) Ltd v GLC*,[3] approving *Daniels v Daniels* [1978] 2 All ER 89). The test to be applied in deciding what are objectionable actions by directors who are also majority shareholders and which may be restrained by the court was explained in *Harris v Harris (A) Ltd*.[4] The test is not whether the actings complained of were fraudulent in

---

1 (1843) 2 Hare 461.
2 [1982] 1 All ER 437 at 443; see also *Rolled Steel Products (Holdings) Ltd v British Steel Corps* [1985] 2 WLR 908 and *Thompson v Barke (J.) & Co (Caterers) Ltd* 1975 SLT 67.
3 For 2 above.
4 1936 SC 183 at 202 per Lord Murray.

55

character but whether they constituted a breach of the fiduciary duty owed to the company by directors.

Cases where the action of a company is *intra vires* but the method adopted to carry out is either illegal or *ultra vires* are subject to the minor irregularity rule in *Macdougall v Gardiner*.[5] If, said Mellish LJ in that case, the thing complained of is a thing which, in substance, the majority of the company is entitled to do, or is something which has been done irregularly but which the majority of the company are entitled to do regularly, or if something has been done illegally, which the majority of the company are entitled to do legally, there can be no use in having a litigation about it, since the ultimate end is only that a meeting has to be called and ultimately the majority gets its wishes. The principle is that all members of the company are bound to agree to accept the decision of the majority, if it is expressed according to law and is within the powers of the company as contained in its articles. The court will not interfere with the management of companies acting legally and within their powers and has no jurisdiction to do so. It will not interfere in matters which require the exercise of discretion unless what is proposed is *ultra vires*, fraudulent or oppressive.[6] A majority of shareholders or members of an association cannot ratify an act which in itself is illegal or *ultra vires* of the company[7] or where the act perpetrated or threatened amounts to a fraud upon the minority shareholders.[8]

The phrase 'a fraud on the minority' and the actions which may constitute it are difficult to define. Thus a resolution may be a fraud on the minority, and subject to restraint, if it is not passed 'bone fide for the benefit of the company as a whole'.[9] Similarly where the effect of the resolution is to discriminate between the majority shareholders and the minority shareholders in such a manner as to give the former an advantage of which the latter are deprived.[10]

Ultra vires actings

Examples of *ultra vires* acts arise where a resolution requiring a specific majority is passed only by a simple majority or a resolution requires a prior ballot[11] or the proceeds of shares issued is applied to

---

5 [1875] 1 Ch 13 at 25. See also as to acts *ultra vires* s 35 of the Companies Act 1985.
6 *Foss v Harbottle* (1843) 2 Hare 461; *Burland v Earle* [1902] AC 83 at 93 per Lord Davey; *Cox v Edinburgh Tramways Co* (1898) 6 SLT 63 per Lord Kyllachy.
7 *Edwards v Halliwell* [1950] 2 All ER 1064; *Parlides v Jensen* [1956] Ch 565.
8 *Brown v Stewart* (1898) 1 F 316; *Harris v Harris (A) Ltd* 1936 SC 183; *Oliver's Trustees v Walker & Sons* 1948 SLT 140.
9 *Allen v Gold Reefs of West Africa* [1900] 1 Ch 656 at 671 per Lindley MR; *Shuttleworth v Cox Bros & Co Ltd* [1927] 2 KB 9 at 18 per Bankes LJ.
10 *Greenhalgh v Ardene Cinemas Ltd* [1950] 2 All ER 1120 at 1126 per Evershed MR; but see *Crookston v Lindsay, Crookston & Co* 1922 SLT 62.

unauthorised purposes[12] or in creating an unauthorised reserve fund;[13] giving effect to invalid resolutions;[14] the wrongful use of proxies[15] and where directors were appointed who were not qualified under the articles, have all been held *ultra vires*.[16]

Appointment and removal of directors

Where shareholders requisitioned an extraordinary general meeting to appoint three new directors and, in the notice calling the meeting, this business was referred to but there was also included therein, but not in the requisition, a resolution to remove an existing director, the resolution to that effect was held invalid and interdict was granted.[17]

But in *Bentley-Stevens v Jones*[18] where a meeting was convened to consider removal of a director and the meeting was irregularly convened but the irregularity was capable of being cured, interim interdict was refused. The court followed the principle laid down in *Browne v La Trinidad*[19] where Lindley LJ said:

> I think it is most important that the Court should hold fast to the rule upon which it has always acted not to interfere for the purpose of forcing companies to conduct their business according to the strictest rules where the irregularity complained of can be set right at any moment.

Transfer of shares

Where a company raised an action against certain shareholders to compel observance of the article of association regarding transfer of shares and those shareholders requisitioned a meeting to have certain directors removed, the company was held entitled to interdict preventing the shareholders from voting at the meeting.[20] An alteration of the articles, made in accordance with the provisions of these articles, cannot be restrained simply because it may have the effect of prejudicing the rights of a particular class of shareholders.[1]

For a discussion of the distinction between acts *ultra vires* of the company under its objects clauses and acts *ultra vires* of the directors

---

11 *Edwards v Halliwell* above.
12 *Wilson v Glasgow & S W Railway Co* (1850) 13 D 227.
13 *Paterson v Paterson (R) & Sons Ltd* 1917 SC (HL) 13.
14 *Quin & Axtens Ltd v Salmon* [1909] AC 442; *Ball v Metal Industries Ltd* 1957 SLT 124.
15 *Cousins v International Brick Co* [1931] 2 Ch 90.
16 *Pollock v Garrett* 1957 SLT (Notes) 8; but see *Spencer v Kennedy* [1926] 1 Ch 125.
17 *Ball v Metal Industries Ltd* 1957 SLT 124.
18 *Bentley-Stevens v Jones* [1974] 2 All ER 653; *Browne v La Trinidad* (1887) 37 Ch D 1 at 17, CA.
19 Fn 18 above.
20 *Lyle & Scott Ltd v British Investment Trust Ltd* 1957 SLT (Notes) 26.
1 *Crookston v Lindsay Crookston & Co* 1922 SLT 62 at 64.

and the tests for determining *ultra vires* acts see *Rolled Steel Products (Holdings) Ltd v British Steel Corpn.*[2]

Interdict in winding up

Interdict is occasionally competent in proceedings for winding up a company. In a petition by one director for compulsory winding up the existence of a debt for directors' fees founded upon was disputed. In considering whether the petition to wind up was an abuse of process, it was held that to invoke the winding up jurisdiction, where the debt was substantially disputed, would amount to abuse and the petition proceedings should be restrained.[3] In an action by a company to restrain a creditor from moving for an order to wind up on just and equitable grounds, it was held there was insufficient available evidence to establish that the winding up order would amount to an abuse of process, and an interlocutory injunction was refused.[4]

Any shareholder may interdict a company in liquidation, and the liquidator, from actions *ultra vires*, as for example where a railway company which had been dissolved, other than for the purpose of winding up and dividing its free funds to creditors and shareholders, proposed to pay out large sums to the chairman, secretary and other officials, as compensation for loss of office.[5] A debenture holder has similar rights against the trustees for the debenture holders.[6]

Where the validity of a resolution to wind up and of the appointment of a liquidator was challenged on the ground that no quorum was present it was doubted whether this could be done in an action of interdict seeking simply to restrain the appointment.[7]

---

2 [1985] 3 All ER 52 at 85.
3 *Mann v Goldstein* [1968] 2 All ER 769.
4 *Bryanston Finance v de Vries (No 2)* [1976] 1 All ER 25, CA.
5 *Clouston v Edinburgh and Glasgow Ry Co* (1865) 4 M 207.
6 *Ellice & Ors v Invergarry & Fort Augustus Ry Co* 1913 SC 849.
7 *Howling's Trustees v Smith* (1905) 7 F 390 at 395 per Lord Kyllachy.

Chapter 9

Protection of intellectual property including commercial, literary and artistic interests

1 GOODWILL

The goodwill of a commercial business or professional practice may be protected contractually by a restrictive covenant preventing the seller of a business from setting up in competition. In such event the extent to which a seller who contravenes the restrictive covenant may be subject to interdict, will depend upon the extent to which the covenant is enforceable in law.[1]

2 ACTIONS TO RESTRAIN PASSING OFF

Nature of passing off

Apart from contract, an action at common law based upon 'passing off' will lie where one party has represented his goods or services as being those of a competitor in such a way as is calculated to deceive the public. In *Haig (John) & Co Ltd v Forth Blending Co Ltd,* a case involving the sale of whisky by the respondents in bottles resembling those of 'Dimple Haig', which was a trade mark registered in the name of the petitioners but of a blend different from that of the petitioners, Lord Hill Watson, in a comprehensive review of the authorities up to that date, and in granting interdict against the respondents, said:

> One man is not entitled to sell his goods under such circumstances by the name or the packet or the mode of making up the article, in such a way as to induce the public to believe that they are the manufacture of someone else.[2]

The rule of as thus laid down was expanded in the later case of *Erven Warnink BV v Townend (J) & Sons (Hull) Ltd*[3] In that case Lord Diplock

---

1 See ch 15 on Breach of Contract.
2 1954 SC 35 at 37; *Cellular Clothing Co v Maxton and Murray* (1899) 1 F (HL) 29; *Singer Manufacturing Co v Kimball & Morton* (1873) 11 M 267; see also *Kinnell & Co v Ballantyne & Sons* 1910 SC 246; *Dunlop Pneumatic Tyre Co v Dunlop Motor Co* 1907 SC (HL) 15; *Dewar (John) & Sons v Dewar* (1900) 7 SLT 462; *Woolley & Son v Morrison* (1904) 6 F 451; cf *Bile Beans Manufacturing Co v Davidson* (1906) 8 F 1181.
3 [1927] All ER 927, HL.

59

(at p 742) identified five characteristics which must be present in order to create a valid cause of action for passing off, viz (i) misrepresentation; (ii) made by a trader in the course of his trade; (iii) to prospective customers of his or ultimate consumers of goods or services supplied by him; (iv) which is calculated to injure the business or goodwill of another trader (in the sense that this is a reasonably foreseeable consequence); and (v) which causes actual damage to a business or goodwill of the trader by whom the action is brought or (in *quia timet* actions) will probably do so. In the same case and in *dicta* differing in substance but not in principle from that of Lord Diplock, Lord Fraser said:

> It is essential for the plaintiff in a passing off action to show at least the following facts, viz: (i) that his business consists of or includes selling in England a class of goods to which the particular name applies; (ii) that the class of goods is clearly defined and that in the minds of the public or a section of the public in England, the trade name distinguished that class from other similar goods; (iii) that because of the reputation of the goods, there is goodwill attached to the name; (iv) that he (the plaintiff) as a member of the class of those who sell the goods is the owner of goodwill in England which is of substantial value; (v) that he has suffered or is really likely to suffer substantial damage to his property in the goodwill by reason of the defendant's selling goods which are falsely described by the trade name to which the trade name is attached. Provided these conditions are satisfied, I consider that the plaintiff is entitled to protect himself by a passing off action.

The extended principles were adopted in Scotland in *Lang Bros v Goldwell Ltd*[4] and in *Flaxcell Ltd v Freedman*.[5] In the former case, in applying the *dicta* in *Erven Warninck BV v Townend (J) & Sons (Hull) Ltd*, the Lord Justice Clerk (Wheatley) said: 'There is ample authority for the proposition that the law of Scotland does not differ from the law of England in this field of law.' These decisions establish that the principle underlying an action for passing off is injury to goodwill by misrepresentation.

The case of *Bollinger v Costa Brava Wine Co Ltd*[6] established the principle of the 'class' action for passing off by a group of traders who shared goodwill in a name of a product (ie champagne) in the same manner as the single trader having personal goodwill.[7]

Descriptive names for goods

But where goods are advertised and sold under a description which is

4 1982 SLT 309.
5 1981 SLT (Notes) 131.
6 [1960] 1 Ch 262.
7 See further as to 'class actions' p 63 below.

aptly and properly used to describe the nature of the goods and is a word of the English language commonly in use, no question of 'passing off' arises. Thus in *Cellular Clothing Co Ltd v Maxton and Murray*[8] the petitioners manufactured cloth of a particular texture which was sold under the description of 'cellular' and they sought interdict to prevent another trader selling cloth under the same description which was not manufactured by the petitioners. It was held they had failed to discharge the onus of showing that the word 'cellular' had been so universally recognised by the trade and the public as denoting the petitioners' goods, that its application to other goods involved misrepresentation. In contrast, in *Singer Manufacturing Co v Kimball & Morton*[9] the word 'Singer' in the particular circumstance of its use by the respondents was held to apply to the sewing machines manufactured by the petitioners and interdict prohibiting its use was granted.

If it is proved that a single feature of what has been judicially referred to as the 'get up' of goods is so peculiar that it, above all else, attracts the eye and is retained in the memory of the purchasing public, and that they recognise the goods of the trader by this one feature alone, then a second trader may be prevented from adopting the peculiar feature of the first trader's 'get up' and so misleading the public.[10] When whisky was labelled 'Bunnabhain Islay' and there was a *prima facie* case of infringement of a trade mark and of 'passing off' interim interdict was granted.[11]

Damages combined with interdict

Damages for 'passing off' as opposed to interdict thereof, will only be awarded where it has been proved that there has been loss arising to the complainer in that custom intended for him has, in consequence of the act of 'passing off' been secured by the competitor. An action confined to interdict will, however, be competent even if no loss of business has been proved, providing the wrong is still continuing.[12]

Fraud and fraudulent intent

In an action of interdict based on 'passing off' it is unnecessary to aver or prove fraud, intent to deceive or negligence. The offender may well be ignorant of his competitors's product and the similarity in name or appearance may be entirely accidental but if it is shown that members

8 (1899) 1 F (HL) 29.
9 (1873) 11 M 267.
10 *Haig (John) & Co v Forth Blending Co* 1954 SC 35 at 38.
11 *Highland Distilleries Co v Speymalt Whisky Distributors* 1985 SLT 85. See also *Macallan-Glenlivet v Speymalt Whisky Distributors* 1983 SLT 348.
12 *Draper v Trist* [1939] 3 All ER 513, CA.

of the public are likely to be misled, interdict will be granted.[13] The test is an objective one and amounts to whether the operations of the defender were such as would be likely to deceive the public.[14]

Examples of 'passing off'

'Passing off' can arise in a multitude of circumstances and, apart from the foregoing principles, each case must depend largely upon the particular operations and circumstances. Marketing goods under the name of another person[15] or presenting goods of which the name or the style or content of packaging of either bottles or labels, or even the marking of a manufacturer's initials on clothing, if likely to induce the belief that they are the goods of another person, have been held actionable,[16] but where the similarity in appearance or style is necessary to describe the function of the goods or where these features are generally found in other goods of the particular class, no action will lie.[17] In *Scottish Milk Marketing Board v Drybrough & Co Ltd*,[18] the petitioners marketed their dairy products under the name 'Scottish Pride'. The respondents were about to market their lager beer under the name 'Scottish Pride' and the petitioners sought interdict. In refusing interim interdict the court expressed the view that, as a matter of common sense, it was unlikely that confusion would arise in the minds of the general public as between the two products and there was nothing to indicate that the petitioners' goodwill would be adversely affected.

Where there has been an infringement of a registered trade mark but no action has been taken under the Trade Marks Act 1938, an action of interdict based on 'passing off' may still be brought; unregistered trade marks cannot be enforced by proceedings under the Act (s 2) but may be protected by interdict if they are transferred under contract as part of the goodwill of a business on the basis of a simple breach of contract.[19]

If the trade name or description under which the complainer markets

---

13 *Haig (John) & Co Forth Blending Co* 1954 SC 35 at 40; *Johnston v Orr Ewing* (1882) 7 App Cas 219, HL; *Cellular Clothing Co v Maxton & Murray* (1899) 1 F (HL) 29 at 31; but see *Boord & Son Inc v Bagots, Hutton & Co* [1916] 2 AC 382 HL; *GNS Railway Co v Mann* (1892) 19 R 1035 at 1041 per Lord MacLaren.
14 *Draper v Trist* above.
15 *Vokes v Evans and Marble Arch Motor Supplies Ltd* (1931) 49 RPC 140, CA.
16 *Haig & Co v Forth Blending Co* above; *Bayer v Baird* (1898) 25 R 1142; *Scottish Milk Marketing Board v Drybrough & Co* 1985 SLT 253; *Macallan-Glenlivet v Speymalt Whisky Distributors* 1983 SLT 348; *Paperchase Products Ltd v Ridlington* 1980 SLT (Sh Ct) 56.
17 *Jamieson & Co v Jamieson* (1898) 14 TLR 160, CA.
18 See fn 16 above.
19 *Singer Machine Manufacturers v Wilson* (1877) 3 App Cas 376, HL; cf *Melrose-Drover Ltd v Heddle* (1901) 4 F 1120 at 1122.

his goods is found to contain false statements, interdict as a measure of protection will be refused. Thus in *Bile Beans Manufacturing Co Ltd v Davidson*[20] where the complainers described their bile bean remedy as the result of investigation by an eminent scientist, Mr Charles Forde, and as containing a special ingredient imported from Australia, and these facts were proved to be untrue, the court refused to grant interdict against a competitor.

Other examples of 'passing off' causing injury to business interests have been found in the use by one manufacturer of another's trade name for his goods; or advertising services offered by one company which may be confused with those offered by another; in the issue of advertisements or trade circulars describing the quality of goods in the same or similar terms as those used by a competitor but only if the public are likely to be confused as between two advertisements;[1] similarly retailing goods of one manufacturer as having been manufactured by another more widely known competitor.[2]

Where a special or fancy name has become long associated with a particular kind of goods, the use thereof by another trader may be restrained if the public are likely to be confused.[3] The position may be otherwise if the trade name is purely descriptive of the goods.[4] In *Flaxcell Ltd v Freedman*,[5] an English trader in jeans, having a considerable market in Scotland, obtained interdict against a Glasgow trader using the pursuer's trade name for the goods.

The use by a competitor of a trade name consisting of a business location (for example 'Palace Hotel'; the 'Sun Foundry' but not 'Golden Lion Hotel') has been restrained by interdict when there was likelihood of the public being confused.[6]

Class actions for passing off

The decision in *Bollinger v Costa Brava Wine Go Ltd*[7] which related to the

---

20 (1906) 8 F 1181.
1 *Henderson & Son v Munro & Co* (1905) 7 F 636.
2 *Thomson & Co v Dailly* (1897) 24 R 1173; *Bass v Laidlaw* (1908) 16 SLT 660; but see *Bass v Laidlaw* (1886) 13 R 898 (where interdict refused in special circumstances); *John Haig & Co Ltd v John D D Haig Ltd* 1957 SLT (Notes) 36.
3 *Premier Cycle Co v Premier Tube Co* (1896) 12 TLR 481; *Crystalite Gramophone Record Manufacturing Co v British Crystalite Co* (1934) 51 RPC 315.
4 *General Radio Co v General Radio Co (Westminster) Ltd* [1957] RPC 471; *Bile Beans Manufacturing Co v Davidson* (1906) 8 F 1181; *Cellular Clothing Co Ltd v Maxton & Murray* (1899) 1 F (HL) 29.
5 1981 SLT (Notes) 131.
6 *GNS Railway Co v Mann* (1892) 19 R 1035: *Cowan v Millar* (1895) 22 R 833: *Crawford's Trustees v Lennox* (1896) 23 R 747: *Montgomerie v Donald* (1884) 11 R 506: but see *Grand Hotel Co of Caledonia Springs v Wilson* [1904] AC 103; see also *Dunnachie v Young & Sons* (1883) 10 R 874.
7 [1960] 1 Ch 262.

marketing of a sparkling wine as 'Spanish champagne' established the right of a group of traders having a common interest in the goodwill attaching to a product to protect that goodwill by an action for passing off. It has been adopted and followed in Scotland for the protection of several important products. See for example, *Argyllshire Weavers Ltd v Macaulay (A) (Tweeds) Ltd*[8] where interdict was granted against mill owners marketing mill spun tweeds as 'Harris Tweed' and *John Walker & Sons Ltd v Douglas McGibbon & Co Ltd* [9] where interdict was granted against a company supplying Scotch whisky bottles and labels for the production and sale in Honduras of a spirit known as 'McGibbon's Special Reserve' which contained a proportion of locally produced alcohol. In the latter case, Lord Avonside said he was in the realm of *Bollinger v Costa Brava Wine Co Ltd*. In granting interdict his Lordship said:

> 'Scotch whisky' as a description has obtained a particular standing in that it may only be applied to a spirit distilled in Scotland from a mash of cereal grain saccharified by the diatase of malt. To such a spirit many individual brand names are applied but, irrespective of that, all producers satisfying the conditions applicable are entitled to describe their product as 'Scotch whisky' and to take action to protect the advantages conferred by such a right from improper use of that trade description.

The most recent case in Scotland where the *Bollinger* and *Erven Warnink*[10] principles have been invoked is *Lang Bros Ltd v Goldwell Ltd*[11] wherein the Court would seem to have gone somewhat beyond the principles to be derived from the previous authorities[12] and opened the door to a further extension of the law.

3 PROTECTION OF BUSINESS AND PROFESSIONAL NAMES AND DESIGNATIONS

Apart from registered trade marks and cases where there is 'passing off', a trader has no exclusive right of property in the name under which he carries on his business or which he applies to his goods. The principle was explained in *Kinnell & Co Ltd v Ballantyne & Sons* [13] by Lord Skerrington thus:

---

8 1965 SLT 21.
9 1972 SLT 128.
10 [1979] All ER 927, HL.
11 1982 SLT 309 (The 'Wee McGlen' case).
12 For a full discussion of *Lang Bros v Goldwell* see Dr Hector MacQueen 'Wee McGlen and the action of passing off' 1982 SLT 225, and 'The *Wee McGlen* case: Unfair Competition'. European Intellectual Property Review 1983, 18.
13 *Williamson v Meikle* 1909 SC 1272; *Kinnell & Co. v Ballantyne & Sons* 1910 SC 246 at 253 (following *Reddaway & Co v Banham & Co* [1896] AC 199).

I have always understood that, at common law, a person cannot acquire an exclusive right to the use of the name under which he has traded, or which he has applied to his goods; and that, the measure of his right is to demand that other persons shall not use the same name in such a way as is likely to deceive the public to his prejudice.

In such cases, the form of interdict to be granted will be of the type described in *Kinnell & Co Ltd v Ballantyne & Sons* [14] (at p 254), namely an interdict against using the name or description in question without clearly distinguishing his goods from those of the complainer. But where the words 'Kelvinside Chemical Company' were used by a competitor of 'Kelvindale Chemical Company' it was held that the use of the name 'Kelvinside Chemical Company' had not been proved to have misled the public and interdict was refused.[15]

In *Scottish Union & National Insurance Co v Scottish National Insurance Co Ltd*[16] the petitioners sought to interdict the respondents from carrying on business under the name of Scottish National Insurance Co. The petitioners carried on general insurance business but the respondents carried on marine insurance only, although they held power under their articles of association to undertake other types of insurance. In refusing interdict, the court held that the businesses of general and marine insurance were very different and the similarity in the names of the two companies was not likely to deceive the public.

Professional organisations

Professional organisations may interdict non-members from using any description or designation which is calculated to suggest that they are members of the organisation. In *Society of Accountants in Edinburgh v Corporation of Accountants Ltd,* the pursuers obtained interdict against the defenders using the letters 'MCA' as a professional designation.[17] And see, in that case, *obiter dicta* by the Lord Justice Clerk as to the right of members of the Society of Writers to Her Majesty's Signet to prevent other solicitors, not being members of the Society, from using the designation 'WS'.

4 PROTECTION OF THE ROYAL WARRANT

Grant and restraint of abuse

The Royal Warrant, which appoints a person or firm to be suppliers of

14 1910 SC 246.
15 *Williamson v Meikle* 1909 SC 1272.
16 1909 SC 318.
17 (1893) 20 R 750; *Corporation of Accountants v Society of Accountants in Edinburgh* (1903) 11 SLT 424.

66 *Protection of intellectual property including commercial, literary and artistic interests*

specific goods to a member of the Royal Family, entitles the holder to describe himself or a firm as such a supplier, and to exhibit at his premises the Royal insignia. Section 12(1) of the Trade Descriptions Act 1968 makes it an offence for any person who, in the course of any trade or business, gives, by whatever means, any false indication direct or indirect that any goods or services supplied by him, or any methods adopted by him, are, or are of a kind, supplied to or approved by Her Majesty, or any member of the Royal Family. Under the Patents Act 1949 s 92 it is likewise an offence to use the Royal Arms insignia in connection with any trade, business or profession in a manner calculated to deceive the public. Any person holding a warrant to use the Royal Arms[18] or one who is authorised by the Lord Chamberlain to take proceedings may by an action of interdict prevent the use of the insignia by any non-entitled person.[19]

Queen's Award for Industry

The use, without the authority of Her Majesty, in the course of any trade or business, of any device or emblem signifying the Queen's Award to Industry, or of anything so nearly resembling such device or emblem as to be likely to deceive, is an offence against s 12(2) of the Trade Descriptions Act 1968.

5 INFRINGEMENT OF TRADE MARKS AND SERVICE MARKS

TRADE MARKS
General Principles

A trade mark is defined by the Trade Marks Act 1938 as a mark used in relation to goods for the purpose of indicating, or so as to indicate, a connection in the course of trade between the goods and some person having the right, either as proprietor or a registered user of the mark, whether with or without any indication of the identity of that person. It includes a device, brand, heading, label, packet, name, signature, word, letter, numeral or any combination thereof.[20] The Trade Marks Act 1938 was amended by the Trade Marks (Amendment) Act 1984,

---

18 *Royal Warrant Holders' Association v Lipman* (1933) 51 RPC 155; *R W H v Robb* 1935 SN 32.
19 *R W H Association v Deane & Beal Ltd* [1912] 1 Ch 10. Trade Marks Act 1938, s 61 as amended by Patents, Designs and Marks Act 1986, Sch 2.
20 Trade Marks Act 1938 s 68(1) and s 68(2) as amended by Trade Marks (Amendment) Act 1984 s 1(5)(b) and Sch 1, para 25.

which introduced a system of registration for service marks. See as to this p 70 below. Except by way of an action for 'passing off' at common law, no proceedings may be instituted to prevent infringement of an unregistered trade mark or for damages in respect of such infringement.[1]

Nature of infringement

Trade marks may be registered in the Register of Trade Marks in either Part A or Part B,[2] each of which carries different rights. When registration has been effected, the common law requirement of proof of long use and association is no longer necessary in any proceedings to prevent infringement.[3]

Registration in Part A confers an absolute right to use the trade mark in relation to the goods in respect of which it is registered. The right is deemed to be infringed by any person who uses an identical mark or one so nearly resembling it as to be likely to deceive or cause confusion. There is no infringement if the trade mark is so used by another in any place or in any circumstances to which the registration does not extend.[4]

In the case of registration under Part B of the Register, which confers the same rights as registration under Part A, no interdict against infringement (except under s 6 which deals with breaches of contract between the proprietor of the trade mark and the purchaser or owner of goods) will be granted if the defender satisfies the court that the use, of which the pursuer complains, is not likely to deceive or cause confusion, or is to be taken as indicating a connection in the course of trade between the goods and some person having right as proprietor or registered user to use the trade mark.[5]

The infringements of trade mark which may be restrained by interdict are set out in the 1938 Act as amended. Registration of a trade mark confers upon the proprietor an exclusive right to the use of the trade mark within the limits prescribed by the entry in the Register.[6] The right is deemed to be infringed by any person who, not being the proprietor of the trade mark or a registered user thereof, uses a mark identical with it, or so nearly resembling it as to be likely to deceive or cause confusion in the course of trade, in relation to any goods in respect of which it is registered and in such manner as to render the use

1 1938 Act s 2 as amended by 1984 Act s 1(5)(a).
2 1938 Act s 4 as amended by 1984 Act Sch 1, para 2.
3 *Boord & Son v Thom & Cameron* 1907 SC 1326 at 1342 per Lord President Dunedin.
4 1938 Act s 4(2) as amended by 1984 Act Sch 1, para 2(3).
5 1938 Act s 5 as amended by 1984 Act Sch 1, para 3.
6 1938 Act ss 4 and 5 as amended by ibid paras 2 and 3.
6a The 1938 and 1984 Acts were amended by the Patents, Designs and Marks Act 1986 which provides for computerisation of the registers and matters connected therewith.

of the trade mark as likely to be taken as imputing a reference to some person having the right, either as proprietor or user, to use the trade mark or to goods with which such person as aforesaid is connected in the course of trade.[7] The criteria to be adopted in approaching the question of infringement was summarised in *Lever Brothers Port Sunlight Ltd v Sunniwite Products Ltd*[8] by Romer J thus:

> You must consider the two words. You must judge of them both by their look and their sound. You must consider the goods to which they are to be applied. You must consider the nature and kind of customer who would be likely to buy the goods. In fact you must consider all the surrounding circumstances and you must further consider what is likely to happen if each of these trade marks is used in a normal way as a trade mark for the goods of the respective owners of the marks.

These criteria were approved and adopted in *Coca-Cola Company v William Struthers & Sons Ltd*[9] where the marks were not identical (being 'Coca-Cola' and 'Koala Cola'), but when pronounced there was similarity in sound. Upon the evidence for the petitioners in that case, which consisted solely of the tape-recorded results of a door-to-door survey, the court held that the petitioners had failed to prove the likelihood of deception or confusion and preferred the evidence led for the respondents from members of the trade who negatived any confusion on the part of customers buying the two soft drinks. The onus of establishing likelihood of deception or confusion rests entirely upon the party seeking the interdict. The question of whether one trade mark so nearly resembles another as to cause confusion, or to deceive, is a question not for the exercise of discretion but for decision upon the facts.[10]

It has been said that the degree of resemblance required to constitute infringement is virtually incapable of definition and the many cases arising on this point must be regarded as examples of infringement pertinent to their own facts.[11] A wide variety of factors have been taken into account in considering whether there has been infringement on account of physical appearance and resemblance of two marks or of similar sounds when spoken.[12] Provided there is even one feature which is distinctive to the proprietor's mark and which specially distinguishes

---

7 1938 Act s 4(1) as amended by 1984 Act Sch 1, para 3.
8 (1949) 66 RPC 84 at 89.
9 1968 SLT 353.
10 *Rysta Ltd, Application* (1943) 60 RPC 87; *Rolls Razor Ltd v Rolls (Lighters) Ltd* (1949) 66 RPC 137; *Aristoc Ltd v Rysta Ltd* [1945] AC 68.
11 *Johnston v Orr Ewing* (1882) 7 App Cas 219, HL; *Price's Patent Candle Co v Ogston & Tennant* (1909) 26 RPC 797; *Andrew & Co v Kuehnrich* (1913) 30 RPC 93; *Birmingham Vinegar Brewery Co v Powell* [1897] AC 710, HL; *Edge & Sons v Nicholls* [1911] AC 693.
12 1938 Act ss 4 and 5 as amended by 1984 Act Sch 1, paras 2 and 3.

his goods, interdict against the use of the offending mark will be granted.[13]

Threatened infringement and threats against infringement

Interdict may also be granted where there is only reasonable ground of apprehension that infringement and consequent injury will take place.[14] Where statement, threats or warnings against the use of a trade mark or the possibility of legal proceedings are used, otherwise than in good faith, they may be restrained by interdict, as also when warnings have continued to be issued after the court has held that there has been no infringement and where allegations under the guise of warnings are issued alleging that a party's goods are not genuine.[15] Such statements, threats and warnings will be protected from interdict or other action if they are made in good faith and under the honest belief that the trade mark has been or is likely to be infringed, notwithstanding that this belief may ultimately turn out to be mistaken or unjustified.[16]

Infringement arising out of contract

Infringement may arise where the proprietor of a trade mark contracts with a purchaser or user of goods to the effect that the latter will not do in relation to the goods any act by which:

(a) the mark is applied to the goods after they have been altered in terms of the contract as regards their state, condition, get-up or packaging;
(b) the trade mark is altered or partly obliterated;
(c) any other trade mark is applied to the goods; and
(d) there is added to the goods any other matter in writing which is likely to injure the reputation of the trade mark, and the purchaser or any user of the goods being in good faith and having notice of the foregoing obligation does any of these acts.[17]

Where no warning was given of infringement of trade mark before a petition for interdict was served, the petitioner's motion for expenses was refused.[18]

---

13 *Jamieson & Co v Jamieson* (1898) 14 TLR 160, CA; *Marshall v Sidebottom* (1900) 18 RPC 43; *Alaska Packers' Association v Crooks & Co* (1901) 18 RPC 129.
14 *Singer Manufacturing Co v Kimball & Morton* (1873) 11 M 267.
15 *Thomas v Williams* (1880) 14 Ch D 864; *London Ferro-concrete Co v Justicz* (1951) 68 RPC 261 CA.
16 *Royal Baking Powder Co v Wright, Crossley & Co* (1889) 18 RPC 95, HL; *Withers & Sons Ltd v Withers & Co Ltd* (1926) 44 RPC 19.
17 1938 Act s 6.
18 *Cellular Clothing Co v Schulberg* 1952 SLT (Notes) 73.

Service marks – Trade Marks (Amendment) Act 1984

This Act set up a system of registration for service marks which is similar in virtually all respects to the registration system for trade marks established by the Trade Marks Act 1938. In the application of the latter Act to service marks, certification trade marks and what are known as defensive registrations have been omitted. The application of the 1984 Act is achieved by the modifications of the 1938 Act set out in Sch 1 to the 1984 Act.

Section 1 of the 1984 Act provides that, subject to the modifications in Sch 1 of the 1984 Act, the Trade Marks Act 1938 shall have effect in the same manner as it affects registration and use of trade marks. A service mark is subject to the 1984 Act if it is a mark used or proposed to be used in relation to services for the purpose of indicating, or so as to indicate, that a particular person is connected in the course of business with the provision of these services, whether with or without any indication of the identity of that person.[19]

The fact that service mark registration may be available does not prevent a complainer exercising his common law right to restrain by interdict a person 'passing off' his business as being that of another person.[20] Where the 1938 Act refers to a near resemblance of marks the 'near' means a resemblance so near as to be likely to deceive or cause confusion.[1]

For the purpose of the 1984 Act, a service mark means a device, name, signature, word, letter, numeral or any combination thereof.[2]

Schedule 2 of the 1984 Act contains provisions which enable owners of existing trade marks to protect their rights against infringement by owners or prospective owners of service marks and similarly vice versa. Schedule 2 with this end in view provides for protection and infringement of what are referred to as associated goods and services.[3]

Section 6 of the 1938 Act which deals with infringement arising out of certain conditions imposed by contract does not apply in relation to infringement of service marks.[4]

---

19 1984 Act s 1(3).
20 1938 Act s 68 as amended by 1984 Act s 2(5)(b) (now s 68(2A)).
1 Ibid now s 68(2B).
2 1984 Act s 2(7).
3 1984 Act Sch 2, para 3.
4 1984 Act Sch 1, para 4. See p 69 above.

6 COPYRIGHT

Nature of copyright

The law of copyright is now contained in the Copyright Act 1956[5] as amended by the Design Copyright Act 1968 s 1 and the Copyright (Amendment) Act 1971.[6] Copyright in relation to a work means the exclusive right, subject to the provisions of the statute, to do, and to authorise other persons to do, certain acts in relation to that work in the United Kingdom or in any other country to which the relevant provisions of the 1956 Act extend. The provisions of the Act as a whole may be extended to other countries by Orders in Council.[7]

Copyright subsists *ipso jure* and without the need for intimation or registration, in every original literary, dramatic or musical work which is unpublished and of which the author was a qualified person when the work was made. It also subsists in such works when published if, but only if, the first publication took place in the United Kingdom or in another country to which the Act has been extended, or the author was a qualified person when the work was first published or the author has died before that time but was a qualified person at the time of his death.[8] The title to copyright passes on the death of the owner to his Executors who may sue for infringement even before Confirmation is obtained.[9]

What is protected by copyright is the original skill or labour in the production of a work and not simply the idea thereof.[10] A literary work includes any written table or compilation. See *Cramp & Sons Ltd v Smythson Ltd*[10] as to necessity for taste and judgment to constitute an original literary work. A computer programme is now protected as a literary work.[11] A musical work is not defined by the Act. A dramatic work includes a choreographic work and mime, and the scenario or script for a cinematograph film.[10]

Copyright subsists in a literary, dramatic or musical work by virtue of s 2 of the 1956 Act until the end of a period of 50 years from the end of the calendar year in which the author died and then expires.[12] If, before death of the author, the work has not been published, performed

---

5 4 & 5 Eliz 2 c 74.
6 19 & 20 Eliz 2 c 4.
7 1956 Act ss 1(1) and 31.
8 1956 Act ss 2(1) and 2(2).
9 *Mackay v Mackay* 1914 SC 200.
10 1956 Act s 2(1) and 48(1); *Alexander v Mackenzie* (1847) 9 D 748; *University of London Press v University Tutorial Press* [1916] 2 Ch 601; *Cramp & Sons v Smythson* [1944] AC 329; *Football League v Littlewood Pools Ltd* [1959] Ch 637; *Wood v Boosey* (1868) LR 3 QB 223; *M'Neil v Rolled Steel Forge Co* 1930 SN 145.
11 Copyright (Computer Software) Act 1985.
12 1956 Act s 2(3).

in public or offered for sale as a record or broadcast, the copyright continues in force for 50 years from the end of the calendar year which includes the earliest occasion when any of these acts was done or the work was adapted for such purpose.[13]

As regards published artistic works, copyright subsists by virtue of s 3 of the 1956 Act only if the first publication took place in the United Kingdom or in a country to which s 3 has been extended, or the author was a qualified person when publication first took place or the author has died before publication but was a qualified person at the time of his death. The copyright continues for fifty years from the end of the calendar year in which the author died. There are exceptions for engravings unpublished at the author's death when the copyright subsists for fifty years from the year of first publication, and for photographs where the copyright expires at the end of fifty years from first publication.

A 'qualified person' for the purpose of the 1956 Act means, as regards an individual, a British subject or a British protected person (under the British Nationality Act 1981) or a citizen of the Republic of Ireland or a person not within these categories who is domiciled or resident in the United Kingdom. A body incorporated under the laws of any part of the United Kingdom or any other country to which the relevant provisions have been applied is also a 'qualified person'.[14]

General principles of infringement

The copyright in a work is infringed by any person who, not being the owner of the copyright and without licence from the owner, does or authorises another to do any of the acts for which the owner of the copyright has the exclusive rights by virtue of s 1 of the 1956 Act.[15] 'Authorise' can mean 'sanction, approve and countenance' or simply 'permit'. For a discussion on the question of whether indifference or mere silence can amount to authorisation see *CBS Inc v Ames Records and Tapes Ltd*.[15] This case dealt with alleged infringement where customers of a record/tape renting shop could make home recordings from the records/tapes which they rented. For a more recent and significant authority see *Amstrad Consumer Electronics v British Phonographic Industry Ltd*.[16]

Infringement of copyright in literary, dramatic and musical works

The acts restricted by the copyright in any of these works consists of

13 Ibid s 2(3).
14 Ibid s 1(5)(a) and (b).
15 Ibid s 1(2), s 2(1) and s 3(1). *CBS Inc v Ames Records & Tapes Ltd* [1981] 2 All ER 812.
16 [1986] FSR 159.

reproducing the work or portions thereof in any material form as in *Leslie v Young & Sons*[17] where portions of a railway timetable were reproduced verbatim; publishing the work as in *Caird v Sime*[17] where a university professor was held entitled to interdict another from publishing his lectures given in his ordinary university course: performing the work in public; broadcasting the work; causing the work to be transmitted to subscribers to a diffusion system; making any adaptation of the work as in *Harpers Ltd v Barry, Henry & Co Ltd*[17] where parts of trade catalogues were copied: or in doing in relation to the adaptation of a work, any of the foregoing acts.[17] Adaptation of a literary or a dramatic work includes conversion of a non-dramatic work into a dramatic work or vice versa; a translation of the work; and the production of a version of the work conveyed wholly or mainly by means of pictures. In relation to a musical work, adaptation means an arrangement or transcription thereof.[18]

The copyright in a literary, dramatic or musical work is also infringed by any person who permits a place of public entertainment to be used for the performance in public of a work where that performance constitutes an infringement of the copyright. It is a defence to show that the person had no reasonable grounds of suspecting the infringement or that he gave the permission gratuitously or for a consideration which was only nominal or for a sum which did not exceed the expenses of use of the place of performance.[19]

Computer programs

The product of a computer program is as much the work of the author as of the computer, the latter being no more than the tool by which the result was produced to the instructions of the author.[20] Under the Copyright (Computer Software) Act 1985, computer programs are now included amongst the works protected by Part I of the 1956 Act.

Where participants in a promotional game were required to match letters on a card with letters in a table, the table was held to be a literary work within the meaning of the 1956 Act.[1] For a case where interim interdict was granted against reproduction of articles in a daily

---

17 1956 Act s 2(5); *Caird v Sime* (1887) 14 R (HL) 37; but see *Francis Day & Hunter v Feldman & Co* [1914] 2 Ch 728, CA; *Philip v Pennell* [1907] 2 Ch 577; *Leslie v Young & Sons* (1893) 21 R (HL) 57; *Harpers v Barry, Henry & Co* : (1892) 20 R 133; *Ladbroke v William Hill (Football) Ltd* [1964] 1 All ER 465, HL (copyright in football coupon).
18 1956 Act s 2(6).
19 Ibid s 5(5).
20 *Express Newspapers plc v Liverpool Daily Post and Echo plc* [1985] 3 All ER 680 per Whiteford J at 684.
1 Ibid.

newspaper but only to the extent of what had been published up to the date of the order, see *Scotsman Publications Ltd v John Edwards Advertising Services Ltd* 1980 SC 308.

Interdict of breach of future copyrights

Doubts have been expressed whether interdict can competently be granted against breach of copyright of a work yet to be published.[2] As in every action of interdict the petitioner must have both title and interest to sue and must have some existing legal right which the anticipated conduct of the respondent will infringe. If the petitioner is not yet the holder of a copyright it is difficult to see how he can be said to be proprietor of the necessary legal right. Future copyrights are however referred to in the 1956 Act s 37 which makes provision for the assignation of the copyright in a work yet to be made or published and for the granting of licences by the prospective owner of a copyright.

Artistic works

'Artistic work' means paintings, drawings, sculptures, engravings and photographs, works of architecture being either buildings or models thereof and works of artistic craftsmanship not falling within the foregoing categories.[3]

Infringement of artistic works

The question of whether a works is 'artistic' within the meaning of the 1956 Act cannot be decided by reference to any preconceived formula or test but must be decided upon the evidence in each particular case. In considering whether a work is one of artistic craftsmanship, the most cogent evidence will be that given either by those who are themselves artistic craftsmen or by those who are concerned with the training of artistic craftsmen. The first essential of a work of art is that it shall have come into existence as the product of an author who is consciously concerned to produce a work of art (*George Hensher Ltd v Restawhile Upholstery Ltd*).[3]

The acts restricted by a copyright of an artistic work consist of reproducing the work in any material form subject to the exception for objects in three dimensions in s 9(8) of the 1956 Act (for examples of these provisions see *Merchant Adventurers Ltd v M Grew & Co Ltd* [1971] 2 All ER 657 and *L B Plastics Ltd v Swish Products Ltd* [1979] RPC 551), publishing work, including the work in a television broadcast, and

---

2 See Dr Hector MacQueen 'Copyright in Future Publications' 1985 JLLS 198, and his commentary on *Scotsman Publications v John Edwards Advertising Services*.
3 1956 Act s 3(1). *George Hensher Ltd v Restawhile Upholstery Ltd* [1974] 2 All ER 420, HL at 437 per Lord Simon and at 483 per Lord Kilbrandon.

causing such a programme to be transmitted on a diffusion service.[4] As to any artistic element in the design and making of a dress, see *Burke v Spicers Dress Designs*.[4]

Where a person commissions the taking of a photograph, or the painting or drawing of a portrait, or the making of an engraving, and agrees to pay for it, that person is entitled to the copyright of the work so commissioned.[5] Where a literary, dramatic or musical work is made by the author in the course of employment under contract with a newspaper, magazine or other periodical, for publication therein, the proprietor of the newspaper, magazine or other periodical is entitled to the copyright but only so far as relating to publication in any newspaper, magazine or other periodical.[6]

Fair dealing

The Act excludes from the protection of copyright fair dealing with literary, dramatic or musical works for the purposes of research or private study,[7] criticism or review, provided in the case of the latter it is accompanied by a sufficient acknowledgment. Other exceptions are made for the use of the work in reporting current events in a newspaper or by broadcasting or showing a film and for reproduction in judicial proceedings. Reading a reasonable extract of a work in public, if accompanied by a suitable acknowledgment, and not used for broadcasting, is also excluded from infringement.[8] A similar exemption applies, subject to certain conditions, to extracts (not being more than two) in a collection intended for but not specifically published for use in schools, provided the collection consists mainly of work in which no copyright subsists.[9]

Cases where copyright excluded on the grounds of public policy

The benefit of copyright will not be granted to a work which is libellous, immoral, obscene or scandalous, or of irreligious tendency.[10] The earlier decisions wherein the question of immorality, obscenity and irreligious tendency were considered can no longer be taken as reliable

---

4 Ibid s 3(5); *Burke v Spicers Dress Designs* (1936) 1 All ER 99; *Hensher v Restawhile Upholstery Ltd* [1974] 2 All ER 420, HL; *Merchant Adventurers Ltd v Grew & Co* [1971] 2 All ER 657; *Infabrics Ltd v Jaytex Ltd* [1981] 1 All ER 1057, HL.
5 1956 Act s 4(3).
6 1956 Act s 4(2).
7 Ibid s 6(1).
8 Ibid s 6(2), (3), (4) and (5).
9 Ibid s 6(6).
10 *Baschet v London Illustrated Standard Co* [1900] 1 Ch 73; *Glynn v Weston Feature Film Co* (1916) 1 Ch 261; *Pasickniak v Dojacek* [1928] DLR 545: see also *Copinger and Skone-James on Copyright* p 221 ff and the older cases there cited.

guides, having regard to the manifest changes in social attitudes to such matters.

Miscellaneous exemptions from copyright

Certain exemptions from infringement are provided for the issuing of copies of an article subject to copyright by certain libraries and archives specified in Regulations made by the Board of Trade;[11] and for the manufacturing of records of musical works where previous recordings have been made or imported into the United Kingdom with the licence of the owner of the copyright, but subject, where records are sold by retail, to the payment of royalties to the owner of the copyright.[12]

As regards unpublished manuscripts which have been deposited in a library or museum, these may be reproduced or published without infringement of copyright provided the author has been dead for fifty years and a hundred years have elapsed since the work was made and the purpose of reproduction is research, private study or for publication.[13]

Exemptions based on fair dealing are also provided in the case of artistic works in relation to the criticism or review thereof.[14] The painting, drawing or engraving of a copyright work of sculpture or artistic craftsmanship as defined by s 3(1)(a) of the 1956 Act permanently situated in a public place or its inclusion in a film or a television broadcast does not amount to infringement.[15] Similar exemptions apply to works of architecture. In relation to infringement of copyright of the construction of a building, where it has already been partly constructed, no interdict may be granted which will prevent completion or require demolition of the building.[16]

Registered industrial designs

The effect of registration of a design used for an industrial purpose and its interrelation with copyright is dealt with later.[17] Exemption from infringement of certain aspects of design copyright is contained in the Registered Designs Act 1949 and the Copyright Act 1956, as amended.[18]

---

11 1956 Act s 7.
12 Ibid s 8(1).
13 Ibid s 7(6).
14 Ibid s 9(2). As to fair dealing see p 75 above.
15 Ibid s 9(3).
16 Ibid s 9(4) and (9), 10 and 17(4).
17 See p 81 below.
18 1956 Act s 10 as amended by the Design Copyright Act 1968.

Published editions of works

Copyright under Part II of the 1956 Act subsists, subject to the provisions of the Act, in every published edition of a literary, dramatic or musical work where the first published edition was in the United Kingdom or another country to which s 10 of the Act extends, or where the publisher of the earlier edition was a qualified person at the date of first publication. The copyright vests in the publisher and expires at the end of 25 years after expiry of the year in which the edition was first published.[19]

Copyright in sound recordings

The making of sound recordings is protected by copyright where the maker was a qualified person when the recording was made and where the first publication of the recording took place in the United Kingdom or in a country to which s 12 of the 1956 Act applies. It continues for fifty years from the end of the year in which the recording was first published.[20] Where a person commissions a sound recording and pays for it he is, in the absence of agreement to the contrary, entitled to the copyright.[1]

The acts which are restricted by the copyright are making a record or tape embodying the recording, causing the recording to be heard in public and broadcasting the recording.[2] In deciding whether a performance has taken place 'in public' each case must be considered upon its own facts. The circumstances may vary widely. As was pointed out in *Performing Right Society v Rangers FC Supporters Club*:[3]

> At one end of the spectrum there is what has been described as the domestic situation. At the other end is the situation where the promoter invites the audience to attend the performance on payment of an entry fee. In between there is a wide range of varying situations.

The reasoning behind the exclusion of domestic or *quasi* domestic performances lies in the relationship between the promoter and his audience. No infringement takes place where a sound recording is caused to be heard in public:

---

19 1956 Act s 15.
20 Ibid s 12(3).
1 Ibid s 12(4).
2 Ibid.
3 Ibid s 12(5); *Harms Inc & Chappell & Co v Martans Club* [1927] 1 Ch 526; *PRS v Hawthorn's Hotel Ltd* [1933] Ch 855; *Jennings v Stephens* [1936] Ch 469; *Phonographic v Pontins* [1967] 3 All ER 736; *PRS v Harlequin Record Shops* [1979] 2 All ER 28; *PRS v Rangers FC Supporters Club* 1974 SLT 151 at 153; *CBS Inc v Ames Records & Tapes Ltd* [1981] 2 All ER 812; *Phonographic Performance v M'Kenzie* 1982 SLT 272.

(a) at any premises where persons reside or sleep and the performance is part of the amenities for residents or inmates; or
(b) it is part of the activities of the club, society or other organisation not established for profit and whose objects are charitable or otherwise concerned with the advancement of religion, education or social welfare.

In the case of (a) no special charge can be made for admission to the area where the recording is to be heard. As regards (b) if a charge is made for admission to the said area the proceeds must be wholly applied for the purpose of the organisation.[4]

A sound recording means the aggregate of the sounds embodied in and capable of being reproduced by means of a record of any description other than a film sound track.[5] 'Record' means any disc, tape, perforated roll or other device in which sounds embodied are capable of being automatically reproduced therefrom.[6]

Where a record company has an exclusive contract to sell a performer's records, the record company and the performer have no civil right of action by interdict against a 'bootlegger' under the Dramatic and Musical Performers' Protection Act 1958. A 'bootlegged' recording is one made of an artiste's performance at a theatre or, concert without the knowledge or consent of the artiste. The Performers Protection Act 1963 and the Performers Protection Act 1972 create only criminal offences and in *RCA Corpn v Pollard*[7] a right of civil action for injunction was held incompetent on the ground that the defendant had not himself interfered with the plaintiff's exclusive contract with the performer (Elvis Presley). For a different view in Scotland see the opinion of Lord Kincraig in *Silly Wizard Ltd v Shaughnessy*[8] where (without expressing a concluded view) his Lordship said that he would have thought an Act (the Dramatic and Musical Performers' Protection Act 1958 s 1) which is designed to protect dramatic and musical performers who would have no control over the question of prosecution, would be one intended to give a right of action to those performers.

Cinematograph films

Subject to the provisions of the 1956 Act, every cinematograph film, of which the maker was a qualified person for the whole or a substantial

---
4 1956 Act s 12(7).
5 Ibid s 12(8) and s 48.
6 Ibid.
7 *RCA Corps v Pollard* [1982] 3 All ER 771, CA.
8 1983 SLT 367.

part of the period within which the film was made, is protected by copyright, provided the first publication of the film took place in the United Kingdom or another country to which s 13 of the Act applies. The copyright subsists for fifty years.[9] The acts restricted by the copyright are making a copy of the film, causing the film's visual images or its sound to be seen or heard in public, broadcasting the film and causing the film to be transmitted to subscribers in a diffusion service.[10]

Copyright in television and sound broadcasts

Copyright subsists, subject to the provisions of the 1956 Act, in every television or sound broadcast by the BBC and ITA from a place in the United Kingdom or in any other country to which s 14 extends.[11] The copyright continues for a period of fifty years from the end of the year in which the broadcast is made.[12] The acts restricted by the copyright and which constitute infringement under the 1956 Act are:

(a) the making of, otherwise than for private purposes, a cinematograph film of the work or copy of such film;
(b) as regards sound broadcast (or a television broadcast so far as it consists of sounds) the making, other than for private purposes, of a sound recording of such broadcast, or a record embodying such recording;
(c) in the case of a television broadcast causing its visual images to be seen or its accompanying sounds to be heard by a paying public; and
(d) rebroadcasting either a television or sound broadcast.

'Pirating' of video tape recordings is struck at by s 21 of the 1956 Act,[13] and radio and television programmes transmitted by cable are now protected by copyright under the Cable and Broadcasting Act 1984 s 22. Schedule 5 para 6(7) of that Act deals with the problems arising from satellite broadcasting.

Proceedings by way of interdict for infringement

Where infringement has taken place, the owner of the copyright or an exclusive licensee of the owner is entitled to interdict the offending party. He may also be entitled in certain circumstances to damages and

---

9 1956 Act s 13(3).
10 Ibid s 13(5); *Milligan v Broadway Cinema Productions Ltd* 1923 SLT 35.
11 1956 Act s 14(1).
12 Ibid s 14(2).
13 Ibid s 14(4); *Rank Film Distributors v Video Information Centre* [1981] 2 All ER 76, HL.

to count reckoning and payment.[14] An exclusive licence in favour of another person must be in writing.[15] While civil proceedings for infringement of copyright, registered trade mark or design are competent against the Crown, under s 3 of the Crown Proceedings Act 1947, the remedy of interdict is excluded by s 21(a) as applied to Scotland by s 43(a). The court will however make an order declaring the rights of parties.

Where there is an owner of copyright and an exclusive licensee and an infringement of copyright is alleged, both the owner and licensee, if both are seeking interdict, must, unless with leave of the court, sue as joint pursuers. Either the owner or the licensee may however apply for interim interdict.[16] Certain organisations exist as assignees to pursue persons performing a literary, dramatic or musical work, sound recordings and television broadcasts without the licence of the copyright owner. These include the Performing Rights Society, Phonographic Performers Ltd and the Mechanical Copyright Protection Society Ltd. An assignation of copyright must be in writing.[17]

Proof of facts in copyright actions

The copyright alleged is presumed to exist unless its existence is put in issue by the defender. Where the existence of the copyright is proved, admitted or presumed under the Act, the pursuer claiming ownership is presumed to be the owner unless the question of ownership is put in issue by the defender. Certain presumptions as to authorship are provided where a name purporting to be that of the author appears on copies of the work.[18]

Crown copyright

A right of copyright vests in the Crown in respect of every original literary, dramatic or musical work made by or under the direction or control of Her Majesty or of a Government Department.[19] The copyright subsists for fifty years.

14 1956 Act ss 1 and 17.
15 Ibid s 19.
16 Ibid s 19(3) and s 24.
17 Ibid s 37.
18 Ibid s 20.
19 Ibid s 39.

7 REGISTERED DESIGNS

General principles

Designs may be registered under the Registered Designs Acts 1949[20] to 1968. 'Design' means feature or shape, configuration, pattern or ornament applied to an article by any industrial process or means, being features which, in the finished article, appeal to and are judged solely by the eye, but does not include a method or principle of construction, or features of shape or configuration which are dictated solely by the function which the article to be made in that shape or configuration has to perform.[1] To be capable of registration the design must be new or original.[2] Articles which are primarily literary or artistic are excluded from the operation of the Registered Designs Acts.[3]

The author of the design is deemed to be the proprietor, except where the design is executed by the author for another person for good consideration. In such circumstances that other person is to be treated, for the purposes of the Acts, as the proprietor.[4]

The registration of a design gives to the proprietor the copyright in the registered design, being the exclusive right in the United Kingdom and the Isle of Man to make or import for sale or for use for the purposes of any trade or business or to sell, hire or offer for sale or hire, any article of which the design is registered.[5]

The copyright in the design extends for five years but may be extended upon application to the registrar for two further periods each of five years.

Nature of infringement

Infringement of the copyright of a registered design is a ground for interdict.[6] Damages and an accounting may also be claimed.

Damages will not be awarded (but interdict may be granted) against a defender who proves that, at the date of the infringement, he was not aware and had no reasonable ground for supposing that the design was registered. A person is not deemed to have been aware or to have had reasonable cause to suppose that the design was registered, by reason only of the marking of the article with the word 'Registered' or any

20 12, 13 and 14 Geo'VI c 88, as amended by Patents, Designs and Marks Act 1986, Sch 3.
1 1949 Act s 1(3).
2 Ibid s 1(2).
3 Design Rules 1949 r 26.
4 1949 Act s 2(1).
5 Ibid s 7(1).
6 Ibid s 9(2).

abbreviation thereof or any words implying registration, unless the number of the design accompanies the word or its abbreviation. This does not however prevent the granting of interdict.[7]

Certification that validity has been contested

Where the validity of a registered design has been the subject of legal proceedings, including interdict, and has been found by the court to be validly registered the court may certify that the validity was so contested.[8] Where such a certificate has been granted, and there are subsequent proceedings alleging infringement, and judgment is given to the registered proprietor, he will, unless the court otherwise orders and excepting any appeal in such proceedings, be entitled to his expenses on a solicitor and client basis. The Court means the Court of Session.[9]

Infringement of unregistered trade designs

Infringement occurs where any act is done, the exclusive right to do which is vested in the registered proprietor. No infringement can arise in the case of unregistered designs except in the conditional cases covered by s 10 of the Copyright Act 1956, as amended by the Design Copyright Act 1968 but an action of interdict at common law may lie on the ground of 'passing off'. The whole question of protection of unregistered designs under s 10 is complex. Thus the law laid down in the most recent authority (*British Leyland v Armstrong Patents*[10]) declares that a design which cannot be registered because, for example, it is wholly functional may still be entitled to copyright as an artistic work.

Similarity of designs

Difficult questions can arise in deciding whether one design resembles a registered design to such an extent as to justify interdict. The fact that two designs may perform a similar function is irrelevant.

Any similarity must be judged visually and must have regard to the shape, configuration, pattern or ornament and whether the design is new or original. For a full discussion of the factors involved in considering these aspects of the design see *Harvey & Co (London) Ltd v Secure Fittings Ltd*.[11]

7 1949 Act s 9(1) and 9(2).
8 Ibid s 25.
9 Ibid s 45(2).
10 [1986] 1 All ER 850. For a previous line of authority see *Dorling v Honnor Marine* [1965] 1 Ch 1: *Amp Inc v Utilux Pty Ltd* [1972] RPC 103, HL.
11 1966 SLT 121; see also *Stenor Ltd v Whitesides (Clitheroe) Ltd* [1948] AC 101; *Hunter & Co v Falkirk Iron Co* (1887) 14 R 1072; *Hecla Foundry Co v Walker, Hunter & Co* (1889) 16 R (HL) 27.

8 PATENTS

Definition and exclusions

As from the passing of the Patents Act 1977 on 29 July 1977, a patent may be granted only for an invention which is new, involves an inventive step and is capable of industrial application.[12] Amongst new material declared not to be inventions for the purpose of the 1977 Act are listed scientific theories and mathematical methods, literary, dramatic and musical and artistic works and any scheme or method for performing a mental act, playing a game or doing business or a programme for a computer and the presentation of information.[13] The Secretary of State may by order vary these provisions.[14]

Patents granted under the Patents Act 1949 are still regulated by that Act. New applications and matters arising from them are dealt with under the 1977 Act and the Patent Rules 1978 (SI 216).

A patent may not be granted for an invention, the publication of which would be generally expected to encourage offensive, immoral or anti-social conduct.[15]

A patent is the grant of letters patent under the seal of the Patent Office in exercise of the Royal prerogative of an incorporeal right of property in the exclusive and monopoly privilege of exploiting an invention.[16] The grant gives to the inventor a right to prohibit all other persons from doing what the inventor has protected by his patent.[17]

The patent continues in force for 20 years beginning with the date of filing the application or such other date as may be prescribed[18] but subject always to the payment of such periodical renewal fees as may be laid down from time to time.

Acts defined as infringement

A person infringes a patent for an invention if, but only if, while the patent is in force, he does any of the following things in the United Kingdom in relation to the invention, without the consent of the proprietor of the patent, namely:

(a) where the invention is a product, he makes, disposes of or offers to dispose of, uses or imports the product or keeps it whether for disposal or otherwise;

---

12 1977 Act s 1.
13 Ibid s 1(2).
14 Ibid s 1(5).
15 Ibid s 1(4).
16 *Steers v Rogers* (1893) 10 RPC 245, HL; *Neilson v Househill Coal & Iron Co* (1842) 4 D 470 at 475.
17 *Hutchison, Main & Co v Pattullo Bros* (1888) 15 R 644 at 657 per LJC Moncreif.
18 1977 Act s 25.

(b) where the invention is a process, he uses the process or offers it for use in the United Kingdom when he knows, or it is obvious to a reasonable person in the circumstances, that its use there without the consent of the proprietor would be an infringement of the patent;
(c) where the invention is a process, he disposes of, offers to dispose of, uses or imports any product obtained directly by means of that process or keeps any such product for disposal or otherwise.[19]

A person also infringes a patent for an invention if, while the patent is in force and without the consent of the proprietor, he supplies or offers to supply in the United Kingdom to a person, other than a licensee or other person entitled to work the invention, with any of the means relating to an essential element of the invention for putting the invention into force, when he knows or it is obvious to any reasonable person in the circumstances, that these means are intended to put the invention into effect in the United Kingdom.[20]

Infringement of a patent may arise by imitation or adaptation of a mechanical process either by adding something to it or by removal of part of the process and substituting an equivalent mechanism so that the offending process differs only colourably from that of the patentee.[1] Where a patent claims to achieve a particular result by a mechanical or other process, it is not infringed by a machine which achieves the same result by a distinct and quite different process.[2] It has been held that the repairing or renovating of an article may amount to an infringement by making of a new article.[3] The conclusion for interdict should refer specifically to the claims of the specification and not merely to an improvement contained therein.[4]

Application may be made to the court by an aggrieved person, in the course of defending an alleged infringement, or in the principal action, where revocation of a patent has occurred, on any of the grounds set out in s 72 of the 1977 Act. If, however, the patent has been in existence for two years, such action is incompetent unless it can be shown that the person registered as the proprietor knew at the time of the grant that he was not entitled to the patent.[5]

---

19 1977 Act s 60(1); *Calman v PCL Packaging (UK)* [1982] FSR 406; *Canon K K's Application* [1982] RPC 549; *British Thomson-Houston Co v Charlesworth Peebles & Co* 1922 SC 680.
20 1977 Act s 60(2); *PCUK v Diamond Shamrock Industrial Chemicals* [1981] FSR 427.
 1 *Dudgeon v Thomson* (1877) 4 R (HL) 88; *Van Berkel v R D Simpson Ltd* 1907 SC 165; *Murchland v Nicholson* (1893) 20 R 1006; *Henderson v Clippens Oil Co* (1883) 10 R (HL) 38.
 2 *John Hastie & Co v Brown* (1906) 8 F (HL) 10; *Stewart and Briggs v Bell's Trustee* (1883) 11 R 236.
 3 *Sirdar Rubber Co Ltd and Maclulich v Wallington, Weston & Co* (1907) 24 RPC 539 at 543.
 4 *Ygris v M'Farlane Bros (Heat) Ltd* 1969 SLT (Notes) 77.
 5 1977 Act s 72.

An act which would otherwise constitute an infringement of patent will not do so if it is done privately, and for purposes which are not commercial, or for any of the other purposes or in the circumstances set out in s 60(5) and s 60(6) of the 1977 Act.

Nature of interdict sought

Civil proceedings for interdict may be brought by the proprietor of a patent in respect of any act alleged to infringe the patent or any apprehended infringement. An exclusive licensee may sue for interdict. There may be combined with the crave for interdict claims for destruction or delivery of the offending articles or any articles in which the product is inextricably[6] comprised together with a claim for damages or count reckoning and payment and the declarator that the patent is valid and has been infringed by the defender.[7]

As soon as application for a patent has been published, and pending the grant of the patent, the application may, subject to certain qualifications, sue for interdict and damages where an infringement has taken place.[8]

References to the Comptroller of Patents

By agreement of parties, questions as to whether a patent has been infringed may be referred to the Comptroller of Patents and, in such a reference, the proprietor of the patent may seek interdict and the other remedies mentioned above.[9] The Comptroller may however decline to exercise his jurisdiction.

Where there is no such reference to the Comptroller, proceedings relating primarily to patents must be brought in the Court of Session.[10] The jurisdiction of the Sheriff in regard to patents was abolished by s 98(1) of the 1977 Act except in relation to questions which are incidental to proceedings otherwise competent in the Sheriff Court.

Where in any proceedings a patent is found to be partially valid, interdict may be granted in respect of that part found valid and infringed.[11] An order for destruction or delivery to the pursuer of the offending articles may be sought but would be granted only on final success in the action.[12]

---

6 Ibid s 61(1).
7 1977 Act s 61(1); *Hawker Siddely Dynamics Engineering v Real Time Developments Ltd* [1983] RPC 395; *Scottish Vacuum Cleaner Co v Provincial Cinematograph Theatres Ltd* (1915) 1 SLT 389.
8 1977 Act s 69.
9 Ibid s 61(3).
10 Ibid s 98(1); see also Act of Sederunt (Patent Rules) 1978, SI 1978, 955.
11 Ibid s 63(1); *Codex Corp v Racal-Milgo* [1983] RPC 369, CA.
12 *Incandescent Gas Light Co v M'Culloch* (1897) 5 SLT 180.

As to the appropriate order where a number of infringements are alleged in regard to particular machines, see *Plasticisers v Stewart*.[13]

Assignation of patents and licences

Special provisions applying to Scotland as to the nature of any transaction in patents, and applications for patents are contained in s 31 of the Act. A patent or an application for patent is declared to be incorporeal moveable property and it may be assigned and security granted over it. Licences or sub-licences may be granted under any patent or application for patent for working the invention which is the subject of the patent and these also may be assigned and may be subject to security. An assignation or security must be in writing and probative of the parties. An assignation of a patent or of an application for patent, or any exclusive licence therefore may confer upon the assignee or licensee the right to bring proceedings for interdict in respect of any alleged infringement.[14]

Interdict of threatened infringement

Where there is averment of a threat of infringement of a patent, or of intention so to do, an action of interdict will be competent.[15] Ignorance of the existence of the patent is no defence, nor is absence of intention to infringe.[16]

Patents under international conventions

In terms of the European Patent Convention 1973 a patent granted under the Convention which designates the United Kingdom as one of the countries to which it applies is, in so far as infringement is concerned, treated as if it were a patent granted under the 1977 Act. The registered proprietor is entitled to all the rights and remedies provided by the Act. The Court of Session may, subject to certain exceptions,[17] entertain actions arising out of patents granted under the Convention.

The European Community Patent Convention 1975 is applicable to the United Kingdom and its provisions have the force of law. Questions arising under this Convention and its application to the United Kingdom may, again with certain exceptions, be tried in the Court of

---

13 1973 SLT 58.
14 *Scottish Vacuum Cleaner Co Ltd v Provincial Cinematograph Theatres* (1915) 1 SLT 389.
15 *Dowling v Billington* (1890) 7 RPC 191; *Bloom v Shulman* (1934) 51 RPC 308.
16 *Proctor v Bennis* (1887) 4 RPC 333 and 336 CA; *Young & Neilson v Rosenthal & Co* (1884) 1 RPC 29. See also *BTH v Charlesworth Peebles & Co* 1922 SC 680.
17 1977 Act s 82.

Session, subject to the residential and other qualifications specified in s 88 of the Act.[18]

Interdict against threats of infringement proceedings

Where a person threatens another with proceedings for infringement of a patent, the party aggrieved by such threats may obtain declarator that the threats are not justified, together with interdict against their continuance and damages where loss can be shown. It matters not that the threats were made in the honest belief that a patent was to be infringed and the manner of making the threats is of no consequence. The pursuer is entitled to the foregoing remedies unless the defender proves that the acts complained of would constitute infringement of a valid patent.[19]

Withdrawal of privileges against self-incrimination in proceedings relating to intellectual property

The problem reflected in *British Phonographic Industry Ltd v Cohen, Cohen, Kelly, Cohen & Cohen Ltd*,[20] which concerned breach of copyright where the pursuers sought *ex parte* an order for production of documents in the respondent's possession under s 1 of the Administration of Justice (Scotland) Act 1972, has now been affected by s 15 and 19 of the Law Reform (Miscellaneous Provisions) (Scotland) Act 1985. In *British Phonographic Industry Ltd v Cohen, Cohen, Kelly, Cohen & Cohen Ltd*, on remit from the Lord Ordinary, the Inner House had given the opinion that where the actions alleged against the respondents would constitute a criminal offence, the court must consider whether compliance with an order for production would require the respondents to incriminate themselves. In such circumstances the proper course was to refuse the order.

Section 15 of the Law Reform (Miscellaneous Provisions) (Scotland) Act 1985, provides that in any proceedings for infringement of rights pertaining to any intellectual property or for passing off, or to obtain disclosure of information relating thereto, or to prevent apprehended infringement or passing off, a person shall not be excused from answering any questions or from complying with any order by reason that to do so would expose him to proceedings for a related offence or for the recovery of a related penalty. Section 15(3) provides however that no statement or admission by a person in the aforesaid proceedings shall in proceedings for any related offence or recovery of a related penalty be admissible in evidence against him.

---

18 See generally as to the whole subject of patents, Walton and Laddie on *Patent Law of Europe and the United Kingdom*.
19 Patents Act 1977 s 70; *Skinner & Co v Perry* (1893) 10 RPC 1, CA.
20 1983 SLT 137.

'Intellectual property' is defined by s 15(5) of the last mentioned Act as amended by Patents, Designs and Marks Act 1986, Sch 2 as any patent, trade mark, service mark, copyright, registered design, technical or commercial information or other intellectual property. The same subsection defines 'related offence' and 'related penalty'.

Section 1 of the Administration of Justice (Scotland) Act, 1972 is amended by s 19 of the 1985 Act to enable the Court of Session and the Sheriff Court to order any person to disclose information as to the identity of any persons who might be witnesses in civil proceedings pending or which are likely to be brought or might be defenders in any civil proceedings which appear likely to be brought.

Interim interdict in the protection of intellectual property

The principles governing the grant or refusal of interim interdict in Scotland, where the action is one for the protection of intellectual property and in actions of passing off, are the same as those applied in other fields of law.[1] In relying upon English decisions involving interlocutory injunctions, care must be taken to distinguish the difference between the Scottish and English approaches to the question of ultimate success and the preliminary pleadings and/or affidavits. The Scottish practice is explained by Lord Fraser in the House of Lords case *N W L Ltd v Woods*[2] (an English case involving industrial relations) where he emphasises that (contrary to the English practice) the Scottish courts will have regard to the relative strengths of the cases put forward in averment and argument at the interim interdict stage. The likelihood of ultimate success for one party or the other may be an element in the balance of convenience. In explaining this difference between the two systems, his Lordship noted that the approach in *American Cyanamid Co v Ethicon Ltd*[3] did not apply in Scotland.

---

1 As to interim interdict generally see Chapter 17 below.
2 [1979] 3 All ER 614, CA at 628.
3 [1975] 1 All ER 504, HL.

Chapter 10

Interdicts and exclusion orders under the Matrimonial Homes (Family Protection) (Scotland) Act 1981

General principles

The Matrimonial Homes (Family Protection) (Scotland) Act 1981, as amended by the Law Reform (Miscellaneous Provisions) (Scotland) Act 1985, introduced three major and long awaited reforms into the law of Scotland. In the first place, by the very fact of marriage it confers upon a spouse, who is neither the tenant nor owner, nor otherwise entitled to occupy the matrimonial home, a right to occupy that home.[1] This right now exists *ex lege* by virtue of the marriage and there is no requirement for registration of the right or any special procedure. Secondly, it extends and greatly strengthens the powers of the court to make orders by way of interdict and otherwise for the prevention of domestic violence and for the preservation and protection of certain matrimonial assets.[2] In the third place, it gives to a cohabiting partner, who has no right of occupancy of the house in which he or she cohabits, the right in certain circumstances to occupy that house.[3] Unlike the case of the spouse, however, the right of the cohabitee does not arise automatically in consequence of the cohabitation,, but must be declared to exist by the court, following an application by the cohabitee in which the provisions of s 18 of the 1981 Act must be satisfied.

Occupancy rights of spouses[4]

Where one spouse is entitled or permitted by a third party to occupy a matrimonial home (known as 'the entitled spouse') and the other spouse is not so entitled or permitted (known as 'the non-entitled spouse'), s 1 of the Act confers upon the non-entitled spouse two rights:

(a) if he or she is in occupation of the matrimonial home, the right not to be excluded from it by the entitled spouse; and

---

1 S 1(1)(a) and (b) as amended by the Law Reform (Miscellaneous Provisions) (Scotland) Act 1985.
2 Ss 3, 4 and 14.
3 S 18.
4 For a full discussion of the 1981 Act and its application see *Nichols and Meston* on the Matrimonial Homes (Family Protection) (Scotland) Act 1981 (2nd edn).

89

Interdicts and exclusion orders

(b) if not in occupation of the matrimonial home, the right to enter into and occupy it.

The definition of 'Matrimonial Home' in s 22 of the Act is wide and means any house, caravan, houseboat or other structure which has been provided or has been made available by one or both of the spouses as, or has become, a family residence and including any garden or other ground or building attached to and usually occupied with or otherwise required for the amenity or convenience of the house, caravan, houseboat or other structure. A caravan means a caravan, either mobile or fixed to the land.

Orders as to occupancy and protection granted by the court

Section 3(1) of the 1981 Act provides that, where there is an entitled spouse and a non-entitled spouse or where both are entitled spouses (as in the case of joint ownership or joint tenancy), either spouse may apply to the court (being either the Court of Session or the Sheriff Court) for an order:

(a) declaring the occupancy rights of the applicant spouse;
(b) enforcing the occupancy rights of the applicant spouse;
(c) restricting the occupancy rights of the non-applicant spouse;
(d) regulating the exercise by either spouse of his or her rights of occupancy; or
(e) protecting the occupancy rights of the applicant spouse in relation to the other spouse. This part of the order may be utilised to prevent by interdict any interference with the occupancy rights in consequence of dealings between the entitled spouse and third parties, whether by sale, lease or otherwise.

Section 3(2) of the 1981 Act provides that, where one spouse owns or hires or is acquiring by hire purchase or conditional sale agreement, furniture and plenishing in a matrimonial home, the other spouse, if he or she has occupancy rights, may apply to the court for an order granting permission to use, in the matrimonial home, any such furniture and plenishing, but subject to the right of any third party where there is a hire purchase agreement or conditional sale agreement.

Under s 3(3) the court, if satisfied that the application applies to a matrimonial home, must grant a declarator of occupancy rights of the applicant spouse. Where an application seeks also orders under para (b), (c), (d) and (e) or under s 3(2) relating to the preservation of furnishing and plenishing the court has a discretion. It may grant only such of these orders as appear just and reasonable having regard to all the circumstances of the case including:

(a) the conduct of the spouses in relation to each other or otherwise;
(b) the respective needs and financial resources of the spouses;
(c) the needs of any child of the family;
(d) the extent (if any) to which:
  (i) the matrimonial home, and
  (ii) in relation to any order under s 3(2) the furniture and plenishing
  is used in connection with the trade or business of either spouse, and
(e) whether the entitled spouse offers or has offered to make available to the non-entitled spouse any suitable alternative accommodation.

None of these provisions under s 3 is designed to exclude the non-applicant spouse from the matrimonial home, and s 3(5) provides that the court shall not make an order under s 3(1) or any interim order under s 3(4) if it appears that the effect would be so to exclude the non-applicant spouse from the matrimonial home. Orders regulating the rights of occupancy under s 3(1) are therefore clearly distinguished from orders under s 4(1) as amended by s 13(5) of the 1985 Act which suspend the occupancy rights of the non-applicant spouse (referred to in the 1981 Act as 'exclusion orders').

A 'child of the family' includes any child or grandchild of either spouse and any person who has been brought up or accepted by either spouse as if he or she were a child of that spouse whatever the age of that child, grandchild or person may be.[5]

Exclusion orders

Where there is an entitled and a non-entitled spouse, or where both spouses are entitled or permitted by a third party to occupy the matrimonial home, either spouse may apply to the court for an order suspending the occupancy rights of the other spouse (an exclusion order).[6] Subject to the provision of s 4(3), the court is required to make an exclusion order if it appears that the order is necessary for the protection of the applicant spouse, or any child of the family, from any conduct or any threatened or reasonably apprehended conduct of the non-applicant spouse, which is or would be injurious to the physical or mental health of the applicant spouse or child.[7]

The court may not however make an exclusion order if so to do

---

5 S 22.
6 S 4(1).
7 S 4(2).

would be unjustified or unreasonable having regard to all the circumstances, including the conduct of the spouses in relation to each other, their respective needs and financial resources, the needs of any child of the family (as previously defined), the extent to which the matrimonial home is used in connection with the trade, profession or business of either spouse and whether any suitable alternative accommodation has been offered.[8]

Ancillary orders and interdicts attached to exclusion orders

In making an exclusion order the court is required, on the application of the applicant spouse, to grant three ancillary orders namely:

(a) a warrant for ejection of the non-applicant spouse;
(b) an interdict preventing the non-applicant spouse from entering the matrimonial home without the express permission of the applicant spouse;
(c) an interdict prohibiting the removal by the non-applicant spouse, except with the written consent of the applicant spouse, of any furniture or plenishing in the matrimonial home.[9]

It is however open to the non-applicant spouse to satisfy the court that the warrant for ejection and the interdict prohibiting removal of furniture are unnecessary.[10]

Four further orders[11] which are not mandatory but within the discretion of the court may be appended to an exclusion order, if sought by the applicant spouse or, in the case of paragraphs (b) and (c) below, if the court considers it reasonable to do so, namely:

(a) interdict preventing the non-applicant spouse from entering or remaining in a specified area in the vicinity of the matrimonial home;
(b) an order directing preservation of the non-applicant spouse's goods and effects which remain in the matrimonial home at the time of his summary ejection;
(c) an order attaching such terms and conditions to the exclusion order, warrant and interdict as the court may prescribe;
(d) such order as may be necessary for the proper enforcement of the warrant, exclusion order and interdict.[12]

---

8 S 4(3).
9 S 4(4).
10 Ibid.
11 S 4(5).
12 As to the attachment of powers of arrest see s 15(1) and p 96 below.

Interim exclusion orders

Pending the making of an exclusion order, the court may make an interim order suspending the occupancy rights of a spouse, and the interdicts under the provisions of s 4(4) and 4(5) will apply to such interim order. The interim order may be made only if the non-applicant spouse has been afforded an opportunity of being heard or represented before the court. Under s 15(1) the court is required, if sought by the applicant spouse, to attach a power of arrest in respect of a breach of the exclusion order or of any of the ancillary interdicts.[13]

Grounds for granting of exclusion orders

Initially, in the interpretation of s 4 and in formulating the test to be applied in deciding whether or not to make an exclusion order, a variety of approaches were adopted by the courts. These disclosed substantial differences of view amongst judges and sheriffs. Many of the early difficulties stemmed from the divergent if not conflicting opinions expressed by the judges in *Bell v Bell*[14] and *Smith v Smith*.[15] Both these cases dealt with applications by non-entitled spouses who had left the matrimonial home. The views expressed by Lord Robertson and Lord Grieve (differing in emphasis if not in principle from those of the Lord Justice Clerk) gave rise to a number of problems. Both Lords Robertson and Greive expressed the view that:

(a) the test of necessity for the exclusion order was a high and severe one and that the applicant must be in real and immediate danger of serious injury and irreparable damage (words which find no place in the Act);
(b) the court should be slow to grant an interim exclusion order where the parties were not living together in the matrimonial home and there was no immediate necessity for protection; and
(c) where the parties were living separately, an interim exclusion order would only be granted in exceptional circumstances.

These views did not however find favour with the court in the subsequent cases of *Ward v Ward*;[16] *Colagiacomo v Colagiacomo*[17] and *Brown v Brown*.[18]

In *Ward*[19] and *Brown*,[20] the applicant spouses were living outwith the

---

13 See fn 12 above.
14 1983 SLT 224.
15 1983 SLT 275.
16 1983 SLT 472.
17 1983 SLT 559.
18 1985 SLT 376.
19 Fn 16 above.
20 Fn 17 above.

matrimonial home in consequence of the husbands' violent conduct towards them. In *Colagiacomo*[1] both parties were living in the matrimonial home but occupying separate portions thereof. In delivering the judgment of the court in *Colagiacomo* the Lord Justice Clerk said:

> If there is any misconception that, following *Bell v Bell*, an interim exclusion order will only be granted if the parties are both occupying the matrimonial home, the sooner that misconception is removed the better. The fact that only one of the parties is occupying the matrimonial home is a factor to be taken into account but it is not *per se* to be regarded as a conclusive one.

The doubts raised by *Bell v Bell* and *Smith v Smith* were largely laid to rest by the decision in *Brown v Brown*[2] where in delivering the judgment of the court, Lord Dunpark adopted the view of the Lord Justice Clerk in *Bell v Bell* on the question of leaving the matrimonial home in preference to those of Lords Robertson and Grieve. Lord Dunpark said:

> That is a factor which can be taken into account but it is by no means a disqualifying factor on the ground that the party does not require protection. A party may leave the matrimonial home for a variety of reasons and the particular reason or reasons can be properly taken into consideration. If the applicant desires to exercise the legal right to resume residence in the matrimonial home the Court has to consider the whole position in the light of what the situation would be if that were done and decide whether an interim order is warranted.

Grounds for granting interim exclusion orders

On the question of harm to the physical or mental health of the applicant spouse or the children of the family and the consequent necessity for an interim exclusion order, the problems raised by the opinions of Lord Robertson and Lord Grieve in *Bell* were finally resolved in *Colagiacomo* where the test to be applied was laid down thus:

> An exclusion order will be granted against a husband *ad interim* only where there are *prima facie* grounds for apprehending as a matter of necessity and urgency that the safety of the wife and children will be jeopardised if he is permitted to remain in the matrimonial home.

It may be noted that in *Colagiacomo*, the court accepted that the pursuer's averments of drunken threats supported by medical certificates constituted *prima facie* evidence that the interim exclusion order was necessary.

---

1 Fn 17 above.
2 1985 SLT 376. For further comment on *Bell v Bell* and *Ward v Ward* see *McCafferty v McCafferty* 1986 SLT 650.

In *Brown* where, on appeal, the court restored the judgment of the Sheriff, the latter had accepted affidavit evidence disclosing what the Sheriff considered to be material and serious violence by the defender against the pursuer and he had considered the factors set out in sub-ss 4(2) and 4(3). In dealing with the discretion to be exercised by the judge of first instance in granting or refusing interim exclusion orders, Lord Dunpark said:

> If the judge granting the interim order has considered all the relevant factors and has applied the Section 4 test and thereupon grants an interim exclusion order, it follows that he is satisfied the order is necessary for the protection of the Pursuer. If he is so satisfied that is enough, unless it can be demonstrated that it was unjustifiable or unreasonable for him, upon the relevant facts before him, to grant the interim order.[3]

It would appear in the light of this dictum and the recent case of *McCafferty v McCafferty*[4] that, provided the judge of first instance has dealt with the application in the manner laid down in *Brown*, an appeal court will hesitate to disturb a decision based upon a discretion *ex facie* properly exercised. For an example of exercise of discretion by suspension of the effective date for three months to meet special factors see *Mather v Mather*.[5]

On the question of whether, in *Brown*, a matrimonial molestation interdict under s 14(2) would have afforded sufficient protection, the court was clearly of the view that it would not. It was pointed out that all the assaults had been drink related and a molestation order would not necessarily restrain the defender when he was in drink.

In the Court of Session affidavit evidence may be submitted in any application under the Act (Rule of Court 188D (15)). In the Sheriff Court however the use of affidavit evidence is limited to cases where applications for interim orders are opposed (Act of Sederunt (Consistorial Causes) 1984 para 3(15)).

Matrimonial interdicts

Section 14(1) of the Act introduces the concept of 'matrimonial interdict' which may be granted notwithstanding that the spouses are living together. Although similar to the interdict which may be attached to an exclusion order the matrimonial interdict is an entirely separate remedy and may be obtained where there is no application for

---

3 *Brown v Brown* 1985 SLT 376 at 378.
4 1986 SLT 650.
5 1986 GWD 51.

an exclusion order. A matrimonial interdict is defined by s 14(2) as an interdict, including an interim interdict, which:

(a) restrains or prohibits any conduct of one spouse towards the other spouse or a child of the family; or
(b) prohibits a spouse from entering or remaining in a matrimonial home or in a specified area in the vicinity of the matrimonial home.

The matrimonial interdict which prohibits a spouse from entering or remaining in the matrimonial home does not suspend and cannot be used as a device which in effect suspends the occupancy rights of that spouse. To do so would avoid the requirement to satisfy the test of necessity and would make s 4 and exclusion orders redundant. An interdict which sought to deny the tenant of a house his legal right to occupy it would alter the whole nature and concept of interdict as a redress for a litigant.[6]

Where, in a divorce action, a wife obtained *inter alia* interim interdict against the husband entering the matrimonial home and interim interdict against his entering and remaining therein, the court recalled the second order as being unnecessary in light of the terms of the first order.[7] As to the power of the court to make orders regulating the occupation of the former matrimonial home after divorce, and excluding one of the parties from it, see the Family Law (Scotland) Act 1985 s 14(2).

The remedy of a common law interdict against ejection of an applicant spouse from the matrimonial home or against interference with the furniture remains undisturbed. It has the advantage that a common law interim interdict may be obtained immediately on *ex parte* averments whereas to obtain an interim matrimonial interdict under the 1981 Act requires notice to the defender and he must be given the opportunity to appear.[8]

Attachment of powers of arrest to matrimonial interdicts

The enforcement of interdicts between spouses has in the past frequently presented much difficulty. The effectiveness of matrimonial interdicts under the 1981 Act has however been greatly strengthened by the provisions providing for the inclusion of warrants for police arrest in cases of breach of such interdicts.

Section 15(1) requires the court to attach power of arrest, when sought by the applicant spouse, to:

---

[6] *Tattersall v Tattersall* 1983 SLT 506 at 509 per the Lord President. See also *McKenna v McKenna* 1984 SLT (SL Ct) 92.
[7] *Cowie v Cowie* (1986) 2 GWD 33.
[8] Rules of Court 188D(9).

(a) any matrimonial interdict which is ancillary to an exclusion order, including an interim exclusion order granted under s 4(6); and
(b) to any other matrimonial interdict where the non-applicant spouse has had the opportunity of being heard or represented before the court, unless it appears to the court that, in all the circumstances of the case, such an order is unnecessary.

The power of arrest, like the interdict and the exclusion order, ceases to have effect on the termination of the marriage.[9] Where the power of arrest is granted, it entitles a constable without warrant to arrest a non-applicant spouse if he has reasonable cause to suspect that spouse of being in breach of the interdict.[10]

As soon as possible after service of an interdict with power of arrest attached on the non-applicant spouse, the applicant spouse must ensure that there is delivered to the chief constable of the police area in which the matrimonial home is situated, and if the applicant spouse resides in another area, to the chief constable of that area, a copy of the application for interdict and of the interlocutor granting the interdict, together with a certificate of service of the interdict.[11] Where any matrimonial interdict has been varied or recalled, the spouse who applied for the variation or recall must ensure that a copy of the application for variation or recall, and of the interlocutor, is served upon the chief constable or chief constables to whom notification of the interdict was made.[12]

Procedure on arrest and powers of police

Where a spouse has been arrested under powers contained in s 15 of the Act in respect of a suspected breach of a matrimonial interdict, he may be released unconditionally if the police are satisfied that there is no longer any risk of violence to the applicant spouse or to any child of the family. In such an event a report will be made to the procurator fiscal.[13] Alternatively, the arrested spouse may be detained pending his appearance in court on the first court day occurring after the date of arrest.[14]

Where the procurator fiscal decides not to initiate criminal proceedings against the arrested spouse, the proceedings become of a *quasi* civil nature. The Sheriff may remand the spouse in custody for a

9 S 15(2).
10 S 15(3).
11 S 15(4).
12 S 15(5).
13 Ss 16(1)(a) and 16(2).
14 Ss 16(1)(b) and 17(2).

period not exceeding two days. During this period, the Sheriff will consider:

(a) whether the facts disclose *ex facie* a breach of interdict;
(b) whether proceedings for such breach are to be brought by the applicant spouse; and
(c) whether there is substantial risk of violence by the arrested spouse against the applicant spouse or any child of the family.

If he is satisfied upon all three points, the Sheriff may detain the arrested spouse for a further period not exceeding two days so that proceedings for breach of interdict may be initiated. If the Sheriff is not satisfied that all three factors are present, the arrested spouse must be liberated.[15] In computing the periods of two days no account is to be taken of Saturday or Sunday or any court holiday.

Interdicts and exclusion orders affecting cohabiting couples

Section 18 of the Act extends to cohabiting couples many of the provisions affecting spouses. A cohabiting couple are a man and a woman living together as though they were man and wife in a house which one of them is entitled or permitted by a third party to occupy ('the entitled partner') and the other ('the non-entitled partner') is not entitled or so permitted.

The occupancy rights of a non-entitled partner do not arise *ex lege* and application for declaration of these rights must be made to the court. Occupancy rights may be granted for an initial period of three months and thereafter may be continued at the discretion of the court for a further period or periods none of which may exceed six months.[16]

In determining whether, for the purposes of s 18(1), a man and a woman are a cohabiting couple the court must have regard to the time for which it appears they have been living together and whether there are any children of the relationship.

So long as an order under s 18(1) granting occupancy rights or any extension of such an order is in force, or where both partners are entitled or permitted by a third party to occupy the house in which they are cohabiting, certain provisions of the Act apply to that couple as though they were spouses and apply to any child residing with the cohabiting couple as they apply to a child of the family.[17] The provisions so applying are those in s 2 granting subsidiary and

---

15 S 17(4) and (5).
16 S 18(1).
17 For definition of 'child of the family' see s 22.

consequential rights for securing the occupancy rights of a non-entitled spouse; s 3 which provides for regulation by the court of rights of occupancy (but excepting s 3(1)(c)); s 4 which relates to the conditions upon which the court may grant exclusion orders and interdicts and interim orders suspending rights of occupancy; s 5 which gives the court power to vary or recall any order for occupancy rights, orders for interim suspension thereof and the various interdicts provided by s 4; s 13 which deals with transfers of tenancy; s 14 which authorises the granting of matrimonial interdicts where spouses are living together as man and wife; ss 15, 16 and 17 which allow the attachment of powers of arrest to matrimonial interdicts and set out the powers of the arresting officer and the procedure after arrest and s 22 which is the interpretation clause. It must be noted that unless and until occupancy rights are granted to a non-entitled partner under s 18, none of these provisions of the Act can be invoked by that partner.

The definition of a house in the context of cohabiting couples is given in s 18(6) as including a caravan (which may be either mobile or fixed to the ground), houseboat or other structure in which the couple are cohabiting and any garden or other ground or building attached to and usually occupied with or otherwise required for the amenity or convenience of the house, caravan, houseboat or other structure.

Chapter 11
Interdict in industrial disputes

Historical background
The mass of complex legislation enacted by successive governments since 1971 has produced far-reaching changes in trade union law. In this process the remedy of interdict has played an important role.

Probably the most controversial issue arising from the statutory provisions has been the vexed question of the immunity from legal proceedings of trade unions and their members and officials and of employees generally, in respect of acts undertaken in the course of industrial action, and alleged to have been committed in contemplation of furtherance of a trade dispute. Until the House of Lords decision in *Taff Vale Railway Co v Amalgamated Society of Railway Servants*[1] it had been generally accepted, upon construction of the trade union legislation of 1871 and 1876, that a trade union could not be sued in delict where the act complained of had been carried out by the union, its officers and members in contemplation or furtherance of a trade dispute. Their Lordships held, however, that there was no such general immmunity. The effect of the *Taff Vale Railway* decision was largely nullified by the passage of the Trades Disputes Act 1906. Section 3 of that Act provided that an act done by a person in contemplation or furtherance of a trade dispute should not be actionable on the ground only that it induced some other person to break a contract of employment, or that it was an interference with the trade, business or employment of some other person, or of the right of some other person to dispose of his capital or labour as he willed. Section 4 went on to declare that no court could entertain an action against a trade union or against any members or officials thereof, acting on behalf of themselves and all other members, in respect of any tortious act alleged to have been committed by or on behalf of a trade union. Sections 3 and 4 of the 1906 Act were repealed by the Industrial Relations Act 1971, but were partially re-enacted with modifications by s 14 of the Trade Union and Labour Relations

---
1 [1901] AC 426·

Act 1974. That section was itself wholly repealed by s 15 of the Employment Act 1982.

Apart from the general principle of immunity from legal proceedings, the growth of the trade union movement brought other problems before the courts involving the definition of a trade dispute; the extent to which particular forms of industrial action should be accepted as having been taken in contemplation or furtherance of a trade dispute; the inducement of workers to break contracts of employment, and the regulation and management of the union's affairs. In particular, the greatly increased political and social influence of the trade unions during the latter part of the present century brought new problems such as mass picketing of employers' premises and secondary industrial action by trade unions and their members against employers not directly involved in the particular industrial dispute.

The repeal of the Industrial Relations Act 1971 by the Trade Union and Labour Relations Act 1974 brought the demise of the shortlived and ill-fated National Industrial Relations Court. The 1974 Act was itself amended by the Trade Union and Labour Relations (Amendment) Act 1976, the Employment Protection (Consolidation) Act 1978, the Employment Act 1980, the Employment Act 1982 and the Trade Union Act 1984. A considerable volume of the legislation contained in these statutes is concerned with the protection of the rights of individual employees arising from unfair dismissal and proceedings before the Industrial Tribunals and is beyond the scope of this work. Interdict has however played an important part in dealing with industrial action by employees, such as picketing, 'sit in' and 'work in' activities, and secondary action aimed at employers not directly concerned in the particular dispute; with inducing employees of such employers to breach their contracts of employment, and with the promotion of strikes and other industrial action by trade unions without the support of a prior ballot of union members.

Immunity from legal proceedings

Section 13(1) of the Trade Union and Labour Relations Act 1974, as substituted by s 3(2) of the Trade Union and Labour Relations (Amendment) Act 1976, replaced the immunity provisions of s 3 of the Trades Disputes Acts 1906. Section 13(1) provided that an act done by a person in contemplation or furtherance of a trade dispute should not be actionable in delict on the ground only:

(a) that it induced another person to break a contract, or interfere or induce another person to interfere with its performance, or
(b) that it consisted in his threatening that a contract (whether one to which he was a party or not) would be broken or its performance interfered with, or that he would induce another to break a

contract or interfere with its performance.[2]

Under s 13(4) of the 1974 Act (which is still operative) an agreement or combination of two or more persons to do or procure the doing of any act in contemplation or furtherance of a trade dispute was declared not to be actionable in tort, if the act was one which, if done without any such agreement or combination, would not have been actionable. This immunity presumably extends to a trade union or members thereof. By s 19(2) of the Employment Act 1982, 'tort' was declared in Scotland to mean 'delict'.

Section 14(1) of the 1974 Act, dealing with the immunity of trade unions, their officials and members acting on behalf of the trade union, replaced the immunity provisions of s 4 of the Trades Disputes Act 1906. Section 14(1) provided that no action would lie against a trade union, its trustees, officials or members in respect of any act threatened or intended to be done by or on behalf of a trade union or alleged to have been done in connection with the regulation of relations between employers and workers or a trade union. From this immunity there was excluded by s 14(2) liability arising from negligence, nuisance or breach of duty resulting in personal injury to any person and of breach of duty by the union or its members in respect of ownership, occupation, possession, control or use of property, heritable or moveable, if not arising from an act in contemplation or furtherance of a trade dispute.

With the passing of s 15 of the Employment Act 1982, s 14 of the 1974 Act was wholly repealed and the immunity of trade unions, their officials, and members acting on their behalf from actions in delict was virtually swept away, except in those cases covered by the limited immunity granted by s 13(1)(a) and (b) of the 1974 Act as substituted by s 3(2) of the Trade Union and Labour Relations (Amendment) Act 1976, and by s 13(4) of the 1974 Act. The effect of this repeal would seem to be that the principles laid down in the *Taff Vale Railway* case are revived and trade unions and their officials and members are now liable to be sued in a wide variety of circumstances.

Vicarious liability of trade unions

Section 15 of the 1982 Act also established the vicarious liability of a trade union for the acts of its officials and members and this must be regarded as supplementary to any liability arising under the common

---

[2] See *Square Grip Reinforcement Co Ltd v Macdonald* 1966 SLT 232 where efforts by a union to induce members not directly involved in a strike to breach contracts by refusing to handle goods destined for an employer involved in a strike by other members, were **held illegal**.

law rules of vicarious liability. Such statutory liability arises however only where the act in question can be shown to have been authorised or endorsed by a responsible person, as defined by s 15(3). No vicarious liability arises where a responsible person, as so defined, repudiates the act in question within a reasonable time and in writing (s 15(4)). The statutory vicarious liability attaches to a union in respect only of the acts specified in s 13(1)(a) and (b) of the 1974 Act as substituted by s 3(2) of the Trade Union and Labour Relations. (Amendment) Act 1976, namely, breach of contract and interference with the performance of contracts, threatening breach of contract or conspiracy to commit a tortious act.

Industrial action without ballots

The restricted immunity remaining to trade unions under s 13 of the 1974 Act was further eroded by s 10 of the Trade Union Act 1984 which declared that nothing in s 13 of the 1974 Act should prevent an act done by a trade union, without the support of a ballot, being actionable in delict on the ground that it induced a person to break his contract of employment or to interfere with its performance or that it induced a person to break a commercial contract.

Peaceful picketing

The original immunity conferred by s 13(1) of the 1974 Act was also substantially restricted by s 16 and 17 of the Employment Act 1980 which dealt with a new formula for 'peaceful picketing' and removed from immunity all the acts specified in s 13(1)(a) and (b) of the 1974 Act where these acts arose out of 'secondary action', as defined by s 17(2) of the 1980 Act, and which did not satisfy the requirements of s 3(4) and (5) of that Act. These provisions were designed to amend the law as laid down in *Express Newspapers Ltd v MacShane*[3] and *Duport Steels Ltd v Sirs*[4] which had determined that secondary action[5] might be covered by the immunity in s 13 of the 1974 Act, where those concerned honestly believed that the acts complained of would further the cause of the persons concerned in the industrial dispute. It is, however, noteworthy that in redefining the meaning of 'a trade dispute' in s 18 of the 1982 Act, care was taken to make it clear that the amendment does not affect the question of whether an act done by a person is done by him in contemplation or furtherance of a dispute. Thus it may well be the case that the principle of 'honest belief' and consequent immunity

---

3 [1980] 1 All ER 65, HL.
4 [1980] 1 All ER 529.
5 See further as to secondary picketing p 109 below.

under s 13 of the 1974 Act established by *NWL Ltd v Woods*,[6] *Express Newspapers Ltd v MacShane*[7] and *Duport Steels Ltd v Sirs*[8] have not been entirely lost and that the test is still the subjective belief of the person concerned.

The Employment Act 1982 ss 12, 13 and 14 carried still further the erosion of the immunities remaining under s 13 of the 1974 Act, as amended. The combined effect of these three complex sections of the 1982 Act is to remove from the immunity of s 13 of the 1974 Act (a) any tortious act *inter alia* designed to breach ss 12 and 13 of the 1982 Act (which deal *inter alia* with conditions in commercial contracts requiring the employment of only union members, refusal to negotiate with one or more unions, and similar matters); and (b) any tortious act where the reason for its commission is the use of non-union labour by an employer. The effect would seem to be that, where an action would have been a delict at common law but is protected by the residual immunity in s 13 of the 1974 Act, that protection will be lost if what is done amounted to an inducement or attempted inducement to breach ss 12 and 13 of the 1982 Act.

Acts in furtherance of trade disputes

The repeal, by s 19(1) of the Employment Act 1982, of the declaratory provision in s 13(2) of the 1974 Act that an act in contemplation or furtherance of a trade dispute should not be actionable in delict, followed upon the decisions in *Hadmor Productions Ltd v Hamilton*[9] and *Plessey Co plc v Wilson*.[10] In both cases the actions complained of had taken place before the repeal of s 13(2) of the 1974 Act. In the *Plessey* case, which involved a 'sit in' by employees at a factory, it was held that the action of the employees in occupying the premises, in the face of a requirement to remove, constituted an illegal act. On the other hand it was admitted that what the employees had done was to occupy the premises in contemplation or furtherance of a trade dispute between them and their employers. The court took the view (relying on *Hadmor Productions Ltd v Hamilton*) that unlawful acts so committed might attract immunity for the wrongdoers under s 13(2) where the only conseqence which could give rise to a claim for reparation for loss or damage by the employer was some form of interference with the trade or business of the complaining employer. Upon this proposition and upon the balance of convenience, the court refused to grant interim interdict against the occupying employees. By contrast, in *Phestos*

6 [1979] 3 All ER 614, HL.
7 Fn 3 above.
8 Fn 4 above.
9 [1982] 2 WLR 322.
10 [1983] SLT 139.
11 [1983] SLT 388.

Shipping Co Ltd v Kurmiawan,[11] which also related to a period prior to the repeal of s 13(2) of the 1974 Act, and which was concerned with the occupation of their ship by seamen involved in a trade dispute with the owners, the court carefully avoided any decision as to whether the unlawful occupation of the ship was covered by the immunity given by s 13(2) (although their Lordships conceded that this might be so) and granted interim interdict against the occupying seamen on the balance of convenience and on the ground that, since the men had been dismissed, the only dispute was as to a claim for additional remuneration under their contracts, which could be resolved by an action for payment.

The case of *Galt v Philip*,[12] a decision of the High Court of Justiciary also relating to the period prior to the repeal of s 13(2) of the 1974 Act, was a criminal prosecution of laboratory staff at a hospital, who had barricaded themselves within the premises and unlawfully prevented access thereto by doctors and others. The employees had undertaken to carry out essential work during this period of industrial action and apparently did so. This was therefore a 'work in' as opposed to a 'sit in' in the *Plessey* case. The prosecution was brought under s 7 of the Conspiracy and Protection of Property Act 1875. On appeal the prosecution was successful, despite a plea by the accused that the immunity conferred by s 13(2) of the 1974 Act applied to both civil and criminal proceedings. Giving judgment, the Lord President (Emslie) and Lord Cameron expressed the view that, had civil proceedings for interdict been brought in order to restrain the 'work in' they would have been successful. In the light of this *obiter dicta*, it is difficult to follow the reasoning which led to the refusal of interdict in the *Plessey* case where there had been no undertaking by the employees to carry out any work.[13]

The demise of s 13(2) of the 1974 Act by its repeal under s 19(1) of the Employment Act 1982, seems, at least for the present, to have removed any possible immunity which might have been enjoyed by employees occupying their employer's premises in contemplation or furtherance of a trade dispute. This view is supported by the decision in *British Airports Authority v Ashton*[14] which, although not binding in Scotland, seems likely to be regarded as persuasive. In that case, a claim for immunity by the defendants in an action for injunction against employees at an airport who had occupied an area of ground and a control post within the airport perimeter was refused and an injunction was granted. Reliance by the workers on a plea that they were merely 'peacefully picketing' within the terms of s 15 of the 1974

12 1984 SLT 28.
13 As to the doctrine of 'honest belief' in furtherance of a dispute, see p 103 above.
14 [1983] 3 All ER 6.

Act as amended by s 16(2) of the Employment Act 1980, found no support from the court.

While the decisions in *Hadmor Productions Ltd v Hamilton* and *Plessey Co plc v Wilson* can no longer be regarded as authoritative, their effect might well be revived and become of importance if s 19(1) of the 1982 Act were to be repealed or amended in the future. In the meantime, however, so long as that section remains in force, it may be said that, if and when a 'sit in' or 'work in' occurs in the course of industrial action:

(a) an action of interdict will lie against any group of employees operating either of these forms of industrial action;
(b) the basis of the employer's right to interdict is that there has been some illegal act such as trespass upon his premises, after a requirement to leave;
(c) the employer must show some loss or injury, even if this amounts only to inability to consult records and other papers within the building; and
(d) before interim interdict will be granted it must be shown that the balance of convenience requires such an order. Since in most cases of 'work in' the employees continue to carry out the work for which they were employed, it may be more difficult to swing the balance of convenience against such employees than against those engaged merely in a 'sit in'.

Definition of trade dispute

Since the organisation and operation of unlawful industrial action must almost inevitably result in some civil wrong such as breach of employment contract or trespass or delict of some kind, liability of those organising or participating in it to interdict at common law is virtually certain, unless the immunity remaining under s 13(1) of the 1974 Act, as substituted by s 3(2) of the 1976 Act or s 13(4) of the 1974 Act, can be invoked.

In order to secure this cloak of immunity it must now be shown *inter alia* that the strike action is taken in contemplation or furtherance of a 'trade dispute'. The definition of a 'trade dispute' is now contained in s 29(1) and (6) of the 1974 Act, as amended by s 18 of the Employment Act 1982. Under these provisions a trade dispute means a dispute between workers and their employer which is relative wholly or mainly to one or more of the matters contained in s 29(1)(a). These matters cover virtually every facet of employment and also freedom of membership or non-membership of trade unions and facilities for union officials. Section 29(6) as amended contains the important definition that 'worker' in relation to a dispute with an employer means a 'worker employed by *that* employer'. The trade dispute, in order to be covered by immunity, must not only be between workers and their employer but must relate wholly or mainly to matters which are specific to that employment. In considering whether a trade dispute, as so defined, in fact exists, the court must have regard to the predominant purpose of the dispute. It is necessary to consider not merely the occasion which caused the dispute to break out but also the reason why there was a dispute (*Mercury Communications Ltd v Scott-Garner*).[15]. Immunity must therefore depend upon whether the industrial action has been taken for a proper purpose within the definition of a trade dispute. Strikes and other industrial action designed to achieve political ends can no longer enjoy immunity under s 13 of the 1974 Act, as amended.

Primary picketing

The operations, commonly called picketing, during a trade dispute are not defined by statute. The Employment Act 1980 s 16 does however define the circumstances in which a person may lawfully carry out those actions which are normally regarded as constituting the act of picketing. That section provides that it shall be lawful for a person, in contemplation or furtherance of a trade dispute, to attend:

(a) at or near his place of work, or
(b) if he is an official of a trade union, at or near the place of work of a member of that union whom he is accompanying and whom he represents,

for the purpose of 'peacefully obtaining or communicating information, or peacefully persuading any person to work or abstain from working'.

The Code of Practice on Picketing under s 3 of the 1980 Act states that pickets and their organisers should ensure that, in general, the number of pickets does not exceed six and frequently a smaller number will be appropriate. The Code may be admitted in evidence and any relevant provisions of the Code may be taken into account by the court in determining the question in issue.

The immunity afforded by s 16 of the 1980 Act will not assist a person committing a criminal act either at common law or under statute. Where picketing is carried out in such a manner as to be beyond the scope of and outwith the immunity conferred by s 16, and whether involving criminal acts or not, civil proceedings by way of interdict may be invoked in order to prevent repetition or continuation of the illegal picketing.

The case law which has been developed since the passing of s 16 of the 1980 Act has been largely concerned with two areas of industrial action, viz:

---

15 [1984] 1 All ER 179 at 216 per Lord Dillon.

(a) the legal rights of non-striking workers to attend at their place of work and continue working, and the attempts of mass pickets to prevent these workers (whether members of the striking union or not) from entering their place of work, and
(b) picketing of premises to prevent the entry or exit of materials destined for the employer involved in the industrial dispute.

Legal rights of non-striking workers against picketing

The problem of protecting the rights of workers seeking to work during a period of industrial action, where a trade union has called for strike action and pickets are being operated, was highlighted in the case of *Thomas v National Union of Mineworkers (South Wales Area)*.[16] In that case a ballot in favour of strike action had been taken under the Trade Union Act 1984, and the legality of the strike was not in question. A number of miners working at five different collieries, who during the subsistence of the strike returned to work, were harassed at the colliery entrances by massed pickets and had to be escorted to work by the police. The working miners sought *inter alia* an injunction prohibiting the Union Branch and its officers from organising unlawful picketing or demonstrations at the five collieries. In granting the injunction sought Scott J held that the working miners were entitled to use the highway for the purpose of going to work and to do so without being unreasonably harassed by others. The evidence had disclosed that there was a daily congregation of between fifty and seventy pickets hurling abuse at the working miners, who required to be taken to work every day in vehicles under police escort. He was of the opinion that the harassment carried out by the pickets constituted per se a tortious act which rendered the method of picketing illegal. The form of the injunction granted is of interest. It restrained the Union Branch and its officers and servants from inciting, assisting, encouraging or organising members of the Union or others to congregate or assemble at or near the entrances to the collieries:

(a) otherwise than for the purpose of peacefully persuading any person to work or to abstain from working, and
(b) otherwise than in numbers not exceeding six.

It will be noted that, for the purpose of fixing a reasonable size of picket, the court adopted the number recommended by the Code of Practice.

The decision in *Thomas v National Union of Mineworkers (South Wales Area)* is probably one of the most far-reaching judgments in the wake of

16 [1985] 2 All ER 1.

statutory restraints placed upon trade unions and their picketing operations. It is a persuasive judgment which will no doubt be given careful consideration in Scotland, although the question of whether harassment as described in *Thomas* would amount to delict in Scotland has not so far been tested. It must also be noted that some doubt was cast upon the decision in *Thomas* in the recent case of *News Group Newspapers Ltd v SOGAT '82*[17] which contains an extensive review of the authorities on picketing.

Primary picketing operations which may be restrained by interdict

Primary picketing at the entrance to a work place, or occupation thereof is not per se actionable but may be restrained by interdict where there are picketing operations:

(a) in the course of industrial action not arising out of a trade dispute as defined by s 29(1) of the 1974 Act as amended by s 18 of the Employment Act 1982;
(b) arising out of a dispute between an employer, other than the employer of the pickets, and his workers;
(c) except in the case of a trade union official, if carried out at a place, other than at or near the pickets' own work place;
(d) which by harassment, force of numbers or threats or other activities amounting to tortious acts or to delict in Scotland, interfere with the right of those wishing to work to enter their work premises;
(e) when picketing has been carried out either by a 'work in' or a 'sit in' and there has been trespass upon the employer's premises and he suffers some loss, injury or damage; and
(f) where the picketing operations being tortious go beyond the limit allowed by common law.

Secondary industrial action

Section 17(1) of the Employment Act 1980 introduced the concept of illegal secondary industrial action. That section provides that nothing in s 13 of the 1974 Act, as amended (which contains the residual immunity privileges) shall prevent an act from being actionable in tort (and therefore subject to interdict) on a ground specified in s 13(1)(a) or (b). This withdrawal of immunity applies only where the contract (as referred to in s 13(1)(a) and (b)) is not a contract of employment and one of the facts relied on in the case is that there has been

---

[17] [1986] 1 IRLR 337, CA at 348, see also at 346. As to the tort of intimidation in England see *Rookes v Barnard* [1944] AC 1129, HL.

secondary action, and that it is not action which satisfies s 17(3), (4) and (5) of the 1980 Act.

Secondary action is defined as taking place where:

(a) a person induces another to break a contract of employment, or
(b) threatens that a contract of employment will be broken, and the employer under the contract of employment is not a party to the trade dispute.

Section 17 of the 1980 Act accepts the legality of secondary action where (subject to various conditions):

(a) the purpose or principal purpose is directly to prevent to disrupt the supply of goods or services between an employer who is a party to the dispute and the employer under the contract of employment of the person carrying out the secondary action; and
(b) the purpose or principal purpose is directly to prevent or disrupt the supply of goods or services between any person and an associated employer of an employer who is a party to the dispute; and
(c) the action constitutes 'peaceful picketing' under s 15 of the Trade Union and Labour Relations Act 1974, as substituted by s 16(1) of the Employment Act 1980.

These provisions were considered in *Marina Shipping Ltd v Laughton*[18] where secondary industrial action by lock-keepers was restrained by injunction. In Scotland, in *St Stephen Shipping Co Ltd v Guinane*[19] the circumstances were analagous to those in *Marina Shipping Co v Laughton* and interim interdict was granted. The recent cases of *News International v SOGAT '82*[20] and *News International v Transport and General Workers Union*[20] demonstrate the rigid nature of the restraints now placed upon trade unions. In the former case, the union, without holding a ballot, had given certain instructions to its members employed by John Menzies, newspaper distributors. The instructions were given in support of industrial action by SOGAT following the dismissal of workers in Fleet Street employed by News International who were members of SOGAT. There was no trade dispute between John Menzies and their employees, and Menzies was not a party to the Fleet Street dispute. There was a commercial contract between Menzies and News International under which the former distributed the latter's newspapers. As a result of the union's instruction, employees of Menzies who were members of SOGAT refused to distribute News

---

18 [1982] 1 All ER 481, CA.
19 1984 SLT 25.
20 (1986) Scotsman 1 February.

International's papers. Holding that the instruction was unlawful, that there had been illegal secondary industrial action and that therefore the union had no immunity from legal proceedings under the 1974 Act, as amended, Lord Sutherland granted interim interdict against SOGAT '82 prohibiting them from inciting, inducing or encouraging their members employed by Menzies to break their contracts of employment by refusing to handle the newspapers.

In *News International v Transport and General Workers Union*,[1] which arose out of the same circumstances, members of the Transport and General Workers Union employed by Roadhaulage Ltd, on instructions from their union, refused to handle News International's papers or to cross picket lines at the latter's plant at Glasgow. The defenders did not oppose an application for interim interdict prohibiting them from inducing their members to break their contracts of employment by refusing to handle the papers and refusing to cross the picket lines.

Secret ballots before industrial action

Section 10 of the Trade Union Act 1984 carried a stage further the withdrawal of immunity of trade unions from legal proceedings. It introduced the concept of a voluntary ballot of union members before industrial action is initiated. The requirement for a ballot is not compulsory but the calling of industrial action by way of a strike or otherwise, of such a nature as to induce a person to break his contract of employment, or to interfere with its performance, without the support of a ballot, has the effect of withdrawing any immunity which the union might have enjoyed under s 13(1)(a) of the 1974 Act, as substituted by s 3(2) of the Trade Union and Labour Relations (Amendment) Act 1976, and renders the action unlawful.[2] Although s 10 of the 1984 Act relates to an act done by a trade union, liability could attach to a trade union official, for whose actions the union would be vicariously responsible under s 15(3) of the Employment Act 1982.

A 'strike' is defined by s 11(11) of the 1984 Act as a concerted stoppage of work. No attempt is made to define 'other industrial action'. The question of how far work-to-rule and 'go slow' activities may be subject to the ballot seems obscure.[3]

The initiation of industrial action by a union or by one of its officials or an individual member, without the support of a ballot, renders the person and may render the union liable in delict, should this arise.

---

1 (1986) Scotsman 1 February.
2 *Taylor & Foulstone v NUM* [1984] 1 IRLR 445.
3 *Secretary of State for Employment v ASLEF (No 2)* [1972] 2 QB 455, CA.

In the absence of a supporting ballot, or if the organisation of the ballot fails to satisfy the requirements of s 11 of the 1984 Act, the immunity of the trade union will be lost and an action of interdict may be raised to restrain any delict or threat of delict arising out of the strike or other industrial action. See for example *Solihull Metropolitan BC v NUT*,[4] where, without a supporting ballot, a union directed its members to refuse to cover for absent colleagues or to engage in extra-mural school activities or supervision of school meals, and thus to break their contracts. In granting an interlocutory injunction, the court held that since the action had been called without a supporting ballot, the union could not claim immunity and could be sued for inducing breach of contract.

Restriction on compulsion to work

Section 16 of the 1974 Act prohibits any court from making an order, whether by way of specific performance or interdict, restraining a breach or threatened breach of contract, the effect of which will be to compel an employee to do any work or attend at any place for the doing of any work.

Ex parte interdicts

Where application for interdict is made to a court in the absence of the defender or his representative and the defender claims, or in the opinion of the court will be likely to claim, that he acted in contemplation or furtherance of a trade dispute, the court shall not grant the interdict unless satisfied that all reasonable steps have been taken to secure that notice of the application and an opportunity of being heard has been given to the defender (1974 Act s 17(1)) as inserted by the Employment Protection Act 1975 Sch 16, Part III, para 6.[5]

---

4 [1985] 1 IRLR 211.
5 *Gouriet v Union of Post Office Workers* [1978] AC 435; *Scotsman Publications Ltd v SOGAT '82* 1986 SLT 646.

Chapter 12

Interdict against abuse of power and government Act

Restraint of the Crown and its Ministers

The court has no jurisdiction to grant interdict against the Crown. Where, however, in any proceedings against the Crown, such relief is sought as might, as between private persons, be granted by way of interdict, the court may, in lieu of interdict, make an order declaring the rights of parties.[1] In *Ayr Magistrates v Secretary of State for Scotland and Anr*[2] the pursuers sought declarator that it was the duty of the Secretary of State to refrain from causing a local enquiry to be held into an order under the Water (Scotland) Act 1946 and for interim declarator and for interdict against the Reporter appointed by the Secretary of State. It was held that the Act did not entitle the court to make a hypothetical declaratory order. And in England an interim declaratory order in any form has been held incompetent.[3] The question of whether an interim declaratory order against the Crown, which is not of a hypothetical nature, may be competently granted does not appear to have been finally decided in Scotland. In *Robertson v Lord Advocate* representing the Central Land Board,[4] Lord Strachan, commenting on *Underhill v Ministry of Food*[5] where Romer J had held that the court had no jurisdiction to make an interim declaratory order, said: 'It is not necessary for me to go so far as that but I am of opinion that, in the circumstances of the present case, I cannot make an order declaratory of the rights of the Board without interpreting the terms of the Regulations and pre-judging the merits of the case'.

The remedy of interdict against any officer of the Crown is also excluded, if the result would be to give any relief against the Crown which could not be obtained by direct action.[6]

Where the Crown and a subject are both called as defenders, a

---

1 Crown Proceedings Act 1947 s 21(a) and s 43(a).
2 1965 SC 394.
3 *Underhill v Ministry of Food* [1950] 1 All ER 591; *International GEC of New York v Commissioners of Customs and Excise* [1962] Ch 784.
4 (1950) at 1965 SC 400.
5 Fn 3 above.
6 Crown Proceedings Act 1947 s 21(a) and s 43(a).

113

declaratory finding may be sought against the Crown and interdict against the subject defender. But in *Prince v Secretary of State for Scotland*[7] voters in the June 1984 elections of the European Assembly sought declarator of their right to a system of proportional representation against the Secretary of State and interdict against the Returning Officer from conducting the election and counting the votes. It was alleged the holding of the election under the existing system was *ultra vires* and contrary to s 2 of the European Communities Act 1972. The court held that until the issue of *ultra vires* had been decided against the defenders, no legal wrong was threatened against the pursuers and in any event the Returning Officer was bound to carry out his duties under the United Kingdom statutes until they were repealed. Interim interdict was refused.[8]

In *Harper v Secretary of State for the Home Department*[9] the plaintiff sought to restrain the submission to Her Majesty in Council of a draft Order approving a redistribution of Parliamentary seats as recommended by the Boundary Commission. In holding that the draft Order was not at variance with the House of Commons (Redistribution of Seats) Act 1949, the Court of Appeal expressed strong doubts as to whether, in any event, the restraining order was competent having regard to the terms of s 21 of the Crown Proceedings Act 1947.

In *Merricks v Heathcot-Amory* where the Minister of Agriculture laid before Parliament a draft Scheme under the Agricultural Marketing Act 1931, and the plaintiff sought an order restraining the Minister from approving the draft Scheme, it was held that the Minister was acting as an officer of the Crown and an order for restraining was excluded by s 21 of the Crown Proceedings Act 1947.[10]

Interdict in judicial review[11]

The Court of Session has for long exercised judicial control of inferior courts, public bodies and public authorities. These powers were supplemented by the statutory powers vested in the court by s 91 of the Court of Session Act 1868,[12] which gave power to order the specific performance of statutory duties, under penalty of fine or imprisonment in the event of default. The remedies available under what is usually called the supervisory jurisdiction of the court were in earlier times

---

7 *Prince v Secretary of State for Scotland and Anr* 1985 SLT 74.
8 Fn 6 above.
9 [1955] 1 All ER 331, CA.
10 [1955] 2 All ER 453.
11 For a treatise on the law and practice of judicial review see *St. Clair and Davidson on Judicial Review in Scotland.*
12 31 and 32 Vict ch 100.

extensively sought but latterly became sadly neglected. In many cases the only remedy against the act of a public authority or body is still by an action of reduction, a process devoid of the speed often essential in the disposal of such complaints. The remedy of interdict in the exercise of the supervisory jurisdiction is specifically excluded where the act complained of is that of the Crown or any of its Ministers. In such cases the power of the court is restricted to granting a declarator of the rights of parties. This is done upon the basis that the Crown or the Minister will voluntarily give effect to the declarator.[13]

The circumstances in which the Court of Session, in the exercise of its supervisory jurisdiction, may review the orders of a government or public authority or body were extensively canvassed in *Watt v Lord Advocate*.[14] This was an action in which the pursuer sought reduction of the decision of the National Insurance Commissioner that the pursuer was disqualified from receiving Unemployment Benefit. The basis of the pursuer's case was that the Commissioner had misconstrued the provisions of s 22(1) of the National Insurance Act 1965, and as a result had asked himself the wrong question. He further maintained that the commissioner had reached his decision as a result of an error in law, and, even if he had not thereby acted *ultra vires*, the decision was still open to reduction. The court upheld these contentions (reversing the Lord Ordinary) and granted decree of reduction. Giving the leading opinion, the Lord President (Emslie) approached the question on the basis that, if the error in construction was one within the powers of the Commissioner to commit, his decision would not be open to review. There was no doubt, said his Lordship, that when a statutory tribunal, which quite properly enters upon an enquiry which it has jurisdiction to carry out, misconstrues the question which it is required to answer (as had been done here), and decides some other question not remitted to it, its decision is a nullity (*Hayman v Lord Advocate*[15] and *Anisminic v Foreign Compensation Commission*[16]). In *Watt v Lord Advocate* the Lord President quoted from the opinion of Lord Reid[17] in *Anisminic* where he said:

> But there are many cases where, although the tribunal had jurisdiction to enter upon the enquiry, it has done or has failed to do something in the course of the enquiry which is of such a nature that its decision is a nullity. It may have given its decision in bad faith. It may have made a decision which it had no power to make. It may have failed to comply with the requirements of natural justice. It may in perfect good faith have failed to deal with the

---

13 Crown Proceedings Act 1947 ss 21 and 43.
14 1979 SC 120.
15 1952 SLT 209.
16 [1969] 2 AC 147, HL.
17 Ibid at 171.

question remitted to it and decided some question not remitted to it. It may have refused to take into account something which it was required to take into account or it may have based its decision upon some matter which, under the provisions setting it up, it had no right to take into account. But, if it decides a question remitted to it, without committing any of these errors, it is as much entitled to decide that question wrongly as it is to decide it rightly.

The decision in such circumstances, although wrongly answering the question, would be *intra vires* since the question answered was that remitted to the tribunal for decision by the provisions setting it up. In *Watt v Lord Advocate*[18] the Lord President went on to say:

> This case is not one where the Commissioner misconstrued certain statutory provisions in the course of attempting to answer the right question remitted to him. He misconstrued that very question and answered a different question as a result of his error. For these reasons I am persuaded that the Commissioner's decision was *ultra vires*.

In the field of interdict as a process of judicial review, the Act of Sederunt (Rules of Court Amendment No 2) (Judicial Review) 1985 now provides specifically that the power of the court in the exercise of its supervisory jurisdiction shall include the grant of interdict and any interim order where this is competent under the existing law.[19] This Act of Sederunt has not so far been supported by legislation and, standing ss 21(a) and 43(a) of the Crown Proceedings Act 1947, the Court of Session has still no power to interdict the Crown either on an interim or permanent basis. The position would seem to be different in England. There the Supreme Court Act 1981 s 31 confers upon the Queen's Bench Division power to make such orders as would be 'just and convenient'. In *R v Governor of Pentonville Prison ex parte Herbage* ((Times) 21 May 1986) Hodgson J expressed the opinion that the court now had jurisdiction to grant injunction against an officer of the Crown, and to grant interim restraint. His judgment seems to have been given on the basis that s 31 of the Supreme Court Act 1981 has by implication repealed or at least amended s 21(a) of the Crown Proceedings Act 1947.

Acts ultra vires of statutory bodies

Where a statutory body is alleged to have acted or to be threatening to act *ultra vires* of the statute under which it operates, it may be restrained by interdict.[20] There are many examples of interdict sought

---

18 1979 SC 120.
19 *Strathkelvin District Council v Secretary of State for the Environment* 1987 GWD No 258.
20 *Campbell v Leith Police Commissioners* (1870) 8 M (HL) 31 at 38 per the Lord Chancellor.

and obtained in such circumstances by those members of the public who have a title and interest to sue.[1] In *Adams v Secretary of State for Scotland and South-Eastern Regional Hospital Board*[2] the pursuers, being women resident in Edinburgh, sought to interdict the defenders from offering the post of consultant physician in two Edinburgh Hospitals dedicated to the treatment of women and children (and whose medical staff in accordance with the Founder's objects were exclusively female) to either men or women. The hospitals had vested in the Secretary of State under the National Health Service (Scotland) Act 1947 under which he was required to ensure, so far as practicable, that the objects for which they were used were not prejudiced by the exercise of the powers conferred. It was held that it was practicable to implement the objects of the hospitals and the defenders were restrained from appointing a male practitioner unless and until the post had been advertised as open only to women and no women suitably qualified had applied.

In *Wilson v Independent Broadcasting Authority*[3] three individuals entitled to vote in the Scottish Referendum sought to interdict the defenders from broadcasting certain party political programmes shortly before voting day, on the ground that the defenders' said programme did not maintain a proper balance within the meaning of s 2(2) of the Independent Broadcasting Authority Act 1973. In an application for interim interdict the court held *inter alia* that it was the duty of the defenders to preserve such a balance and that they were *prima facie* in breach of that duty and that *prima facie* the pursuers were qualified by title and interest to sue and interim interdict was granted.

But where the actions of a statutory body are *intra vires* of that body by virtue of the statute under which they operate and where the procedure undertaken is per se valid, the court will not interfere to restrain the actions of the body in operating their statutory rights. See, for example, *Central Regional Council v Clackmannan District Council*[4] where interim interdict against the issue of a stop notice following a valid enforcement notice under s 84(1) of the Town and Country Planning (Scotland) Act 1972 was refused.

Abuse of power by public authorities and public bodies

A public body invested with statutory powers and an administrative

---

1 *Wakefield v Renfrew Commissioners of Supply* (1878) 6 R 259; *Stirling County Council v Falkirk Magistrates* 1912 SC 1281; *Farquhar & Gill v Aberdeen Magistrates* 1912 SC 1294; *Malloch v Aberdeen Corpn* 1974 SLT 253; *Innes v Kirkcaldy Burgh* 1963 SLT 325; *Nicol v Dundee Harbour Trustees* 1915 SC (HL) 7: *Brock v Forth Pilotage Authority* 1947 SN 41.
2 1958 SC 279. As to title and interest generally see Ch 3 above.
3 1979 SLT 279 (distinguishing *Grieve v Douglas-Home* 1965 SLT 186 at 193).
4 1983 SLT 666.

discretion must take care not to abuse its powers. It must act in good faith and act reasonably, that is, with judgment and discretion.[5] Interdict may be invoked whenever a public body fails to comply with these standards and as a result the legal rights of an individual having title and interest are endangered.[6] Where a discretion is by statute conferred upon a public body, the exercise of that discretion can only be challenged if it is exercised in a manner which is outside the powers of the body in question or is exercised in bad faith.[7]

Where a statutory remedy remains against an alleged infringement of statutory powers or against alleged denial of natural justice, such as failure to hear a party, interdict will be refused so long as the statutory remedy remains unexhausted.[8]

Where a schoolmaster was dismissed and an enquiry into the merits of the dismissal was ordered and before the result was known, the Education Authority sought to appoint a candidate to the vacant post, interim interdict was granted.[9] But where a school teacher's appointment in a particular post had been terminated and the local authority sought to transfer her to an inferior post, it was held interdict was not appropriate.[10] And where Traffic Commissioners sought to vary the conditions of an operator's licence, and questions were raised as to whether an Order by the Minister of Transport was valid under the Road Traffic Act 1934, interim interdict was refused pending final decision of the merits, since the Commissioners were a public body acting in the public interest.[11]

In *Hamilton v Lanarkshire County Council*[12] where a petitioner under the Temperance (Scotland) Act 1920 averred that he had not been heard by the clerk to the authority on his objection to the requisition for a poll, interim interdict was refused. And where a student was suspended in respect of an offence which he did not deny and the University Authority failed to give him the opportunity of being heard, it was held

---

5 *Westminster Corpn v London & North Western Railway Co* [1905] AC 426, HL; *Brock v Forth Pilotage Authority* 1947 SN 41; *Rennie v Scottish Milk Records Association* 1985 SLT 272.
6 *Campbell v Leith Police Commissioners* (1870) 8 M (HL) 31.
7 *Pollok School Co v Glasgow Town Clerk* 1946 SC 373 and 1947 SC 605; *Anisminic v Foreign Compensation Commision* [1969] 2 AC 147, HL at 171. For a full discussion of the factors contributing to abuse of power and bad faith (in the context of housing management) see *Edinburgh District Council v Parnell* 1980 SLT (Sh Ct) 11 and a leading authority *Associated Provincial Picture Houses v Wednesbury Corpn* [1947] 2 All ER 680, CA at 685 per Lord Greene MR.
8 *Hamilton v Lanarkshire County Council* 1971 SLT (Notes) 12.
9 *Trapp v Aberdeenshire County Council* 1960 SC 302.
10 *Murray v Dumbarton County Council* 1935 SLT 239.
11 *Alexander & Sons v Southern Scotland Traffic Commissioners* 1936 SN 38.
12 1971 SLT (Notes) 12.

he had suffered no injustice by the breach of the rules of procedure and interdict was refused.[13]

Abuse of power by actions *ultra vires* of public bodies can arise in a multitude of circumstances. Amongst recent examples interim interdict was granted against a local authority which, as part of a local election campaign, sought to support a publication known as the *Lothian Clarion*.[14] And where the same local authority[15] proclaimed its intention of allowing employees time off with pay in order to attend a lobby of Parliament, interim interdict was granted.

Acts ultra vires of trade unions

The expulsion of members of a trade union by the governing body of the union may be restrained by interdict. For examples of acts *ultra vires* of the unions in this connection see *Partington v NALGO*[16].

---

13 *Glynn v Keele University* [1971] 2 All ER 89.
14 *Meek v Lothian Regional Council* 1983 SLT 494.
15 Ibid 1980 SLT (Notes) 61.
16 1981 SLT 184.

Chapter 13
Interdict in personal relationships

Interdict against defamation and personal molestation

Interdict although granted infrequently is competent where clearly defamatory statements have been made and there is serious threat or apprehension that they will be repeated.[1] In *Fairbairn v SNP*[2] interim interdict was granted at common law against the circulation of pamphlets defamatory of a Member of Parliament who, it was alleged, had failed to collect large quantities of mail from the House of Commons Post Office. But where there is a defence of justification or qualified privilege interim interdict will not be granted unless it is shown that the defender intends maliciously to publish information that he knows is false.[3]

Statements calculated to mislead third parties may be restrained if there are reasonable grounds for apprehending repetition.[4]

Where personal molestation or assault is seriously threatened interdict may competently be sought.

Interdict against contracting a marriage

Actions of interdict seeking to prevent a marriage taking place in Scotland normally arises where one or both of the parties are, according to the law of their domicile, prohibited from marrying when they are below a certain age. Different considerations apply where (a) the impediment alleged is simply that one or both are incapable of contracting a marriage under the law of their domicile unless with parental consent, and (b) where one of the parties, being under the age of marriage, has been made the subject of an order by a competent court in a non-Scottish domicile prohibiting his or her marriage.

Thus in *Pease v Pease*[5] the father of an American domiciled daughter

---

1 *Shinwell v National Sailors' and Firemen's Union* (1913) 2 SLT 83; *Martin v Nisbet* (1893) 1 SLT 293.
2 *Fairbairn v SNP* 1980 SLT 149.
3 *Harakas v Baltic Mercantile and Shipping Exchange Ltd* [1982] 2 All ER 701; *Herbage v Pressdram Ltd* [1984] 2 All ER 769 (publication of spent convictions).
4 *Henderson & Son v Munro & Co* (1905) 7 F 636.
5 1967 SC 112.

daughter craved interdict preventing his daughter from contracting a marriage in Scotland with the second defender, Myers. It was averred that, while the daughter and Myers had been living in London, she had, on the application of her father, been made a ward of court in the Chancery Division of the High Court in England. The daughter and Myers fled to Glasgow. Following the established practice but without entering upon the merits, the court, on appeal from the decision of the Lord Ordinary, continued the interim interdict which he had granted in order to maintain the status quo.

By contrast, in *Hoy v Hoy and Ramsay*[6] a girl aged sixteen left her home in England, where she was domiciled, and came to Scotland with the intention of marrying Ramsay, who was domiciled there. Thereafter on the application of her mother, the girl was made a ward of court in the Chancery Division and an order was made preventing her from contracting a marriage with Ramsay. This was an order which, since neither the girl nor Ramsay were then resident in England, the Chancery Court had no power to make. The mother then sought interdict in Scotland to prevent the marriage from taking place there. On appeal from the Lord Ordinary, who had refused to grant interim interdict, the court held that, in the exceptional situation arising from the fact that the English court had no jurisdiction to pronounce the order made, there were no grounds for interfering with the Lord Ordinary's discretion in refusing the interim interdict. Giving the leading opinion the Lord President (Clyde) emphasised that, when a valid order of the Chancery Court restraining a marriage is made while a girl is resident in England, the court in Scotland will not aid or abet a party seeking to evade that order. Where such a valid order has been made in England, that order is a factor, although not necessarily a conclusive factor, in favour of granting interim interdict. In *Bliersbach and Another v MacEwan*[7] where objection had been lodged to the issue of a Registrar's certificate, under the Marriage Notice (Scotland) Act 1878 s 10, the court considered at length the nature of impediments constituted by the laws of foreign domiciles which may prevent the solemnisation of a marriage in Scotland. The Lord President (Clyde) emphasised the difference between the *impedimentum dirimens* or irritant impediment, and the *impedimentum impeditivum* or prohibitive impediment. The former is so fundamental (as in the case of prohibited degrees of relationship) as to render the marriage null *ab initio*. The latter is not fundamental but prevents the marriage being celebrated, unless and until the impediment is removed. The court held that lack of parental consent, necessary according to the law of the domicile but not

6 1968 SC 179.
7 1959 SC 43.

according to the law of Scotland, was merely an irritant impediment and granted decree allowing the Registrar's certificate to be issued.

Against removal of property in divorce

In *Johnstone v Johnstone*[8] interdict was granted against a defender in a divorce action prohibiting him from making a disposition of his property to a third party or removing it from the jurisdiction, contrary to the Succession (Scotland) Act 1964 ss 26 and 27, now repealed. Similar provisions were contained in the Divorce (Scotland) Act 1976 s 6 now also repealed by the Family Law (Scotland) Act 1985. For circumstances in which interdict may be granted against avoidance transactions, see s 18 of that Act.

Right of wife to have abortion

In England, as between husband and wife, the right of a wife, who held the required medical certificates, to have an abortion contrary to the wishes of the husband was upheld and his application for injunction was refused.[9] Under Roman law the consent of the father to an abortion was essential. The Abortion Act 1967 contains no such requirement.

Removal of children from the jurisdiction

Under s 13 of the Matrimonial Proceedings (Children) Act 1958, the removal of children from the jurisdiction of the Scots courts may be prevented by interdict. At any time after the commencement of an action in which the court would have power to regulate the custody, maintenance or education of a child, either party to the action, or the guardian of the child, or any person who wishes to obtain under an order of the court, the custody or care of such child, may apply to the Court of Session to grant interim interdict prohibiting the removal of the child furth of Scotland or out of the control of the person having custody of the child. The procedure for such applications is now regulated by Rules of Court 1965 para 170c, as substituted by SI 1976/1994.[10]

---

8 1967 SLT 248.
9 *Paton v Trustees of BPAS* [1978] 2 All ER 987; Abortion Act 1967 s 1.
10 See also the Child Abduction and Custody Act 1985.

Chapter 14.
Damages for wrongful interdict

General principles

A claim for damages for wrongful interdict is competent where a decree of interdict whether interim or permanent is wrongfully obtained and, having become operative, is subsequently recalled. Where interdict has been granted subject to conditions, but the conditions have not been implemented, the decree has never become operative and no claim for damages will lie. Thus in *Wilson v Gilchrist*[1] where the defender in an action of interdict, in the knowledge that the interdict granted against him was subject to caution being lodged, and that it had not been lodged, chose to comply voluntarily with the interdict, his subsequent claim for damages for wrongful interdict was excluded upon the principle that any loss suffered by the defender in the interdict was due to his own voluntary act and was not attributable to the interdict. And where interdict against diligence was recalled but the creditor did not then enforce his diligence for three months thereafter, a claim for loss was refused.[2]

So long as the decree of interdict remains in force, and no change of circumstances justifying recall has occurred, any claim for damages is excluded, the defender's remedy being by way of appeal, if this is still open, failing which he must take action to reduce the decree. In any event any claim for damages can apply only to the period during which the decree of interdict was in force. Loss occurring after the date of recall or following expiry of the decree will be excluded.[3]

Interdict must have been wrongful

A further and obvious limitation of the right to claim damages for wrongful interdict is that the interdict must in fact have been wrongful. If the interdict was granted to prevent the defender doing something which he had no right to do, he can have no justifiable claim for

---
1 (1900) 2 F 391.
2 *Buchanan v Douglas* (1853) 15 D 365.
3 *Daw v Eley* (1867) LR 3 Eq 496.

damages in respect of the restraint placed upon him, even though the action may, for example, have been misconceived. There are numerous examples of this principle. In *Jack v Begg*[4] the pursuer had removed a wall and proceeded to erect a building gable on the ground which belonged to the defender. When the gable was almost finished and negotiations had failed the defender sought and obtained from the Sheriff an order for restoration of the wall and interdict against proceeding with the building of the gable. On appeal the interdict was recalled on the ground that the application was too late and the action was 'inappropriate'. In an action by the pursuer (being the party interdicted) for damages for wrongful interdict it was held that, although withdrawn, the interdict would have been justified if timeous and the claim was refused.

Invasion of legal right essential to claim

To succeed in an action of damages for wrongful interdict it must be shown that the pursuer has, by the operation of the interdict, suffered some invasion of his legal rights. Thus in *Aird v Tarbert School Board* the pursuer, a schoolmaster, was dismissed by the defenders. Interdict was subsequently granted against Aird preventing him from continuing to act as schoolmaster but was later recalled on the ground that the dismissal had been irregular. Aird was then suspended by the School Board under their statutory powers and he sustained loss of emoluments. Aird then brought an action for damages for wrongful interdict. This was dismissed on the ground that Aird, having been suspended under statutory powers, had not, by operation of the interdict, suffered any invasion of legal right, notwithstanding that the interdict had been irregularly obtained.[5] And in *Macdonald Ltd v Lord Blythswood*[6] a tenant obtained interdict against a firm of timber merchants prohibiting erection of a sawmill on ground allegedly let to the tenant. The interdict was recalled on the ground that the tenant was not in possession. The timber merchants, although admitting they had no legal right to enter the land, sued the tenant for damages for wrongful interdict. The claim was refused on the ground that, having themselves no legal title, the timber merchants had suffered no invasion of legal right by reason of the interdict.

Recall of interdict

Where interdict is recalled this is conclusive that it was wrongfully

---

4 (1875) 3 R 35.
5 1907 SC 305.
6 1914 SC 930.

obtained, unless the ground of recall is a change of circumstances occurring subsequent to the date of the decree.[7] But the mere recall of the interdict will not, as has been explained, ground a claim for damages unless it can be shown that in consequence of the interdict some loss had been occasioned by invasion of a legal right.

Damages for interim interdict

Special considerations apply to actions of damages for wrongfully obtaining interim interdict. Since it is a remedy granted, generally speaking, upon the *ex parte* statements of the pursuer, interim interdict is obtained *periculo petentis*. Where the party obtaining interim interdict is ultimately unsuccessful in having it declared perpetual, this is conclusive evidence that the interim interdict was wrongfully obtained. If the party interdicted can prove some loss or that he was, by reason of the wrongfully obtained interim interdict, deprived of some right which he would have been entitled to exercise, he may recover damages. Averment of malice is unnecessary.[8] On the other hand, where interim interdict has been granted to secure a pursuer in his existing possession of property, and a competing title is produced by the defender which is subsequently preferred after proof, the latter will be entitled to damages, only if he can show that the pursuer in the interdict action acted maliciously, and without probable cause.[9]

Inversion of present position

Where the result of an application for interim interdict has been an order which inverts the possession of property by removing the existing possessor and substituting in possession the pursuer in whose favour the interdict has been granted, that pursuer is liable for the strict truth of his averments. He will be liable for damages if averments are shown to be unfounded and the interim decree is recalled or after inquiry the court refuses to grant perpetual interdict, no matter what is the reason. In such cases no averments of malice are required.[10]

---

7 *Miller v Hunter* (1865) 3 M 740.
8 *Abel's Executors v Edmond and Edmond* (1863) 1 M 1061 at 1065.
9 *Kennedy v Fort-William Police Commissioners* (1877) 5 R 302 at 307 and 308; *Glasgow City and District Railway v Glasgow Coal Exchange Co* (1885) 12 R 1287 at 1292.
10 *Kennedy v Fort-William Police Commissioners* (1877) 5 R 302 at 306.

Chapter 15
Interdict against breach of contract and breach of confidence

General principles

Where a contract contains a clause under which one party is taken bound to refrain from a particular course of action any breach or threatened breach of that undertaking may give rise to an action of interdict. Where however the breach of contract consists of one single act which has already been completed and there are no averments of reasonable apprehension of further breach, interdict is incompetent. Clauses containing negative obligations of this kind are frequently found in contracts for the sale of a business, where the seller is taken bound not to carry on the same or a similar business; and in contracts of employment where an employee undertakes not to engage, after termination of his employment, in the same type of business as that of his former employer. Negative obligations involving restraints are also frequently found in feu contacts and building agreements, where a party is taken bound not to erect a particular type of building or to refrain from encroaching beyond specified building limits or obliges himself to use premises only for particular purposes. In all these cases, provided the clause is legally enforceable, any breach of the undertaking may be restrained by interdict. A party seeking to enforce such a clause must, however, as in all cases of interdict, be able to show that he has a title and interest to enforce the restriction and that he will be prejudiced by its breach.[1] Thus, where the employer sells the business, a restrictive covenant against his former employee will not generally be enforceable unless the employee has consented to assignation of the covenant, or possibly where no additional burden is placed upon the employee.[2] But a restraint against a seller in a contract for the sale of a business is assignable and may be enforced unless the terms of the restraint are such as to render it entirely personal in which case it may not be assignable.[3]

---

1 *Ballachulish Slate Quarries Co v Grant* (1903) 5 F 1105.
2 *Berlitz School of Languages v Duchene* (1903) 6 F 181; *Methven Simpson Ltd v Jones* (1910) 2 SLT 14.
3 *Rodger v Herbertson* 1909 SC 256.

Contracts in restraint of trade and employment

In order to be enforceable by interdict a covenant in restraint of trade or employment must be shown to be reasonable between the parties in the circumstances and not contrary to the public interest. Failure to pass either of these tests renders the covenant void and unenforceable.[4] The court will not substitute a new contract for one which it holds unreasonable or against the public interest, nor can it simply be left to the court to enforce a restriction so far as it considers it reasonable.[5]

Contracts containing severable restraints

Where however the contract contains what are, in effect, two separate restraints, and it is possible to sever one found unreasonable from one found to be reasonable, the principle of severance may be applied and the former declared void, while the latter is upheld. In such event interdict may be granted as regards the latter. Thus in *Mulvein v Murray*[6] where a covenant prohibited a shoe salesman from canvassing the petitioner's customers and from selling or travelling (on unspecified business) in any district in which the petitioner traded, the court held that the unduly wide prohibition against selling or travelling in any of the towns traded in by the pursuers was severable from the remainder and could be struck out leaving the first covenant enforceable. In *Chill Foods (Scotland) Ltd v Cool Foods Ltd*[7] where several petitions for interdict, arising out of alleged breach of the same covenant, were presented, some were granted and others refused; but in *Rentokil Ltd v Hampton*[8] Lord Stewart held that, in the circumstances of that case, the principle of severance could not be applied so as to reduce a prohibition which might be unreasonably wide and thus invalid to one which would be reasonable in the circumstances. In that case averment was made of breach of two covenants within one agreement but interim interdict as regards one covenant was not contested.

Distinction between restraints on employment and restraints on trading

Following upon the decision in *Mason v Provident Clothing & Supply Co Ltd*[9] it has been accepted that a restraint, in the case of a sale of a business, may be more widely stated and more readily upheld than one

---

4 *Mason v Provident Clothing & Supply Co Ltd*[1913] AC 724.
5 *Baker v Hedgecock* (1889) 39 Ch D 520; *Dumbarton Steamboat Co v MacFarlane* (1899) 1 F 993.
6 1908 SC 528: *Mason v Provident Clothing & Supply Co Ltd* above.
7 1977 SLT 38.
8 1982 SLT 422.
9 [1913] AC 724 at 731 per Viscount Haldane.

regulating post-employment activities, where the sole object is to protect the interest of the employer. An employee when undertaking such an obligation may well be in a poor bargaining position.

A distinction must be drawn between contracts made freely between parties bargaining on equal terms and those which are imposed upon an employee and have not been the subject of negotiation nor approved by an organisation representing the weaker party. Contracts of the former nature between parties on equal terms carry a strong presumption that they are fair and reasonable. In contracts of the latter kind no such presumption exists and their provisions must be examined to see whether they are fair and reasonably necessary for the protection of the legitimate business interests of the complaining party.[10]

The same general principles apply in the case of agreements between the manufacturer and the distributor where the latter is taken bound, usually for a consideration, to sell only the manufacturer's products.[11]

Basis of validity

Area, duration and public interest

The validity or otherwise of a contract in restraint of trade or employment will depend upon whether, in the particular circumstances,

(a) it is reasonable between the parties as to area, duration and the nature of the interest to be protected, and
(b) whether the public interest is affected by operation of the restraint.

Geographical area of the restraint

A covenant following the sale of a business and restraining trade on a worldwide basis may in special circumstances be valid. It may be upheld where a very large consideration has been paid and the establishment of a worldwide competitor would seriously erode the goodwill of the business sold.[12] It was at one time considered that such a wide geographical restraint could have no place in a contract in restraint of employment. The decision in *Bluebell Apparel Ltd v Dickinson*[13] indicates however that in the light of modern commercial practice, and the activities of multi-national companies, a worldwide restriction on employment may be upheld, if coupled with a

---

10 *Schroeder Music Publishing Co v Macaulay* [1974] 3 All ER 616, HL.
11 *Esso Petroleum Co v Harper's Garage (Stourport) Ltd* [1969] AC 268; *Shell UK v Lostock Garage Ltd* [1977] 1 All ER 481, CA.
12 *Nordenfelt v Nordenfelt (Maxim) Guns and Ammunition Co* [1894] AC 535, HL.
13 1980 SLT 157.

comparatively short period of restriction and if it is directed at preventing trade secrets of a company operating worldwide from falling into the hands of competitors.

It was pointed out in *Bluebell Apparel*,[14] which concerned the manufacture and sale of 'jeans', that the risk of trade secrets coming to the knowledge of a rival concern, whether deliberately or unwittingly, arises whenever the former employee under restraint joins the ranks of a competitor, in any capacity, anywhere in the world. In that case, the court held the worldwide restriction not to be *prima facie* unreasonable and that, since the balance of convenience strongly favoured enforcement, interim interdict should be granted. An area of exclusion comprising the United Kingdom for a year was upheld in *A & D Bedrooms Ltd v Michael;*[15] and of a quarter of a mile in *SOS Bureau Ltd v Payne*.[16] For further examples of restraints where the areas have been held not to be unreasonable see *Meikle v Meikle*[17] and the cases cited below.

The employer is however bound to show in the case of a restrictive covenant against an employee that, in the circumstances of a particular business, the prohibition is not wider than is necessary to protect his legitimate interest.[18]

For an example of a case where a company, which was a member of a group, imposing upon one of its employees a prohibition against *inter alia* dealing with clients of associated or subsidiary companies within the group, and where interim interdict was refused, see *Bowring (UK) Ltd v Smith*.[19] The prohibition, while subject to one year limitation, contained no limitation as to the nature of the dealings struck at nor was there any specified geographical limit. The prohibition was held to be too widely expressed. A further ground of refusal was that the pursuers had failed to show that, in the particular circumstances, they were the employers of the defender.

In the recent case of *Randev v Pattar*[20] the seller of an hotel was taken bound not to carry on business as a hotelier within one mile of the premises sold for a period of five years. Although interim interdict was refused on the ground that the duration rendered the validity of the

---

14 Ibid.
15 1984 SLT 297; see also *Forster & Sons v Suggett* (1918) 35 TLR 87; *Commercial Plastics v Vincent* [1964] 3 All ER 546 and *Littlewoods Organisation v Harris* [1978] 1 All ER 1026.
16 1982 SLT (Sh Ct) 33.
17 (1895) 3 SLT 204; *Stewart v Stewart* (1899) 1 F 1158; *Williams & Son v Fairbairn* (1899) 1 F 944; *Taylor v Campbell* 1926 SLT 260; *Anthony v Rennie* 1981 SLT (Notes) 11.
18 *Scottish Farmers' Dairy Co (Glasgow) Ltd v M'Ghee* 1933 SLT 142 at 145 per Lord President Clyde.
19 (1987) 7 GWD 207.
20 1985 SLT 270.

clause doubtful, the geographical limit imposed does not appear to have been regarded as unreasonable.

There have been many cases where the restraint relating to area has been regarded as too wide and interdict has been refused and as to these see the cases noted below.[1]

Duration and nature of the restraint

An acceptable period of restraint must depend upon the circumstances of each case, and the period may to some extent be linked to the interest to be protected. Generally speaking, long periods of restraint, particularly against employment in a particular field, are no longer favoured. In exceptional circumstances, however, long periods have been accepted as reasonable. These include 'for life',[2] 'for 25 years',[3] and 'for 21 years'.[4] On the other hand, in *Mulvein v Murray*,[5] five years was held to be too long. For discussion of circumstances of reasonable space and time see the cases undernoted.[6]

Protection of trade secrets under contract

The nature of the restraint under contract in employment cases is frequently concerned with the protection of so-called trade secrets. The phrase has been variously interpreted and it is not easy to reconcile the *dicta* in some cases. In *Commercial Plastics Ltd v Vincent*[7] it was stated that the plaintiff's scheme of organisation and methods of business were not to be counted as trade secrets. A different view seems to have been taken in Scotland where the system of work, the nature and prices of the petitioner's products, the pricing policy and lists of customers present and potential have all been declared to be trade secrets, or

---

1 *Allsopp v Wheatcroft* (1872) LR 15 Eq 59; *Remington Typewriter Co v Sim* (1915) 1 SLT 168; *Dumbarton Steamboat Co v MacFarlane* (1899) 1 F 993; *Leng (Sir WC) & Co v Andrews* [1909] 1 Ch 763; *Empire Meat Co v Patrick* [1939] 2 All ER 85, CA; *Pratt v Maclean* 1927 SN 161.
2 *Eastes v Russ* [1914] 1 Ch 468, CA; *Wyatt v Kreglinger & Fernau* [1933] 1 KB 793, CA.
3 *Nordenfelt v Nordenfelt (Maxim) Guns and Ammunition Co* [1894] AC 535, HL.
4 *Esso Petroleum Co v Harper's Garage (Stourport) Ltd* [1968] AC 269.
5 1908 SC 528; *Mason v Provident Clothing & Supply Co* [1913] AC 724; *Attwood v Lamont* [1920] 3 KB 571, CA.
6 *Williams & Son v Fairbairn* (1899) 1 F 944; *Ballachulish Slate Quarries & Co v Grant* (1903) 5 F 1105; *Taylor v Campbell* 1926 SLT 260; *Scottish Farmers Dairy Co v M'Ghee* 1933 SC 148; *Rentokil v Kramer* 1986 SLT 114; *Reed Stenhouse (UK) Ltd v Brodie* 1986 SLT 354: *A & D Bedrooms v Michael* 1984 SLT 297; *Group 4 Total Security v Ferrier* 1985 SLT 287; *Steiner v Breslin* 1979 SLT (Notes) 34; *Rentokil v Hampton* 1982 SLT 422; *Fellowes v Fisher* [1975] 2 All ER 829.
7 [1964] 3 All ER 546, CA. See also as to breach of confidence in respect of trade secrets p 132 below.

information similar thereto which could properly be protected by interdict.[8]

Where an employer seeks by a conventional restraint on an employee merely to protect himself against competition,[9] the restrictive clause will almost inevitably be regarded as unreasonable and therefore unenforceable. He must show that he has some exceptional proprietorial interest either of trade connection or trade secrets.[10]

Public interest

Apart from cases arising under the Restrictive Trade Practices and the Fair Trading legislation, the question of whether a restraint is reasonable in the public interest seems seldom to arise. The point was considered in *Kores Manufacturing Co v Kolok Manufacturing Co*[11] where two companies agreed not to employ any person who had been employed by the other during the five years prior to the agreement. The agreement was declared void as going beyond any restraint necessary to prevent misuse of trade. But in *Deacons v Bridge*[12] a five year covenant applied to a partner in a firm of solicitors was upheld as reasonable between the parties and also being in the public interest. In some cases, the doctrine of protection of the public interest merges into protection of the general right of the individual to have freedom of action. Thus in *Greig v Insole*[13] the court refused to hold as reasonable a retrospective ban on cricketers who had participated in the World Series Cricket, from taking part in Test Matches. As to the weight to be given to public interest in considering commercial contracts in restraint of trade see *Esso Petroleum Co Ltd v Harper's Garage (Stourport) Ltd*.[14]

Interdict in miscellaneous contracts

Interdict is competent to halt conduct which is in breach of a wide variety of agreements. In *Exchange Telegraph Co v Giulianotti*[15] the petitioners, under agreement, supplied the respondent exclusively for his Dundee office, with up-to-date racing information. When the

---

8 *Chill Foods (Scotland) Ltd v Cool Foods* 1977 SLT 38; *A & D Bedrooms v Michael* 1984 SLT 297; *Rentokil v Kramer* 1986 SLT 114. See also *Faccenda Chicken Ltd v Fowler* [1986] 1 All ER 617, CA; *Saltman Engineering Co Ltd v Campbell Engineering Co Ltd* [1963] 3 All ER 413, CA; *Dowson & Mason v Potter* [1986] 2 All ER 418, CA.
9 *SOS Bureau v Payne* 1982 SLT (Sh Ct) 33; *A & D Bedrooms v Michael* above.
10 *Morris v Saxelby* [1916] 1 AC 688, HL.
11 [1958] 2 All ER 65, CA. But see *BMTA v Gray* 1951 SC 586 and *Macrae & Dick v Philip* 1982 SLT (Sh Ct) 5.
12 [1984] 2 All ER 19, PC.
13 [1978] 3 All ER 449.
14 [1968] AC 269, HL at 321 per Lord Hodson.
15 1959 SC 19.

respondent passed the information also to his Perth branch office, interdict was granted. Where a professional searcher carried out work under agreement and for payment, and the petitioner, who was the employer, sought to prevent transfer of the searcher's original notes to a third party, interdict was refused on the ground that, in the absence of express stipulation, the notes remained the property of the searcher and there was no evidence of invasion of a legal right.[16] For cases involving breach of lease conditions see the cases noted.[17]

Breach of feuing or building conditions may be restrained by interdict as when a villa was in course of being converted in part to a school in defiance of a condition that the houses on the feu must be used only as self-contained dwellings.[18]

Inducing a breach of contract

Conduct by a third party which knowingly induces a breach of contract may be prevented by interdict. In *British Motor Trade Association v Gray*[19] in consequence of the post-war shortage of motor cars the petitioners instituted a scheme whereby every purchaser of a new motor car undertook not to sell the car within a specified period. The respondent, who was not a party to the agreement, sought to induce purchasers to sell their cars in breach of their covenants. In an action of interdict, the court held that the covenants were not illegal as they were reasonable in the circumstances and at the time were in the interest of the public, and interdict was granted.

As to inducing parties to break a contract in contemplation or furtherance of an industrial dispute, see p 104 above.

Interdict in breach of confidence

Aside from the matters arising in breach of contract, a simple breach of confidence by disclosure of information may be the subject of interdict at common law. Where a person stands in a confidential relationship to another and that person imparts or threatens to impart to a third party information which he should, because of the relationship and the nature of the information, have withheld, a cause of action arises.[20] There is, however, frequently difficulty in deciding whether in

---

16 *Earl of Crawford v Paton* 1911 SC 1017; *Gold v Houldsworth* (1870) 8 M 1006; *Duke of Argyll v M'arthur* (1861) 23 D 1236.
17 Ibid.
18 *Colquhoun's Curator Bonis v Glen's Trustee* 1920 SC 737.
19 1951 SC 586. See also *British Industrial Plastics v Ferguson* [1940] 1 All ER 479, HL and *Morris Motors v Lilley (trading as G & L Motors)* [1959] 3 All ER 737.
20 *Mushets Ltd v Mackenzie Bros* (1899) 1F 756 at 762 per Lord Moncrieff.

particular circumstances the relationship of confidentiality exists. Professional persons such as solicitors and accountants[1] and medical practitioners[2] stand in a well-established confidential relationship with their clients and patients. Any employee is under an implied obligation to his employer not to disclose confidential information obtained during his employment,[3] and which is a trade secret or is so confidential that it requires the same protection as a trade secret.

In deciding whether a particular piece of information is a trade secret regard must be had to the nature of the employment, the status of the employee in the firm, the true nature of the information and its possible value to a competitor in the same field, and the number of employees in the firm who actually handled the information. In *Faccenda Chicken Ltd v Fowler*,[4] where these tests were applied, lists of customers and prices charged and methods of distribution of frozen chicken were held not to fall into the class of confidential information which, by implication, an employee was bound not to disclose.

The general nature of confidential information, apart from a trade secret, was defined by Lord Greene MR in *Saltman Engineeering Co Ltd v Campbell Engineering Co Ltd:*[5]

> The information to be confidential, must, I apprehend, apart from contract, have the necessary quality of confidence about it, namely, it must not be something which is public property or public knowledge. On the other hand, it is perfectly possible to have a confidential document, be it formula, plan or sketch or something of that kind, which is the result of work done by the maker on materials which might be available for use by anybody: but what makes it confidential is the fact that the maker of the document has used his brain and has produced a result which can only be produced by somebody who has gone through the same process.

An employee cannot be prevented from using the ordinary skill and knowledge he acquires during his employment but he may be prevented from making use of a secret process the knowledge of which he acquired during that employment.[6] While he remains in the employment, the employee is, apart from contract, under an implied obligation of fidelity and good faith. This will be breached if, for example, he makes lists of customers or records or memorises lists for use after he leaves the employment.[7]

---

1 *Brown's Trustees v Hay* (1898) 25 R 1112.
2 *A B v C D* (1905) 7 F 72.
3 *Bents Brewery Co v Hogan* [1945] 2 All ER 570; *Thomas Marshall (Exports) v Guinie* [1978] 3 All ER 193.
4 [1986] 1 All ER 617, CA; but see *A & D Bedrooms v Michael* 1984 SLT 297.
5 [1963] 3 All ER 413, CA at 415 (approved in *Dowson and Mason Ltd v Potter* [1986] 2 All ER 418, CA).
6 *Cranleigh Precision Engineering v Bryant* [1964] 3 All ER 289.
7 *Faccenda Chicken Ltd v Fowler* [1986] 1 All ER 617, CA at 625.

Where a manufacturer grants to another an exclusive licence to manufacture an article and the licensee uses the information to manufacture goods which are similar and which compete with the licensed goods, interdict will be granted.[7] And the remedy has been granted where a confidential report was disclosed to a third party even though the information therein was already public knowledge.[8] But where a partner disclosed information as to arrangements for a dissolution of partnership to a third party it was held that there was no relationship between the other partners and the third party giving rise to confidentiality.[9]

---

8 *Peter Pan Manufacturing Corpn v Corsets Silhouette Ltd* [1963] 3 All ER 402.
9 *Levin & Farmers Supply Association of Scotland* 1973 SLT (Notes) 43.
10 *Roxburgh v Seven Seas Engineering* 1980 SLT (Notes) 49.

Chapter 16
Enforcement of interdict and proceedings for breach of interdict

General principles

Breach of interdict constitutes a challenge to the authority and supremacy of the court and is punishable by admonition, censure, fine or imprisonment.[1] A complaint of breach of interdict, whether initiated by petition and complaint or by minute in the process under the Administration of Justice (Scotland) Act 1933 s 6(4), requires the concurrence of the Lord Advocate, since in some cases the facts relied upon may well involve liability for criminal prosecution.[2] The measure of proof required is beyond reasonable doubt.[3] A person not named in the decree granting interdict cannot be found guilty of breach of the interdict.[4] Notice of the interdict to the party restrained is essential to found proceedings for breach of interdict. Where there are no averments of sufficient knowledge by the defender, the action may be dismissed.[5]

Misnomer of defender

A misnomer of the person charged with the breach, either in the interlocutor granting interdict or in the complaint of breach, may invalidate the breach proceedings but each case will be judged upon its own circumstances. Thus in *Overseas League v Taylor*[6] a defender was designed in the interdict as 'Miss Lilly Taylor (otherwise known as Miss Bunty Taylor)' and in the complaint of breach of interdict as 'Miss Lilly Taylor (sometimes known as Miss Bunty Taylor)'. The defender was commonly known as Bunty Taylor but her christian name was not Lilly and in fact Lilly Taylor was a different person. In

---

1 *Johnson v Grant* 1923 SC 789: *Macleay v Macdonald* 1928 SC 776.
2 *Gribben v Gribben* 1976 SLT 266.
3 *Eutectic Welding Alloys Co v Whitting* 1969 SLT (Notes) 79; approved in *Gribben v Gribben* above.
4 *Pattison v Fitzgerald* (1823) 2 S 536.
5 *Anderson v Moncrieff* 1966 SLT (Sh Ct) 28. See also *Borland v Lochwinnoch Golf Club* 1986 SLT 13 at 16.
6 1951 SC 105.

refusing a motion to have the defender summoned to the bar, the court referred to the serious consequences for the defender and it was emphasised that the misnomer could not be regarded as a mere technicality. By contrast, in *Anderson v Stoddart*[7] also a case of interdict, an irregularity in address and designation was condoned.

Defect in jurisdiction of interdict

Any defect in jurisdiction in the granting of interdict is fatal to the enforcement of the order. In *Calder Chemicals Ltd v Brunton*[8] the defender was cited at his residence within the Sheriffdom. On appeal it was held that the Sheriff's jurisdiction to grant interdict did not extend beyond his Sheriffdom (distinguishing *Home Drummond v Thomson* 1907 15 SLT 524). But also on the question of jurisdiction to interdict outwith the Sheriffdom and for what appears a contrary view, see *McKenna v McKenna*[9] where a common law interdict was sought contemporaneously with a matrimonial interdict under s 14(2) of the Matrimonial Homes (Family Protection) (Scotland) Act 1981. The principles of jurisdiction involved where the breach is alleged to have taken place abroad are discussed in *Allen & Leslie (International) Ltd v Wagley*.[10]

Duration of enforcement

So long as an interdict remains in force, the defender is bound to comply with it. It is no defence to allege in the proceedings for breach that the interdict should never have been granted.[11]

Induciae in breach of interdict

The period of *induciae* is within the discretion of the court and may depend upon the remoteness or otherwise of the defender's residence.[12]

Caution against repetition of breach and as condition of interdict

A crave for caution to be lodged against repetition of breach of interdict is competent. An order for interim interdict may be made subject to the petitioner lodging caution sufficient to cover any loss arising from stoppage of the defender's activities in consequence of an interdict.[13]

---

7 1923 SC 755.
8 1984 SLT (Sh Ct) 96. See also Civil Jurisdiction and Judgments Act 1982.
9 1984 SLT (Sh Ct) 92.
10 1976 SLT (Sh Ct) 12.
11 *Dick v Fleshers of Stirling* (1827) 5 S 268; *Stark's Trs v Duncan* (1906) 8 F 429 at 433.
12 *Costa v Costa* 1929 SN 62.
13 *Williams & Son v Fairbairn* (1899) 1 F 944.

Conversely interim interdict was refused where caution was found sufficient to satisfy any loss which the petitioner would sustain through continuance of the defender's activities of which he complained.[14] Where a grant of interdict, whether interim or perpetual, is made conditional upon the lodging of caution by the petitioner, the order operates only from the date upon which caution is found and cannot previously be enforced.[15]

Procedure in defended cases

Where the breach of interdict is denied a record is made up and the case proceeds as an ordinary civil action. Proof will be led and the defender is a competent witness since, in this sense, the proceedings are not criminal.[16] If the petitioner fails to prove the breach the defender will be *assoilzied* and may be found entitled to expenses.[17]

Postponement of interdict order

Where the grounds for interdict of a defender's operations are established but the immediate grant of interdict, interim or perpetual, would cause grave public inconvenience or result in greater loss to the defender than would be caused to the petitioner by the continuance of the wrong of which he complains, the court may occasionally simply declare (for example) the existence of a nuisance. Any further order will, in such circumstances, be deferred to give the defender an opportunity of remedying the situation complained of. Alternatively, interdict may, in cases involving the public interest, simply be refused, as in the case of *Forth Yacht Marina Ltd v Forth Road Bridge Joint Board*.[18] Such cases arise frequently in connection with the pollution of water or air caused by the operations of statutory or local authorities.[19] Where any further order is deferred it is normally conditional upon an undertaking by the defender to carry out remedial measures immediately.[20]

Procedures where breach admitted or proved

If the breach is admitted or proved, the defender is required to appear at the bar of the court. Should he fail to do so warrant for his apprehension may be granted to officers of court. But personal

---

14 *Fergusson-Buchanan v Dumbarton County Council* 1924 SC 42.
15 *Wilson v Gilchrist* (1900) 2 F 391.
16 *Christie Miller v Bain* (1879) 6 R 1215.
17 *Menzies v Macdonald* (1864) 2 M 652.
18 1984 SLT 177.
19 *Hands v Perth County Council* (1959) 75 Sh Ct Rep 173.
20 *Clippens Oil Co v Edinburgh and District Water Trustees* (1897) 25 R 370.

appearance may, in certain circumstances, be dispensed with. In *Walker v Junor*[1] where the defender failed to appear but a medical certificate of inability to attend was produced, the court proceeded to impose a fine in the absence of the defender. And in *Starks Trustees v Duncan*[2] where the defender had failed to appear at the bar, without excuse or explanation, and the Sheriff had imposed a fine in his absence, the defender's appeal was refused. It is thought that, in line with criminal procedure, a sentence of imprisonment cannot competently be imposed in the absence of the defender. The proper course in such circumstances is to grant warrant for the defender's apprehension and adjourn the diet.[3]

As to fines imposed on a trade union for breach of interdict where the union was vicariously liable for the acts of its officials under s 15 of the Employment Act 1982, see *Express Newspapers plc and Star v NGA*.[4]

Wilful disregard of court order

Where there has been no intention wilfully to disregard the orders of the court, the defender may be found liable only in expenses.[5] Where the breach is more serious the defender may be required to find caution against repetition thereof[6] or he may be ordered to make restoration or restitution at his own expense.[7] In *Campbell v Mackay*,[8] a case involving interdict against straying sheep, proof was led of no effective measures to prevent straying but it was held that was insufficient evidence to establish deliberate disregard of the order of the court, and in any case the interdict was too wide and of doubtful validity.

Remission of imprisonment

Where imprisonment has been imposed remission may be granted on cause shown but application must be made to the court which imposed the penalty. The factors which may influence the court in considering remission were explained in *Johnson v Grant*.[9] Appeal against the interlocutor imposing the sentence is however competent in the normal way. The marking of an appeal postpones the sentence and liberation may be granted pending the disposal of the appeal.[10]

---

1 (1903) 5 F 1035.
2 (1906) 8 F 429.
3 *Welsbach Incandescent Gas Light Co v M'Mann* (1901) 4 F 395.
4 CLY 1985.
5 *Fraser's Trustees v Cran* (1879) 6 R 451.
6 *Gray (Lord) v Petrie* (1848) 10 D 718.
7 *Blantyre (Lord) v Dunn* (1845) 7 D 299.
8 1959 SLT (Sh Ct) 34.
9 1923 SC 789.
10 *Mcleay v Macdonald* 1928 SC 776.

Enforcement where change of circumstances

A change of circumstances arising after the order for interdict has been granted may affect the right of a pursuer to enforce the order. Thus where interdict is obtained in respect of breach of contract and the pursuer ceases to have any enforceable interest in the contract, the interdict cannot be enforced.[11] Even where an interdict has been made perpetual, the Court of Session, in exercise of the *nobile officium*, may permit something to be done which would be contrary to the interdict previously granted.[12]

---

[11] *Berlitz School of Languages v Duchene* (1903) 6 F 181.
[12] *Bowie, Petitioner* 1967 SC 36.

Chapter 17
Interim interdict

Nature of the remedy

Interim interdict is a discretionary remedy granted to regulate, and where possible preserve, the rights of parties, pending the final determination of the matter in issue. The discretion of the court is exercised not arbitrarily but in accordance with, and upon the application of, certain well-established principles. The order is frequently made upon the basis of *ex parte* averments and before the defender has been called into court. In such cases, however, usually after notice of the interim interdict has been served upon the defender, and sometimes after defences have been ordered and lodged, a motion for recall of the interim interdict may be made and the matter decided upon a somewhat fuller consideration of the averments of parties. Even when the question is not decided until defences have been lodged, little more than a rough *prima facie* view of the facts is generally available and the discretionary element is of great importance. The question at this stage is not so much the absolute relevancy of the case, as the seeming cogency of the need for interim interdict.[1]

As the Lord Justice Clerk (Inglis) explained in *Rankin v M'Lachlan*.[2]

> It is a very easy thing for a party to make a case on averment. There are cases where the admitted facts are sufficient to justify the granting of interim interdict and in some cases there may be material averments which admit of instant verification, but mere relevancy of averment is not enough.

Thus there may be instances where the whole basis of the pursuer's case is challenged, as when the very existence of a patent alleged to have been breached is denied,[3] and the pursuer's case does not afford *prima facie* a ground for interim interdict. Again, in cases of interdict against libel and slander, where there is a stated defence of *veritas* or qualified privilege, the court will rarely make an order for interim

---

1 *Burn Murdoch on Interdict* para 143 approved in *Deane v Lothian Regional Council* 1986 SLT 22.
2 (1864) 3 M 128 at 133.
3 *Brown v Kidston* (1852) 14 D 826.

interdict, unless it can be shown that the defender dishonestly and maliciously proposes to say or publish information which he knows to be untrue.[4]

Prima facie case on declaratory judgment

A declaratory judgment bearing upon the matter in issue will always found a *prima facie* case for interim interdict. It will also found *prima facie* against new defenders called in the case, even if the declaratory judgment is not *res judicata* against them.[5]

Competing titles to heritage

In cases involving heritable rights, where possessary questions are in issue, the complainer seeking interdict must be able to show, as against a party pleading a competing title, that he has been in possession, properly established by virtue of his title, for at least seven years prior to the date of the attempt to innovate upon it.[6]

Documentary evidence

It is frequently the case that one or perhaps both parties will produce documentary evidence in support of their averments, such as title deeds, plans, commercial documents and contracts and the like. Such productions at this early stage are rarely the subject of proof in the technical sense. They can, however, be, and frequently are, examined at length to ascertain whether *prima facie* the pursuer has a title to sue and has set out a case to try. Productions such as these can, however, at this stage, be taken only at their face value.[7]

Affidavit evidence

In England it is normal practice for parties to lodge affidavits in support of their averments at hearings upon interlocutory injunctions but except in proceedings under the Matrimonial Homes (Family Protection) (Scotland) Act 1981 the practice has not found favour in Scotland. Here the courts rely upon the veracity of the averments of parties and upon the submissions made by counsel and solicitors at the bar. While *ex facie* the production of sworn affidavits in support of averments may appear to have some advantages, in giving the court the

---

4 *Harakas v Baltic Mercantile and Shipping Exchange & Anr* [1982] 2 All ER 701, CA, but see *Fairbairn v SNP* 1980 SLT 149.
5 *Free Church General Assembly v Rain* (1904) 12 SLT 387; *Burn Murdoch on Interdict* para 143.
6 *Colquhoun v Paton* (1859) 21 D 996 at 1001.
7 *Burn Murdoch* para 143.

benefit of much additional information, it has led sometimes to decisions being made prematurely upon the merits. This tendency was criticised in *American Cyanamid Co v Ethicon Ltd*,[8] where it was pointed out in an appeal by the plaintiffs to the House of Lords that what the Court of Appeal had done was to try the issue of an infringement of patent upon conflicting affidavit evidence, as it stood without oral testimony or cross examination.

Question of competency

A question of interim interdict may be dealt with notwithstanding a plea by the defenders that interdict is incompetent. The question of competency may be left over for decision at a later stage.[9]

Granted periculo petentis

Interim interdict is awarded without prejudice to the respective rights of parties as ultimately decided. It is granted *periculo petentis*. If a complainer secures interim interdict but places upon the defender, by reason of the interdict, too great a restraint, the defender will, in the final result, be entitled to damages to compensate for his loss through the excessive interim interdict restraint.[10]

Interim interdict may subsist for a fixed period, as is usual in applications granted upon *ex parte* averments only, or may be continued in operation until further orders of the court. Should a change of circumstances occur and the change materially affect the position of the parties, application may be made for the recall of an interim interdict previously granted. And in *Crawford v Paisley Magistrates*[11] interim interdict against the demolition of a church steeple was recalled upon it being shown that there was adequate justification for the demolition complained of.

Factors affecting the grant or refusal of interim interdict

The pursuer must be able to aver and satisfy the court that he has a title and interest to sue the principal action; that *prima facie* he has suffered some wrongful act at the hands of the defender, or is seriously threatened therewith, and that there is in fact a case to try. Once the court has been satisfied upon these matters, it will proceed to consider whether, upon the balance of convenience, the pursuer has averred sufficient facts to establish a cogent need for immediate protection by the grant of interim interdict. As was explained by the Lord Justice Clerk in *Deane v Lothian Regional Council:*[12] 'The test at the stage of

---

  8 [1975] 1 All ER 504 HL, at 511.
  9 *Scottish Milk Marketing Board v Paris* 1935 SC 287.
  10 *Fife v Orr* (1895) 23 R 8.
  11 (1870) 8 M 693.
  12 1986 SLT 22.

interim interdict is not so much the absolute relevancy of the case as the seeming cogency of the need for interim interdict.' The factors which emerge at this stage are those which truly involve the element of discretion. In many cases these factors are finely balanced and frequently interrelated, but sometimes mutually exclusive. The vital importance of the proper exercise of discretion, and one of the peculiar features of interim interdict, is that, while it is not decided upon the merits of the case, the grant or refusal of the order may in some cases virtually mean the end of the principal action. This is particularly so in certain matrimonial interdicts, in cases involving picketing and other forms of industrial action, and in cases of interdict against the repetition or threat of libel or slander.

Examples of cases where interim interdict may be granted

The circumstances in which interim interdict may be granted cover a wide spectrum. The following list, which is by no means exhaustive, is indicative of the fact that interim interdict can impinge upon almost every branch of our law. In all cases, the basic principles of title and interest to sue, a proper case to try and a cogent need for the granting of the order, must be present before the order will be granted.

(1) To prevent some danger to the complainer that would be manifest *injuria,* and that is also imminent or threatened, such as apprehension or personal injury or danger to life or great and perhaps irreparable material harm.[13] If the harm would be irreparable, this is a strong ground for interim interdict.[14]

(2) To prevent inversion of the existing state of possession[15] particularly in cases involving unlawful encroachment upon heritable subjects, including water rights and salmon fishings.

(3) In order temporarily to preserve the status quo where this would be innocuous, or simply to preserve matters entire.[16]

(4) To restrain a public authority or body from doing some act which is *ultra vires* or a manifest abuse of power and which is likely to cause immediate and irreparable harm to any person.[17]

(5) To prevent a public authority or body from doing any act which is *prima facie* a breach of its statutory authority.[18]

(6) To restrain or regulate numerous domestic relationships, including marriage, custody of children, matrimonial disputes

---

13 *Burn Murdoch on Interdict* para 145.
14 *Baird & Co v Monkland Iron & Steel Co* (1862) 24 D 1418 at 1425 per Lord Justice Clerk Inglis.
15 *Burn Murdoch* para 132, *Brown v Lee Constructions Ltd* 1977 SLT Notes 61.
16 *Glen v Caledonian Railway Co* (1868) 6 M 797 at 800 per Lord Ardmillan.
17 *Deane v Lothian Regional Council* 1986 SLT 22; *Meek v Lothian Regional Council* 1983 SLT 494; *Meek v Lothian Regional Council* 1980 SLT (Notes) 61.
18 *Wilson v IBA* 1979 SLT 279.

and protection of spouses, and the removal of children outwith Scotland.[19]

(7) To prevent breach of contract and inducing breach of contract, imminent or continuing, including employment contracts, covenants restrictive of employment, agreements in restraint of trade, and contracts pertaining to heritable property containing obligations or restrictions.[20]

(8) In company and partnership matters, to restrain breaches of the Companies Act 1985 and of the memoranda and articles of companies and of partnership agreements, and actions *ultra vires* of directors and share holders.[1]

(9) To prevent the creation or continuance of nuisance or breach of servitude or withdrawal of lateral or vertical support.[2]

(10) To restrain wrongs against reputation, involving libel and slander and the publication of statements calculated to mislead.[3]

(11) To restrain trespass upon heritable property and illegal fishing, poaching, and shooting even without actual trespass.[4]

(12) To prevent obstruction of public or private rights of way and access by employees to places of employment in the face of picketing by trade unions.[5]

(13) To deal with infringement of copyright, trade marks, patents, registered designs and to prevent activities involving 'passing off'.[6]

(14) To restrain unlawful execution or enforcement of diligence.[7]

(15) Under the heading of miscellaneous cases where the remedy may be invoked are:
    (a) disclosure of trade secrets by employees;[8]

19 *Brown v Brown* 1985 SLT 376; *Tattersall v Tattersall* 1983 SLT 506; *Pease v Pease* 1967 SC 112; *Hoy v Hoy* 1968 SC 179; Matrimonial Proceedings (Children) Act 1958 s 13; *Johnstone v Johnstone* 1967 SLT 248.

20 *Ballachulish Slate Quarries Co v Grant* (1903) 5 F 1105; *Bluebell Apparel Ltd v Dickinson* 1980 SLT 157; *Randev v Pattar* 1985 SLT 270; *BMTA v Gray* 1951 SC 586; *Colquhoun's Curator Bonis v Glen's Trustee* 1920 SC 737; *Square Grip Reinforcement Co Ltd v Macdonald* 1966 SLT 232; *News International v SOGAT '82* (1986) Scotsman 1 February.

1 *Foss v Harbottle* (1843) 2 Hare 461; *Estmanco (Kilner House) v GLC* [1982] 1 All ER 437; *MacDougall v Gardiner* (1875) 1 Ch D 13; *Ball v Metal Industries Ltd* 1957 SLT 124; *Cousins v International Brick Co* [1931] 2 Ch 90; *Pollock v Garrett* 1957 SLT (Notes) 8.

2 *Giblin v Lanarkshire County Council* 1927 SLT 563; *Watt v Jamieson* 1954 SC 56; *Inglis v Shotts Iron Co* (1881) 8 R 1006; *Caledonian Railway Co v Sprot* (1856) 2 Mac 449, HL; *White v Dixon* (1883) 10 R (HL) 45 at 52.

3 *Fairbairn v SNP* 1980 SLT 149.

4 *Inverurie Magistrates v Sorrie* 1956 SC 175; *Orr Ewing & Co v Colquhoun's Trs* (1877) 4 R (HL) 116.

5 *Mcfie v Scottish Rights of Way Society* (1884) 11 R 1094; *British Airports Authority v Ashton* [1983] 3 All ER 6; *Thomas v National Union of Mineworkers* [1985] 2 All ER 1; *News International v SOGAT '82* (1986) Scotsman 1 February.

6 See the cases cited in ch 10 above.

7 See the cases cited in ch 5 above.

8 *Cranleigh Precision Engineering v Bryant* [1964] 3 All ER 289.

    (b) destruction of evidence required in legal proceedings;[9]
    (c) in certain circumstances breaches of confidence by the publication of letters;[10]
    (d) to regulate ownership of moveable property;[11]
    (e) to restrain the appropriation of land reclaimed from the sea.[12]

Cases where interim interdict may be refused

(1) Where averments sufficient to satisfy any one or more of the three basic principles namely (a) title and interest to sue; (b) a proper case to try; and (c) cogency of the need for interim interdict are lacking.

(2) Where the order would be contrary to the public interest.[13]

(3) Where there has been undue delay in applying for the remedy.[14]

(4) Where the act complained of has been completed and there is no reasonable likelihood of repetition or continuation.[15]

(5) Where the basic claim made by the complainer is challenged upon *ex facie* valid grounds, as in copyright and patent cases where the validity or very existence of the copyright or patent is attacked; and in libel and slander cases where a plea of *veritas* or qualified privilege is taken.[16]

(6) Where, although there is title and interest and a proper case to try, the balance of convenience is against granting interim interdict.[17]

(7) Where an alternative remedy, by way of appeal or otherwise, is available to the complainter.[18]

(8) Where the rights of parties can be fairly and reasonably preserved by the imposition of conditions, or a requirement for caution against damages or by undertakings to keep account of money

---

9 *Grieve v Kilmarnock Motor Co* 1923 SC 491.

10 *Brown's Trustees v Hay* (1898) 25 R 1112 but see *White v Dickson* (1881) 8 R 896.

11 *Wilson v Shepherd* 1913 SC 300.

12 *Irvine v Robertson* (1873) 11 M 298 but see *Hagart v Fyfe* (1870) 9 M 127.

13 *Trainer v Renfrewshire Upper District Committee* 1907 SC 1117 at 1120; *Southern Bowling Club v Ross* (1902) 4 F 405; *Forth Yacht Marina v Forth Road Bridge Joint Board* 1984 SLT 177.

14 *Ayala & Co v Dowell* (1893) 1 SLT 374; *Express Newspapers plc v Liverpool Daily Post and Echo plc* [1985] 3 All ER 680 at 687; *William Grant & Sons v William Cadenhead* 1985 SLT 291 at 293.

15 *Crooke v Scots Pictorial Co Ltd* 1906 43 SLR 723 at 726; *Glen v Caledonian Railway Co* (1868) 6 M 797; *Begg v Jack* (1874) 1 R 366.

16 *Harakas v Baltic Mercantile & Shipping Exchange Ltd* [1982] 2 All ER 701; *Riddel v Clydesdale Horse Society* (1885) 12 R 976 at 981; *Phonographic Performance v MacKenzie* 1982 SLT 272; *William Grant & Sons Ltd v William Cadenhead Ltd* 1985 SLT 291 at 292.

17 *Randev v Pattar* 1985 SLT 270 and cases cited at p 146 below.

18 Burn Murdoch on Interdict para 123; *George Packman & Sons v Young* 1976 SLT (Notes) 52; *London Borough of Hammersmith v Magnum Automated Forecourts Ltd* [1978] 1 All ER 401, CA; *Cumming v Inverness Magistrates* 1953 SC 1 (but see *Innes v Kirkcaldy Magistrates* 1963 SLT 325).

Interim interdict

received or goods sold or even, in exceptional cases by undertakings to refrain from the course of conduct complained of.[19]

The balance of convenience

In questions of interim interdict the relative inconvenience resulting to either party from its grant or refusal is a dominating consideration and must fall upon one side or the other. It is assumed that one party or the other will ultimately be successful and the balance is estimated upon that assumption.

> The object is to regulate interim possession in such a way as to do least damage in the meantime to either party, at the same time to provide sufficiently for proper restitution being made for any damage suffered by the party who shall be found to have been in the right when the case is over.[20]

> The question always comes to be a balance of advantages and disadvantages on the two sides. If there is irreparable injury to be sustained by either recalling or keeping on the interdict, then this is a very important consideration. If there is irreparable injury to both sides then this raises a very delicate question indeed. Still, it will be a balance of convenience and injury; upon which side is the balance? But if, on one side you see an unquestionable irreparable injury, then I think there will be no doubt upon which side the balance should turn.[1]

In cases involving alleged breach of duty by public authorities, it is necessary to look more widely at the balance of convenience, and to consider the balance, not only between the complainer and the authority, but also between the authority and the public at large.[2] There may, in other cases, be special factors to be taken into consideration, as where, on the facts available and as to which there is no dispute, the strength of one party's case is disproportionate to the other.[3] This has for long been the practice in Scotland and was referred to with approval by Lord Fraser in *NWL Ltd v Woods*.[4] In England however it has been laid down that the court in exercising its discretion in granting or refusing an interlocutory injunction ought not to weigh up the relative strengths of the parties' cases on the evidence of affidavits then available.[5]

---

19 *Burn Murdoch* para 162; *Brown v Edinburgh University Court* 1973 SLT (Notes) 55.
20 *Tennant & Co v Thomson* (1870) 8 SLR 15 per Lord President Inglis.
1 *Baird & Co v Monkland Iron & Steel Co* (1862) 24 D 1418 at 1425 per Lord Justice Clerk Inglis; see also *Scottish Milk Marketing Board v Paris* 1935 SC 287 at 296 per Lord President Clyde; *Chill Foods (Scotland) Ltd v Cool Foods* 1977 SLT 38.
2 *Smith v Inner London Education Authority* [1978] 1 All ER 411, CA; *Forth Yacht Marina v Forth Road Bridge Joint Board* 1984 SLT 177.
3 *American Cyanamide Co v Ethicon Ltd* [1975] 1 All ER 504 HL at 511.
4 [1979] 3 All ER 614, CA at 628.
5 Fn 3 above.

Chapter 18
Procedure in actions of interdict

1 IN THE COURT OF SESSION

Commencement of the action

Action for interdict is initiated in the Outer House of the Court of Session by petition which must contain a statement in the form of an articulate condescendence of the allegations in fact which form the grounds of the prayer of the petition. There must be annexed to the petition a note of the petitioner's pleas in law.[1] Other actions in which there is included a conclusion for interim interdict may be initiated by summons.[2] Where the true nature of the remedy sought in the petition is specific implement, interdict is incompetent.[3]

The petition must conform to the style set out in Form No 28 annexed to the Rules of Court, and may be signed by the petitioner's counsel or solicitor.[4] The petition need not make any offer of caution or consignation.[5] It must be brought before a Lord Ordinary in the Outer House in court or in chambers.

Interdict may be combined with other remedies or may be sought as a single conclusion.[6]

Induciae

The normal *induciae* for service of the petition is 14 days but if the respondent resides outside Europe, the *induciae* for personal service is three weeks and if served by post, six weeks.[7] Intimation is made by serving a full copy of the petition and of the interlocutor ordering intimation.[8]

---

[1] Administration of Justice (Scotland) Act 1933 s 6.
[2] RC 79.
[3] *Grosvenor Developments (Scotland) v Argyll Stores Ltd* 1987 GWD 251.
[4] RC 235.
[5] RC 234.
[6] *Exchange Telegraph Co v White* 1961 SLT 104.
[7] RC 192
[8] RC 236. As to shortening *induciae* for interim interdict see RC 236(a).

Further procedure

Subject to certain special requirements applicable to interim orders,[9] the further procedure of entering appearance, lodging answers, making up the open record, adjustment of pleadings and closing the record follows the usual procedure for ordinary actions in the Court of Session.[10]

Similarly, the procedure for enrolling and opposing motions,[11] for applications for commission and diligence for obtaining documents,[12] and the optional procedure,[13] applications for presentation of documents under s 1 of the Administration of Justice (Scotland) Act 1972[14] and lodging productions for the proof[15] follow the usual pattern.

Special procedure for obtaining interim interdict

(a) Where interim interdict is sought, the petitioner's counsel or solicitor must attend upon the Lord Ordinary at the presentation of the petition.[16]

(b) The Lord Ordinary orders intimation and the lodging of answers on such *induciae* as he thinks expedient. He may also pronounce such interim orders as may be meet and convenient in the circumstances, with or without caution or consignation and upon such conditions as he sees fit.[17]

(c) The time for lodging answers begins to run from the date of intimation of the interim interdict to the respondent. If the interlocutor granting the interim order and ordering intimation contains a requirement for caution or consignation by the petitioner and such caution or consignation has not been lodged by the date intimation is made to the respondent, the time for lodging answers does not begin to run until the caution has been lodged or consignation made. If the conditions as to caution or consignation have not been implemented within 14 days from the date of intimation, the petition may be refused, but the court has power to prorogate the time for implementation.[18]

---

9 See below.
10 Se RC 90, 90A, 91, 92.
11 RC 93.
12 Commission and diligence may be granted *ex parte* in an interlocutor ordering intimation and interim interdict. For the test to be applied see *British Phonographic Industry v Cohen, Cohen, Kelly, Cohen & Cohen* 1983 SLT 137.
13 RC 95, 96.
14 RC 95A.
15 RC 107.
16 RC 236(a).
17 RC 236(a). Where motion enrolled for interim interdict notice of motion must be given to the opponent. See *Anderson v Sutherland (Peterhead) Ltd* 1940 SLT 361.
18 RC 236(d).

(d) After hearing parties on the petition and answers (if lodged) and on the question of interim interdict, or after any hearing upon a caveat lodged for the respondent, the Lord Ordinary may make such interim order or further interim order as may be meet and convenient in the circumstances, with or without caution, consignation or special conditions.[19]
(e) The Lord Ordinary may at this stage refuse the petition in whole or in part or declare any interim interdict already granted to be perpetual or may appoint the cause to the adjustment roll.[20]
(f) A motion for recall of interim interdict is competent after a record has been made up and during adjustment.[1]

Caveats

If a caveat has been lodged for the respondent, the Principal Clerk of Session will, upon presentation of the petition, fix a hearing upon the petition and caveat as soon as reasonably practicable and must intimate the date to both parties.[2]

Caution generally

Where caution has been ordered, the bond must be in proper form and contain all the necessary clauses. The Deputy Principal Clerk must consider the sufficiency of the caution lodged and may seek further information.[3]

The party entitled to the benefit of caution may object to the terms of caution and must do so by letter to the Deputy Principal Clerk specifying his objections.[4]

The court has power to order a respondent to find caution and may do so as a condition of refusing the petitioner's application for interim interdict.[5]

Where objections to the amount or quality of caution required of a petitioner have been intimated to the Deputy Principal Clerk, he may consider and himself dispose of the objections or refer the matter to the

---

[19] RC 236(c). An interlocutor which merely reserves the question of interim interdict pending answers being lodged is not a refusal of the crave and cannot be appealed. *Gauldie v Arbroath Magistrates* 1936 SC 861.
[20] RC 236(e) but see *Arneil v Paisley Town Council* 1948 SLT (Notes) 46.
[1] *National Cash Register Co Ltd v Kinnear* 1948 SLT (Notes) 83.
[2] RC 236(b).
[3] RC 238(a).
[4] RC 238(d).
[5] *Wilson v Gilbert* (1863) 1 M 663; *Fergusson-Buchanan v Dumbarton County Council* 1924 SC 42.

court. Any party aggrieved by the decision of the Deputy Principal Clerk may by motion bring the matter before the court.[6]

If a cautioner becomes insolvent or dies without representatives, a note may be presented seeking fresh caution, in which event the court will pronounce such order thereon as the justice of the case may require.[7]

Where a petition is refused upon failure to lodge caution, or upon any grounds not on the merits of the case, it is competent, on payment of the previous expenses, to present a second petition.

Juratory caution

In an offer of juratory caution (where the party ordered to find caution offers to assign his estate in lieu of caution), the Lord Ordinary, when ordering answers, will name a commissioner and make orders as to the preparation of a full inventory of the estate.[8]

Productions in interim orders

Where any paper is lodged by a party prior to the interlocutor appointing the cause to the adjustment roll, or refusing the petition, the solicitor for the party lodging the production must, on the same day, give notice of lodging to the solicitor for the other party and must lodge in the Petition Department a certificate of such intimation.[9]

Certificates of refusal

A certificate of refusal of a petition cannot be issued until the expiry of 48 hours after the entry of the court's refusal in the Minute Book.[10]

Appointment to adjustment roll

Where a petition is appointed by interlocutor to the adjustment roll in cases where caution has to be found, consignation made or conditions fulfilled, the interlocutor does not take effect until caution has been found, consignation made or the conditions implemented.[11]

In such cases the party benefiting from the caution, consignation or conditions shall not be entitled to a certificate of non-fulfilment, without intimating to the other party that he is to apply to the Deputy

---

6 RC 238(e).
7 RC 238(f).
8 RC 240.
9 RC 241.
10 RC 244.
11 RC 245(a).

Principal Clerk for such a certificate; and the Deputy Principal Clerk cannot give out the certificate until 24 hours after such intimation has been made.[12]

Not later than seven days after the date on which

(a) the Lord Ordinary's interlocutor appointing the cause to the adjustment roll has been pronounced and
(b) any caution or consignation has been found or conditions have been implemented,

the solicitor for the petitioner must deliver six copies of the open record (consisting of the petition and answers) to the solicitor for each respondent and must lodge two copies in the Petition Department. The case will then appear in the adjustment roll and the pleadings will be adjusted under RC 90, and thereafter the case will proceed as an ordinary action.[13]

Decrees in absence

Where a petition for interdict has been lodged and no appearance has been entered and no answers have been lodged, the Lord Ordinary has power to pronounce a final judgment granting in whole or in part the prayer of the petition, and declaring any interim interdict previously pronounced to be perpetual and may award expenses against the respondent.[14] Where proceedings are commenced without prior warning against repetition of the wrong complained of, expenses may be withheld.[15]

Interdict against removal of children

Applications under s 13 of the Matrimonial Proceedings (Children) Act 1958 for interdict against removal of a child furth of Scotland or out of the custody of the person in whose care he is, require to be made by motion.[16]

Interdict against infringement of patents and registered designs

In any proceedings where it is alleged that a patent has been infringed, the person alleging infringement must aver in the petition or summons particulars of the infringement relied on showing which of the claims in the specification of the patent are alleged to have been infringed and

---

12 RC 245(b).
13 RC 247.
14 RC 246.
15 *Cellular Clothing Co v Schulberg* 1952 SLT (Notes) 73.
16 RC 170(c).

giving at least one instance of each type of infringement relied upon.[17]

If, as a defence to an allegation as aforesaid, it is averred that, at the time of the infringement there was in force a contract or licence relating to the patent, made by or with the consent of the person alleging the infringement and containing a condition or term void by virtue of s 44 of the Patents Act 1977, the person stating that defence must aver particulars of the date of and the parties to such contract or licence and particulars of each such condition or terms.[18]

Breach of interdict

Where a process in which interim interdict was granted is still subsisting and a breach of that interim interdict occurs, the breach may be dealt with by simple enrolment of the cause, without the necessity for a petition and complaint for breach.[19]

A petition and complaint for breach of interdict, or the note in the case where the case is still subsisting, must contain sufficient averment that notice of the interdict has been given to the offending party or at least that he had knowledge of it.[20]

IN THE SHERIFF COURT

Actions of interdict in the Sheriff Court are ordinary actions and follow the procedure laid down in the Act of Sederunt (Ordinary Cause Rules, Sheriff Court) 1983.[1]

Commencement of the action

The action of interdict is commenced by initial writ as nearly as may be in accordance with Form A in the appendix to the Rules. The writ must be signed by the pursuer or his solicitor.[2] The crave for interdict may be combined with a declarator or a claim for damages.

Citation

The inducing or period of notice to the defender is 14 days where the defender is resident or has a place of business in the United Kingdom,

---

17 RC 255(1).
18 RC 255(2).
19 Administration of Justice (Scotland) Act 1933 s 6(4).
20 *Anderson v Moncrieff* 1966 SLT (Sh Ct) 28 (distinguishing *Henderson v Maclellan* (1874) 1 R 920). See also ch 16.
1 SI 1983 747 (S 66) amended by SI 1984/255, SI 1986/1230 and SI 1986/1946.
2 Rr 3 and 4.

the Isle of Man, the Channel Islands or the Republic of Ireland; 28 days where the defender is resident or has a place of business outwith the foregoing areas but within Europe; and 42 days when he is resident or has a place of business outside Europe. The sheriff may, on cause shown, shorten the *induciae* to not less than two days.[3]

Further procedure

Thereafter the procedure for lodging notice of intention to defend, tabling, lodging defences, making up the record, closing the record and fixing the proof follow the normal rules.[4]

Interim interdict

If interim interdict is sought it must be craved in the writ which must contain averments sufficient to establish a title and interest to sue and a cogent need for interim interdict upon the balance of convenience.[5]

Upon the presentation of the writ for warrant for service, the Sheriff may grant interim interdict on *ex parte* averments and at the same time fix an early diet for hearing parties on interim interdict. Alternatively, he may defer any grant of interim interdict until parties have been heard in which case the diet for hearing will be fixed in the interlocutor ordering service and intimation.

Where interim interdict has been granted on *ex parte* averments and in absence of the defender, the order will not become effective until notice thereof has been given to him by service of the copy writ and a copy of the interlocutor. It has however been held sufficient that notice of the interdict has been given informally, for example by letter.[6]

The question of whether the Sheriff may grant interim interdict in respect of wrongs occurring or apprehended outwith his sheriffdom is not entirely clear. For discussion of this matter see *McKenna v McKenna*.[7]

If interim interdict is refused the application may be renewed at any stage of the case, as for example where there has been a change of circumstances.

An interlocutor granting or refusing an application for interim

---

[3] R. 7.
[4] Rr 33 to 84.
[5] For detailed consideration of the averments necessary to support a crave for interim interdict see ch 17 above.
[6] *Henderson v MacLellan* (1874] I R 920; *Neville v Neville* (1921) 40 Sh Ct rep 151; *Matheson v Fraser* 1911 2 SLT 493. As to notice where the defender is an unincorporated association see *Borland v Lochwinnoch Golf Club* 1986 SLT (Sh Ct) 13.
[7] 1984 SLT (Sh Ct) 92, distinguishing *Home Drummond v Thomson* (1907) 15 SLT 524. See also *Burn Murdoch on Interdict* p 24, and the Civil Jurisdiction and Judgments Act 1982 Sch 4, art 5(3); ch 2 above.

interdict may be appealed to the Sheriff Principal within 14 days from its date in the case of refusal and within 14 days from intimation when the interim order has been granted, if not sooner extracted following a motion for early extract.[8] An appeal will lie even before tabling or the lodging of defences.

Caution

In granting interim interdict, the Sheriff may order the pursuer to lodge caution for any damage the defender may sustain if he ultimately proves successful in his defence.[9] Caution may also be required from a defender as a condition of refraining from an award of interim interdict. As in the Court of Session, interdict granted upon condition of caution being found by the pursuer does not operate until caution is lodged. A similar rule applies where the Sheriff grants interim interdict subject to the fulfilment of specified conditions.

Caveat

The practice of the Court of Session in regard to caveats against interim interdict applies generally in the Sheriff Court.

Productions

At any time after tabling of the cause, the Sheriff may grant a commission and diligence for the recovery of such documents as he deems relevant to the cause.[10]

---

8 R 91. Sheriff Court (Scotland) Act 1907 s 27 as amended by Law Reform (Miscellaneous Provisions) (Scotland) Act 1980 Sch 3. As to early extract see r 90(3).
9 *Home Drummond v M'Lachlan* 1908 SC 12.
10 R 78(3).

Appendix

Appendix

Digest of cases involving grant and refusal of interim interdict

The question of whether interim interdict should be granted or refused will always depend upon the particular circumstances of the case. The relative weight to be given to the established principles by which the court exercises its discretion will vary according to the subject of the dispute and the circumstances surrounding it.

The following examples indicate the approach taken by the court in recent times to the questions of interest and title to sue, averment of a case to try, the cogency of the need and the balance of convenience.

1 CORMACK v McILDOWIE'S EXORS 1972 SLT (Notes) 40

Arbitration Plea of no jurisdiction in arbiter: interdict competent as alternative to allowing arbiter to decide procedural matter.

Executors of a deceased tenant, who had been given notice to quit a farm, applied for the appointment of an arbiter under the Agricultural Holdings (Scotland) Act 1949 for the purpose of *inter alia* fixing compensation for disturbance. The landlord sought to interdict the respondents (the executors) from insisting in the arbitration proceedings on the ground that the deceased tenant's interest had not passed to his executors and therefore the arbiter had no jurisdiction. Holding that the defenders had made out a *prima facie* case that they were tenants within the meaning of the Agricultural Holdings (Scotland) Act 1949 and the Succession (Scotland) Act 1964, Lord Keith said (following *Christison's Trustees v Callender-Brodie* (1906) 8 F 928) that the arbiter might himself consider a procedural plea against the respondents of 'no jurisdiction' but interdict was still a competent remedy. There were however in the present case no circumstances making it inappropriate for the arbiter to deal with the question of the respondents' title. There were no grounds for apprehending that the arbiter would not deal judiciously with the question and, in any event, his decision would be open to review by way of appeal to the sheriff and to the Inner House. It had not been made out that the balance of convenience favoured interim interdict and the motion was refused.

2 BROWN v EDINBURGH UNIVERSITY COURT 1973 SLT (Notes) 55

Abuse of power: disruptive action Interim interdict against exclusion from meetings: attachment of conditions.

Gordon Brown, Rector of Edinburgh University, and Robert Drummond, President of the SRC, brought an action against the University Court craving *inter alia* interdict against the respondents from obstructing or interfering with Drummond's right to attend meetings of the University Court, which he had been doing upon an invitation basis. The said Robert Drummond had, along with other students, carried out militant activities, including occupation of the Senate Hall and the planning of disruptive action within the University. At a meeting of the University Court, at which Drummond was present, it was proposed that the invitation to Drummond to attend the meeting should be withdrawn. Later Drummond was invited to apologise for his militant conduct but declined to do so. The invitation to attend meetings was then withdrawn by the University Court. In an application by Drummond for interim interdict against his exclusion from meetings, Lord Keith took the view that the matter rested upon a balance of convenience. The grant or refusal of interim interdict was, he said, a matter for the discretion of the court, exercised according to the correct principles. It was material to take into account the degree of harm which might be suffered by either party, according to which way the discretion was exercised. With a view to minimising the harm, it was competent to adject conditions either to a grant or to a refusal of interim interdict. Drummond had, through his counsel, expressed his intention of acting responsibly in future. Interim interdict against Drummond's exclusion from the meetings was granted subject to the conditions that he would not incite disruptive action in the University and would not disclose to the press or to the media the proceedings of the University Court.

3 WHEELER v LEICESTER CITY COUNCIL [1985] 2 All ER 1106, HL

Abuse of power Local authority banning Rugby Football Club from use of ground: judicial review.

Leicester Rugby Football Club, which the plaintiffs represented, had a licence from the defendants to use a recreation ground belonging to the defendants. Three members of the club were invited to join the English rugby football side for a tour of South Africa. They accepted the invitation and took part in the tour. The defendants supported a Commonwealth Resolution to discharge sporting links with South Africa as a means of condemning apartheid. The defendants, after failing to obtain from the plaintiffs affirmative answers to four questions relative to the matter, passed a resolution banning the club and its members from using the recreation ground for twelve months. The Club applied for an order for judicial review of the defendants' resolution and for *inter alia* an injunction restraining the defendants from implementing the resolution. The application was refused by the judge of first instance and by the Court of Appeal (by a majority). The Club appealed to the House of Lords.

In allowing the appeal, the House of Lords held that the manner in which the defendants took their decision was unreasonable and unfair (*Associated Provincial Picture Houses Ltd v Wednesbury Corporation* [1947] 2 All ER 680, CA and *Council of Civil Service Unions v Minister for Civil Service* [1984] 3 All ER 935, HL applied). The defendants had formulated the four questions with a view to forcing upon the Club their own policy (however worthy that policy might have been) on their own terms. This was either so unreasonable as to contravene the principles in *Associated Provincial Picture Houses Ltd v Wednesbury Corporation* or a fundamental breach of duty to act fairly. The situation was one in which the court must intervene. The defendants' defence that they were acting in implement of s 71 of the Race Relations Act 1976 (which they were fully entitled to do) did not bar the intervention of the court. The defendants' resolution was quashed.

4 CUTSFORTH v MANSFIELD INNS LTD [1986] 1 All ER 577

Procuring breach of contract Amusement machines: breach of EEC rules: injunction to restrain breach.

The plaintiffs, a firm installing and maintaining amusement machines, had contracts with tenants of fifty-seven public houses owned by a brewery firm. As a result of a takeover, the defendants sought to terminate the contracts. The plaintiffs sought an injunction restraining the defendants from procuring breach of the foresaid contracts and from interfering with the plaintiffs' contracts and machines. The plaintiffs contended *inter alia* that the defendants' actions restricted or distorted competition in breach of art 85A of the EEC Treaty and/or was an abuse of dominant position in breach of art 86B of the Treaty, and they craved an interlocutory injunction.

The court held that, for reasons stated, the pleadings did not disclose an arguable case of procuring breach of contract and that, on this head, the plaintiffs were not entitled to an interlocutory injunction. They had however raised a serious question to try under art 85A (but not under art 86B) *inter alia* on the grounds that the object and effects of the defendants' actings was to restrict and distort competition within the Common Market and specifically within the area within which the plaintiffs' operations occurrred. Damages would not be an adequate remedy for the plaintiffs because denial of interim relief would virtually put an end to their business: and since the plaintiffs would be well able to pay the defendants any damages for losses due to the granting of interim relief, it was appropriate to grant an interlocutory injunction.

5 J A & D S RENNIE v SCOTTISH MILK RECORDS ASSOCN 1985 SLT 272

Natural justice: bias Members of Disciplinary Committee drawn from Council of Association previously involved in adjudication.

The petitioners carried on business as dairy farmers and were members of the respondents' Association, which *inter alia* recorded and published milk yields of cattle belonging to its members. Acting upon certain information (alleged by the petitioners to be inaccurate) the respondents' Council, without giving the petitioners an opportunity of being heard, resolved to cancel the lactation records of the petitioners' business. The petitioners, aggrieved by this decision, referred the matter to arbitration under the Rules of the Association. The arbiter upheld the petitioners' submissions and directed the respondents to withdraw their resolution. Notwithstanding this award the respondents declared their intention to refer the matter to their own Disciplinary Committee.

The petitioners sought to interdict the respondents from proceeding further with their complaint, *inter alia* upon the ground that the Disciplinary Committee comprised nine members of the Council of the Association which had already adjudicated upon the matter and had acted unconstitutionally. In granting interim interdict, Lord Davidson said that although at the disciplinary hearing an opportunity for further evidence would be available this did not detract from the fact that, as Council members, the members who would form the Disciplinary Committee had acted unconstitutionally and in breach of natural justice when adjudicating upon the matter as a Council. The rules of natural justice could be contravened in a wide variety of circumstances. In disputes involving allegations of bias, before pronouncing interim interdict, the court must be satisfied that there is sufficient material available for a *prima facie* view to be expressed as to whether a reasonable man, with no inside knowledge, might well think that a tribunal might be biased. The petitioners had satisfied this test.

The balance of convenience, particularly the fact that prejudice might be occasioned to the petitioners, outweighed that suffered by the respondents and favoured interim interdict, especially in the face of the allegations of bias for which a good *prima facie* case had been made.

6 MEEK v LOTHIAN REGIONAL COUNCIL 1983 SLT 494

Local authority: breach of statutory duty Local Government (Scotland) Act 1973 s 63.

The petitioner, a member of a minority political party of Lothian Regional Council, sought interdict prohibiting the Regional Council from distributing, shortly before an election, a publication called *The Lothian Clarion* on the grounds:

(a) that it was in breach of s 63(1)(b) and (c) of the Representation of the People Act 1949, which prohibits the incurring of expenses of an election (other than by the candidate and his agent) for publications presenting the candidate's views or disparaging the views of his opponents; and

(b) that it was in breach of s 88(2)(a) of the Local Government (Scotland) Act 1973 which authorises local authorities to publish, within their areas, matters relating to local government.

Interim interdict as regards (b) was refused on the ground that s 88(2)(a) did not restrict the local authority to publishing purely factual information. Interim interdict was however granted on the ground that, since the publication was to take place immediately before an election, and the majority party in the Regional Council controlled the publication, it must be concluded that the publication was designed to promote the majority party's candidate and to disparage the minority party's candidate, notwithstanding that no names were mentioned. Held that, on the balance of convenience, interim interdict should be granted. The petitioners, said Lord Ross, had made out a *prima facie* case under s 63(1) since the publication sought to discredit the policies of the minority parties and therefore of their candidates, while praising the actions of the candidates of the majority group. Stopping the circulation of a pamphlet containing material *prima facie* contrary to statute was preferable to allowing publication with all the consequences that might have on the election, and also having regard to the fact that, after the election, the publication could still be distributed and no money would have been wasted (distinguishing *R v Tronoh Mines Ltd* [1952] 1 All ER 697 and *DPP v Luft* [1977] AC 962, HL).

7 WILSON v INDEPENDENT BROADCASTING AUTHORITY
1979 SLT 279

Public authority Breach of statutory duty: broadcasts by political parties: Independent Broadcasting Authority Act 1973.

The petitioners, as members of the public, sought to interdict the respondents from broadcasting certain party political broadcasts a few days before the holding of a Referendum on 1 March 1979 under the Scotland Act 1978 on the ground that, by so doing, the respondents would be in breach of their statutory duty to maintain a proper balance of programmes under ss 2 and 22 of the Independent Broadcasting Authority Act 1973. The petitioners moved for interim interdict on 15 February 1979 and this was opposed on the grounds that:

(a) all parties had not been called since no service had been made upon the political parties concerned;
(b) the petitioners had no title to sue; and
(c) in any event thay had not relevantly averred breach of statutory duty.

In granting interim interdict upon an amended crave, the Lord Ordinary (Ross) held:

(a) the presence of the political parties was not necessary for the decision of the question at issue; and
(b) the petitioners were voters and the Referendum gave them a choice of replies. If the programmes in question were likely to influence the electorate, the petitioners had an interest to see that the respondents did not act in breach of their statutory duty. The petitioners had both title and interest to sue; and
(c) the petitioners' averments were sufficient to establish a *prima facie* case of breach of statutory duty. The Act of 1973 did not provide any means of enforcing the duty, and in such circumstances the court had power to interdict the continuance of the breach of duty. The balance of convenience was in favour of granting the interim interdict. If not granted, the lack of balance in the programme would be maintained and perpetuated. Interim interdict would not prevent the respondents from broadcasting other programmes relating to the Referendum provided they maintained a proper balance. The fact that the BBC were also to broadcast the same programmes was not sufficient to justify depriving the petitioners of their right to interdict the respondents from breaching a statutory duty imposed upon them.

8 MEEK v LOTHIAN REGIONAL COUNCIL 1980 SLT (Notes) 61

Local authority Actions *ultra vires*: employees allowed time off to lobby Parliament without loss of pay.

Lothian Regional Council on 26 November resolved by a majority, to allow certain of their employees who had been nominated by their trade union, to take time off with pay, in order to attend a national rally for the purpose of lobbying members of Parliament upon a particular issue. The rally was due to take place on 28 November. Members of a minority group on the Regional Council sought to interdict the Council from implementing the decision, in so far only as it allowed absence without loss of pay. The respondents, in support of the resolution, relied upon financial powers conferred upon them under s 69(1) of the Local Government (Scotland) Act 1973 and the powers contained in s 28 of the Employment Protection (Consolidation) Act 1978. The petitioners based their case upon pleas of *ultra vires* and *male fides*. While declining at that stage to express any view upon the effect of the Employment Protection (Consolidation) Act 1978, Lord MacDonald considered that the petitioners had raised two issues which justified investigation (following *Innes v Kirkcaldy Burgh* 1963 SLT 325) and there was a case to try.

The balance of convenience, said his Lordship, lay in granting the interim order because (a) even if the petitioners' averments and pleas were erroneous, the payments could still be made to the employees after the event, and (b) the fact that (as the respondents contended) some employees might not attend the rally if pay were not to be issued, was not an argument which impressed the court. The employees were therefore at liberty to attend the rally but, under the terms of the interim interdict to be granted, they would not be paid for the time off duty.

9 PRINCE v SECRETARY OF STATE FOR SCOTLAND 1985 SLT 74

Election European Assembly Elections Act 1978: proportional representation: duty of returning officer.

The petitioner and others were voters in the Lothian constituency of the European Assembly. They raised an action of declarator that their rights as voters were violated by the European Assembly Elections Act 1978 which provides for majority voting at elections; that the Act was in conflict with the Treaty of Rome and therefore a system of proportional representation voting should be operated at the June 1984 election; and for interdict against the holding of the election and the counting of the votes by the Returning Officer. As regards this branch of the case, the court took the view that the Returning Officer was required by the said Act to carry out a statutory duty. Unless and until it could be shown that what the Returning Officer would do was *ultra vires* under the Act, the petitioners had suffered no legal wrong. The law was laid down for the Returning Officer in the 1978 Act and he could not be accused of acting *ultra vires* as long as he obeyed the law. There was no averment of urgency and the balance of convenience was tilted against any interference with the election proceedings at that stage. The petitioners had not stated a *prima facie* case for interim interdict, and it was refused.

10 HAMILTON v LANARKSHIRE COUNTY COUNCIL 1971 SLT (Notes) 12

Breach of statutory duty: alternative remedy Grounds for refusal of interim interdict.

The pursuer sought interdict against the first defenders and their clerk. He averred that under reg 7 of the Temperance (Scotland) Act 1920 Regulations, the clerk to the local authority was bound to hear parties who objected to a requisition for a poll and that he, the pursuer, had not been heard. Refusing interim interdict, the Lord Ordinary (Thomson) held that, having regard to ss 113 to 118 of the Licensing (Scotland) Act 1959 and the Temperance (Scotland) Act 1920, and the decision in *Anderson v Kirkintilloch Magistrates* 1948 SLT 199, he was bound to refuse the application for interim interdict and allow the case to proceed. The pursuer's proper remedy was to seek to have the poll declared null and void as provided for by s 118 of the Licensing (Scotland) Act 1959.

11 LONDON BOROUGH OF HAMMERSMITH v MAGNUM AUTOMATED FORECOURTS LTD [1978] 1 All ER 401, CA

Injunction against continuing breach of statutory provisions Control of Pollution Act 1974: inherent power of High Court.

The defendants operated a twenty-four hour 'taxi care' service in a quiet street. It provided service for taxis and food vending machines etc. Local residents complained of noise and the plaintiffs, being the local authority, served a notice under the Control of Pollution Act 1974, requiring the defendants to cease operations between 11 p.m. and 7 a.m. The defendants appealed to the magistrates' court against the notice. The notice remained in force pending disposal of the appeal. The defendants, however, in defiance of the notice, continued to operate throughout the night. Before the appeal had been dealt with by the magistrates, the plaintiffs applied to the High Court for an injunction under s 58(8) of the 1974 Act restraining the defendants from using the service station between 11 p.m. and 7 a.m. The plaintiffs, in their capacity as local authority, had an alternative remedy by way of summary prosecution of the defendants under s 54(4) of the Act. On appeal, on a motion, by the plaintiffs for an interlocutory injunction (an interim interdict) the court held (per Lord Denning MR at p 405) that, in the circumstances, the plaintiffs were entitled to bring proceedings for injunction. The defendants were committing a plain breach of the law. The plaintiffs had given an undertaking in damages, in case they were wrong at the end of the day. The High Court had an inherent power to secure by injunction obedience to the law by everyone in the land, whenever a person with sufficient interest brought the case before the Court. The interlocutory injunction was granted. (See also *Stafford Borough Council v Elkinford Ltd* [1977] 2 All ER 519).

12 PHONOGRAPHIC PERFORMANCE LTD v McKENZIE 1982 SLT 272

Copyright Sound recordings: public broadcast in hotel: interim interdict granted but operation suspended.

The petitioners sought to interdict the respondent, a hotelier in Elgin, from infringing the petitioners' copyright in sound recordings by permitting public performance thereof in his hotel. The petitioners wrote repeatedly over a period of some nine months requiring the respondent to complete an application for a licence to permit the performance of the recordings. The application form was finallly returned by the respondent and the petitioners issued an invoice for the licence fee. Despite reminders no payment was made and the unauthorised performances, which were open to the public at a charge, continued. The petitioners then applied for interim interdict upon *ex parte* averments. In pronouncing the interim interdict but suspending the operation for seven days, Lord Wylie said a strong *prima facie* case of infringement had been made out. The petitioners had sought interim interdict under the terms of s 17(1) and (6) of the Copyright Act 1956. In view however of the length of time during which the infringement had continued, he doubted the necessity for interim interdict in the absence of a contradictor. If the order were to be granted immediately, the respondent would have to terminate the discotheque performances at the hotel at once. He would sustain substantial loss of income and inconvenience. The loss of licence fees to the petitioners on th eother hand would be minimal. In these circumstances, the balance of convenience pointed strongly against granting the order until the respondent had been able to enter the process. He might then be able to challenge the infringement on the merits or resolve the matter by paying the licence fee. The appropriate course was to grant the order but suspend its operation for seven days.

13 EXPRESS NEWSPAPERS PLC v LIVERPOOL DAILY POST AND ECHO PLC [1985] 3 All ER 680

Copyright Literary work: newspaper game: delay in bringing proceedings.

The plaintiffs, newspaper publishers, devised a game which required distribution of cards and a code and a daily grid containing a set of numbers which required to be matched to the card. Prizes were offered for correct solutions. The defendants, also newspaper publishers, copied the grid and code sequences. The plaintiffs averred that the grid and sequences were a literary work within the meaning of the Copyright Act 1956, and that the defendants were in breach of the copyright. The plaintiffs had written to the defendants on 26 September 1984, requiring them to cease the infringement but did not receive a satisfactory reply. They had, at the same time, written to various other parties alleged to be infringing the copyright and several undertook to desist. On 10 December 1984, the plaintiffs moved for an interlocutory injunction. The defendants alleged *inter alia* that, in view of the delay in raising proceedings, and the obvious lack of urgency, the interlocutory injunction should be refused. In granting the order sought, Whiteford J held that it was not unreasonable in the circumstances for the plaintiffs to delay proceedings in the hope that the matter might be settled without litigation, as indeed they had succeeded in doing with other alleged infringers to whom they had written.

14 LORD DUNCAN SANDYS v HOUSE OF FRASER PLC 1985 SLT 200

Company Conduct of internal affairs: Board of Directors not called as respondents: balance of convenience.

The petitioners, two directors of the respondent company, sought interdict against the company refurbishing certain of their stores unless all necessary information, including financial details, had been furnished to the Board of Directors. A working party appointed by the Board had reported on the project to an executive committee of the Board. There had been no decision of the Board approving the proposal. A meeting of the full Board to approve the actions of the executive committee, which included the appointment of a design consultant and a press release, was however imminent. The respondents opposed the interdict on the ground that it would cripple the management of the company and, in any event, there was in fact no detailed scheme. The court, in refusing interim interdict, held that what the respondents sought was the intervention of the court in the exercise by the Board, who were not parties to the action, of the functions and duties of management of the company as provided by the Articles of Association. The powers of the directors thereunder were very wide. *Prima facie,* the grant of interim interdict in the wide terms sought would necessarily interfere with the wide powers conferred upon the directors. There was a serious question in dispute and it would be rash and premature to grant interim interdict. The balance of convenience tilted heavily in favour of the respondents. The interdict sought would necessarily interfere with the daily and routine conduct of the company's business and might well have crippling and damaging effects. The petitioners would still, as the action progressed, have the opportunity of renewing their motion as regards the contention of 'one off' profits of refurbishment.

15 HARAKAS v BALTIC MERCANTILE AND SHIPPING EXCHANGE LTD [1982] 2 All ER 701

Defamation Plea of *veritas*: interlocutory injunction: principles to be applied.

The second defendants, International Maritime Bureau, were established to combat maritime frauds, which were prevalent. The Bureau were in course of making enquiry into the plaintiffs' activities and caused a notice to be exhibited by the first defendants intimating that anyone doing business with the plaintiffs could apply to the second defendants for certain unspecified information held by them. The plaintiffs sought an injunction against the second defendants prohibiting publication by them of any information alleging that the plaintiffs had been engaged in fraudulent dealings. The plaintiffs contended that the information referred to in the notice was unfounded. The second defendants contended they had reasonable grounds for honestly believing that the information was true.

The plaintiffs sought an interlocutory injunction. The court held that where there was defence of justification or qualified privilege an interlocutory injunction should not be granted, unless it could be shown that the defendants dishonestly and maliciously proposed to say and publish information which they knew to be untrue. There was nothing to suggest that this was so in the present case. The interlocutory injunction granted at first instance was discharged.

16 FAIRBAIRN v SCOTTISH NATIONAL PARTY AND OTHERS 1982 SLT 149

Defamation Averments against Member of Parliament as to failure to perform his duties.

The petitioner, a Member of Parliament standing for re-election, sought interdict against the Scottish National Party and their candidate to prohibit the publication of a pamphlet containing a statement which inferred that the petitioner had failed to collect a large quantity of his mail from the House of Commons Post Office. The grounds of the petition were:

(a) that this statement was false and defamatory at common law and was deprived of qualified privilege by s 10 of the Defamation Act 1952, and
(b) the publication was a contravention of s 91 of the Representation of the People Act 1949.

As regards (b), Lord Ross said that s 19 of the 1949 Act related to cases of attack on the personal character of a candidate, while the words complained of in the present case reflected upon the character of the petitioner as a political representative. He had not made out a *prima facie* case on this ground. As to (a) the court would only intervene to grant interdict of slander in clear cases. To do so was, to some extent, taking the case away from the jury. The words complained of here were however capable of bearing the innuendo put upon them by the petitioner and there was no doubt he had made out a *prima facie* case. Turning to the balance of convenience, his Lordship said the constituency for which the petitioner was standing, and in which he had been the sitting member, was a marginal one. Some 5,000 copies of the pamphlet containing the alleged defamatory statements were still available for distribution. If this were to be done there would be a risk that the petitioner would be defamed in the eyes of the electors. It would be impossible to 'blackout' the offending words. The advantage lay in stopping a possible slander, even if there was a risk that the statement complained of might ultimately prove to be true.

17 WADDELL v BBC 1973 SLT 246

Defamation Subsequent action of damages available to petitioners: fine balance of convenience: interim interdict refused.

The petitioner sought interdict prohibiting the BBC from transmitting, by radio or television, a programme in which suggestions were made that the petitioner had stated to the respondents' reporters certain facts which indicated that he (the petitioner) had been involved in a murder committed by one Patrick Meehan. The petitioner averred that he had not made such statements. It was conceded that the statements attributed to the petitioner, if false, were slanderous. Held (affirming the Sheriff Principal) that, in the application for interim interdict, the basic matter was the balance of convenience. The Lord Justice Clerk (Wheatley), giving the leading opinion, said that it came to a balancing of advantages and disadvantages on both sides. If irreparable harm would be done by granting or refusing the interim interdict, then that was a most important consideration. But the petitioner here had open to him the remedy of an action of damages upon exactly the same grounds as those in the present application. The decision on a balance of convenience was often a difficult and delicate one. Here the balance was in favour of allowing the programme to proceed and interim interdict was refused.

18 NATIONAL ASSOCIATION OF SCHOOL TEACHERS v SCOTTISH JOINT NEGOTIATING COMMITTEE FOR TEACHING STAFF (1987) 8 GWD 246

Title and interest Education: teachers' remuneration.

The petitioners, a teachers' union, sought to interdict the respondents from discussing at a meeting on 22 January 1987 a settlement of the teachers' salaries dispute. At a meeting on 19 December 1986 the respondents had resolved to allow the various unions to ballot on proposals. The result of the petitioners' ballot would not have been known until 24 January 1987. Although notification of the meeting of 19 December had been timeous, notification of the business then to be discussed had not. The petitioners alleged that, lacking the result of their ballot, they would not be able properly to represent the views of their members at the meeting on 22 January. In refusing interim interdict, the court held that the petitioners should have known that the matter in issue would be discussed, that they had only one member representative on the SJNC and he was unlikely to affect the outcome and that the petitioners had failed to demonstrate any appreciable wrong. The balance of convenience was againt interim interdict. In any event it would in due course be open to the petitioners to challenge the legality of any decision taken by the respondents.

19 DEANE v LOTHIAN REGIONAL COUNCIL 1986 SLT 22

Education (Scotland) Act 1980   Closure of denominational school: *prima facie* case: wrong to decide the relevancy at this stage.

A local authority, with the consent of the Secretary of State under s 22D of the Education (Scotland) Act 1980, determined to close a Roman Catholic denominational school. Parents sought an interdict pending an action of reduction of the Secretary of State's consent. The vacation judge refused the application on the ground that there was no issue to try. The Scottish Hierarchy of the Roman Catholic Church were then sisted and the petitioners reclaimed. Held, allowing the reclaiming note, and granting interim interdict, that the test here was whether there was a *prima facie* title to sue and whether a case had been made warranting the interim order. The Lord Justice Clerk, quoting *Burn-Murdoch on Interdict* para 123 said, 'The question at this stage is not so much the absolute relevancy of the case as the seeming cogency of the need for interim interdict.' The court approved the approach of Burn-Murdoch to the difference between interim and final interdict. The vacation judge was wrong to decide upon relevancy at that stage. The petitioners had made out a *prima facie* case and had a title to sue.

20 SMITH v INNER LONDON EDUCATION AUTHORITY [1978] 1 All ER 411, CA

Education: abuse of power   Cessation of maintenance of grammar school in pursuance of a policy approved by the Secretary of State: authority discharging a public duty.

The defendants, as Education Authority, proposed to cease to maintain a grammar school in pursuance of a policy approved by the Secretary of State for comprehensive education and elimination of selection (Education Act 1944 ss 1(1) and 8(1)). On 27 January 1977 the judge of first instance granted an interlocutory injunction restraining the defendants from implementing their proposals on the grounds:

(a) the plaintiff (a parent) had established there was a serious issue to try on whether the defendants had misused their powers under the 1944 Act; and

(b) the balance of convenience favoured the granting of the injunction.

The defendants appealed. The court allowed the appeal and discharged the interlocutory injunction. In doing so it was held that, on the information available, it was impossible to say the defendants had acted unlawfully. They had consulted with parents and those involved and had obtained reports on the proposals. The result was that the plaintiff had no real prospect of final success, if the case went to trial. The question of balance of convenience did not therefore arise. On that point however the court held that, where the defendants were a public authority, performing duties to the public, one must look at the balance of convenience more closely and take into account the interest of the public in general and not merely the balance between plaintiff and defendant. A public authority should not be restrained, even by interlocutory injunction, from exercising its statutory duty to the public at large, unless the plaintiff showed that he had a real prospect of succeeding in obtaining a permanent injunction at the trial. There were here special factors in the balance of convenience, as described in *American Cynamid Co v Ethicon Ltd* [1975] 1 All ER 504, HL at 511.

21 MEADE v LONDON BOROUGH OF HARINGEY [1979] 2 All ER 1016, CA

Education: abuse of power Schools closed in sympathy with trade union strike action.

Following a trade union call for strike action by school caretakers and ancillary staff, all schools in the defendants' area, as Education Authority, were closed. Parents complained to the Secretary of State under s 99(1) of the Education Act 1944 that the defendants had failed to discharge their statutory duty to make schools available for full-time education under s 8 of the Act. The Minister refused to direct the defendants to discharge their duty because, in his view, they were not in breach of it. After the schools had been closed for four weeks, the plaintiff (a parent), applied for *inter alia* an interlocutory injunction prohibiting the continued closure of the schools. The application having been refused on the ground that the remedy lay in s 99(1) of the Act and not by action in the courts, the plaintiff appealed. The trade union called off the strike and, at the date of the appeal, all the schools were open. The court nevertheless heard the appeal on the question of principle. It was held that, if the decision to close the schools was taken without just cause or excuse, it was *ultra vires*. The decision to close the schools in sympathy with a trade union's claim, when the closure could have been avoided, was a misuse of power, if it was a decision affected by considerations not relevant to the educational field. On the other hand, if the defendants had genuinely thought that in order to carry out their duty, it was better to close the schools, or if they had compelling and reasonable grounds for failing to keep the schools open, they would not be in breach of duty. The reasons for the defendants' decision was a matter of fact to be determined at the trial, but the plaintiff had in the meantime made out a clear *prima facie* case of breach of statutory duty. The schools had been closed at the behest of the trade union. If the strike had been continuing an interlocutory injunction would have been granted.

22 MURRAY v DUMBARTON COUNTY COUNCIL 1935 SLT 239

Education   Right of Education Authority to transfer headmaster to another school in their district, under reserved power: interdict sought pending action of reduction by pursuer: completed acts.

The defenders, as Education Authority, had, under the terms of an agreement with the pursuer, power to transfer him from his present appointment as headmaster of Lenzie Academy to another secondary school in their district. On 29 November 1934 the defenders, by Minute, resolved to transfer the pursuer to Vale of Leven School. On 17 December 1934, the pursuer raised an action to reduce the resolution. He was instructed by the defenders to report to Vale of Leven School on 3 January 1935. On 2 January, the pursuer raised an action of interdict to preserve the status quo pending decision of his action of reduction. In refusing interim interdict, the Lord Ordinary (Pitman) said the application was incompetent. It was, he said, out of the question that an Education Authority should be coerced by an order of the court into continuing, as headmaster of a school, a master whom they had already transferred to another school, and that in exercise of a reserved right to transfer.

Even if interdict were the competent remedy, the defenders could not be interdicted from passing the Minute and acting upon it, for they had already passed and acted upon it more than a month before the pursuer applied for interdict.

23 TRAPP v ABERDEENSHIRE COUNTY COUNCIL 1960 SC 302

Education   Dismissal of rector: Secretary of State's inquiry: appointment of new rector during inquiry proceedings.

The defenders, as Education Authority, dismissed the petitioner from his post as rector by resolution of 30 November 1959, and with effect from 14 February 1960. The petitioner, on 15 December 1959, applied to the Secretary of State for an inquiry under s 81 of the Education (Scotland) Act 1946. Notice thereof was given to the defenders, despite which on 25 February 1960 they resolved to advertise the post of rector of the petitioner's school and an advertisement duly appeared. On 3 March 1960 the Secretary of State intimated that he was to hold an inquiry. If, as a result of the inquiry, the Secretary of State was of opinion that the dismissal of the petitioner was not justified, he had power to require the defenders to reconsider their resolution. The petitioner sought interdict to prevent the defenders appointing a new rector until they had considered the opinion of the Secretary of State. He enrolled a motion for interim interdict and, at first instance, the interim order was granted and the defenders appealed.

The court on appeal refused the defenders' plea based on the alleged irrelevancy of the petitioner's case. In considering the balance of convenience, the court took note of the practical disadvantages arising from delay in deciding who was to be the permanent rector of the school. More important however was the fact that, if no interim interdict were granted and the position of rector were to be filled, this would prevent for all time the possibility of reinstatement of the petitioner. This option the defenders would be bound to consider if the Secretary of State were to find the pursuer had been unjustifiably dismissed. The interim interdict was continued.

24 C R SMITH (GLAZIERS) (DUNFERMLINE) LTD v MCKEAG 1986 GWD 39

Restrictive covenant   Employee: severance of covenants.

The respondent, an agent of the petitioners, was bound by contract, after the termination thereof, not to divulge confidential information as to the petitioners' business; not to become, within six months of termination, involved, in his former agency area, with another firm supplying substantially the same goods and services as the petitioners and not to solicit in relation to such goods and services any customer of the petitioners, within one year after termination of the respondent's agency. Subsequent to termination, in an action at the instance of the employers against the agent alleging contravention of said undertaking, interim interdict was granted *ex parte* on all three points. On a motion for recall of the interim interdict, the order was recalled only as regards involvement with another similar concern during six months following termination of the agency, on the ground that the nature of the business made repeat orders within the six month period unlikely.

25 CAMPBELL v CENTRAL REGIONAL COUNCIL 1981 SLT (Notes) 69

Employment Closed shop: trade union

A local authority sought to introduce a 'closed shop' agreement for 'white collar' workers, and for this purpose to enter into an appropriate agreement with a trade union. The petitioner, one of the employees but not a trade union member, sought to interdict the respondents from entering into such an agreement with the trade union concerned. The petitioner alleged a lack of consultation and that such an agreement would constitute a unilateral change of his contract employment. Only trade union members were to be balloted upon the question and only such members would have a vote. The court, in granting interim interdict, held that, if the order were not to be granted the petitioner would be seriously injured, whereas it was not suggested that the respondents would be prejudiced.

26 FELLOWES v FISHER [1975] 2 All ER 829, CA

Restrictive covenant Employee as legal assistant: a question to try: balance of convenience.

The defendant had been employed by the plaintiffs as a legal assistant under an agreement containing a restrictive covenant against his undertaking legal work for a period of five years, after termination of his employment, in Walthamstow and Chingford, an area six miles long and two miles wide. The defendant, within the said time limit, took employment with a law firm practising in a street in Walthamstow next to that in which the plaintiffs had their office. The plaintiffs sought an injunction and an interlocutory injunction.

In the Court of Appeal, Lord Denning MR and Sir John Pennycuik were critical of the decision in *American Cyanamid Co v Ethicon Ltd* [1975] 1 All ER 504, HL but felt constrained to apply the principles there laid down. The plaintiffs had established there was a serious question to try. But, on the balance of convenience, and the relative strengths of the parties' cases, one factor was the possibility that the covenant was too wide. If the order were not granted, there was the possibility the plaintiffs might lose a few clients. If it were to be granted, the defendant would lose his job and might have difficulty in getting employment with another solicitor while the action was pending. The balance of convenience was in favour of refusing the interlocutory injunction.

27 RENTOKIL LTD v HAMPTON 1982 SLT 422

Restrictive covenant Employee: prohibition against engaging in marketing, sale, etc. of goods and services for one year in Tayside region, coupled with prohibition against soliciting customers.

The respondent, who had been employed by the petitioners as a timber infestation surveyor, left their employment and joined the staff of a company which carried on a business similar to that of the petitioners. The respondent's employment contract with the petitioners had contained two restrictive covenants. The first (cl 20 (a)) prohibited him, for a period of one year, from engaging directly or indirectly in the marketing, sale or supply of products or services for the eradication of wood-boring insects and wood-rotting fungi in all types of buildings. The geographical limit was the local authority region of Tayside. The second covenant (cl 20(c)) was against soliciting customers of the petitioners. An *ex parte* interim interdict was granted following the lines of both clauses. The respondent then sought recall of the interim interdict granted under the first covenant (cl 20(a)) but did not contest the interim interdict under the second covenant (cl 20(c)). The petitioners did not aver a case of possible misuse of confidential information but averred that the respondent was a person through whom the petitioners' goodwill and business connections had been developed and maintained. The Lord Ordinary (Stewart) held that cl 20(a) was wide enough to be used simply to defeat competition and its validity was questionable. Once the question of confidential information was excluded, the petitioners' complaint was that a surveyor formerly employed by them had gone into the employment of a competitor. On the balance of convenience and weighing the possible hardship to the respondent if he were to be deprived of his current employment, against the legitimate business interests of the petitioners, he was of opinion that the petitioners would be adequately protected by the interdict already granted under cl 20(c). The interim interdict under cl 20(a) would be recalled.

28 M'GREGOR v NALGO 1979 SC 401

Employment Expulsion from trade union: balance of convenience.

The petitioner was a member of NALGO. In consequence of his alleged strike-breaking, the respondents took steps to expel him from the union. In doing so they failed to comply with certain rules regarding the expulsion of members. The question of the petitioner's expulsion was to be before a forthcoming union conference. The petitioner sought interdict against the respondents prohibiting them from performing any deed in furtherance of the pretended expulsion of the petitioner. In granting interim interdict, the court held that the balance of convenience was heavily weighted in favour of interim interdict. If not granted the union conference might proceed to ratify a decision to expel the petitioner when no such valid decision had been made. The matter was of much greater importance to the petitioner than it was to the respondents.

29 STEINER v BRESLIN 1979 SLT (Notes) 34

Restrictive covenant Employee: restriction on taking employment for six months within three-eighths of a mile: and against enticing or canvassing customers for six months: hardship to employee: legitimate protection of business interest.

The petitioner employed the respondent as a hairdresser in his salons at Gordon Street and the Central Hotel, Glasgow, under a contract containing two restrictive covenants. The first obliged the respondent not to take employment within six months of the termination of her contract within three-eighths of a mile of either of the salons where she had been employed. The second prohibited the respondent, within the like period, from canvassing, soliciting or enticing away any customers of the petitioner. The respondent left the petitioner's employment on 16 December 1978 and took employment as a hairdresser within two hundred yards of the Central Hotel. The petitioner sought interim interdict under both covenants. He averred that twenty of his customers had failed to keep appointments and he believed that the respondent had enticed these customers away. On 28 December, both interim interdicts were granted *ex parte*. Thereafter defences were lodged and the respondent moved for recall of the interdicts. The Lord Ordinary recalled the interdict under the first covenant (following the *dictum* of Lord Clyde in *Scottish Farmers' Dairy Co (Glasgow) Ltd v M'Ghee* 1933 SC 148) on the ground that to grant the interdict would severely damage the respondent's capability to earn a livelihood (she being then unemployed). There was no clear indication that the interim order was necessary to protect the business interest of the petitioner. The clause was not in itself objectionable on the ground of time. The petitioner did not and could not aver that he had lost customers to a nearby competitor because the respondent had taken employment there. The balance of convenience tipped in favour of recalling the first interim interdict because of hardship to the respondent.

As regards the second interdict, different considerations applied. It was *prima facie* reasonable that an employee engaged in business of such a personal nature as hairdressing should be prevented, for a limited period, from enticing away customers to whom she had rendered services while in the petitioner's employment. The second covenant was more clearly related to the legitimate preservation of the petitioner's business. The recall of the second interdict was therefore refused.

30 GROUP 4 TOTAL SECURITY LTD v FERRIER 1985 SLT 287

Restrictive covenant   Employee: only short period of restriction to run.

The respondent's contract of employment with the petitioners contained a restrictive covenant. It provided that, during one year following termination of his employment, the respondents would not, within fifty mile radius of Aberdeen, be concerned in any business activities which were in direct competition with those of the petitioners or any of their associated or subsidiary companies. The respondent left the petitioners' employment and joined a competitor as regional director, Scotland. His responsibilities then embraced the whole of Scotland, although initially he was to be based in Aberdeen. Two months before expiry of the restriction period the petitioners sought interdict. Interim interdict was granted by the Lord Ordinary and the respondent appealed. Allowing the appeal and recalling the interim interdict, the court held (a) it was too early to reach a concluded decision upon the nature and width of the restrictive covenant; (b) in any case the covenant had only two months to run; and (c) if the petitioners eventually succeeded and could prove they had suffered loss by breach of the covenant, they would have a remedy in damages.

31 A & D BEDROOMS LTD v MICHAEL 1984 SLT 297

Restrictive covenant against employee   Geographical restriction applying in the United Kingdom not unreasonable: possibility of irreparable damage to petitioners' business.

The petitioners sought interdict against the first respondent from commencing or carrying on a contract of service with the second respondents for twelve months from 31 July 1983, and against the second respondents from entering into any contract of employment with the first respondent during that period. The first respondent was an interior designer who had been employed by the petitioners and was subject to a restrictive covenant. In granting interim interdict on both counts, Lord Cowie held (a) that the restriction which applied to the United Kingdom was not unreasonable in the circumstances, and (b) that the balance of convenience was in favour of granting interim interdict. If the first respondent was to be allowed to take up employment with the second respondents, untold damage could be caused to the petitioners' business by disclosure of confidential information as to price structure and in regard to existing and potential customers. Such damage would be difficult if not impossible to remedy. This must be prevented, even if it meant the first respondent losing her job with the second respondents and being unable to exercise her specialised skills for twelve months. (See *Chill Foods (Scotland) Ltd v Cool Foods Ltd* 1977 SLT 38 and cf *Commercial Plastics Ltd v Vincent* [1964] 3 All ER 546, CA).

32 REED STENHOUSE (UK) LTD v BRODIE 1986 SLT 354

Restrictive covenant against employee Availability of action of damages to employers: employee handicapped by not knowing how far he could go in commercial activities.

An employee's contract prohibited him from soliciting, for the next two years, persons who had been clients of the petitioners within a period of two years prior to the termination of the employee's contract. 'Clients' were deemed to include 'prospective clients' whose business was the subject of negotiation within six months of the termination of the respondent's employment. Held that the balance of convenience turned upon which party would suffer most if interim interdict were refused. An action of damages would be available to the employers. The respondent would be handicapped in seeking employment or carrying out a future job if in doubt how far he could go in making commercial contacts. Interim interdict was refused on the balance of convenience. (*Group 4 Total Security Ltd v Ferrier* 1985 SLT 287 followed).

33 RENTOKIL LTD v KRAMER 1986 SLT 114

Restrictive covenant against employee Entitlement of employers to protect business interests: balance of convenience and difficulty of quantifying final loss.

An employee was prohibited by contract, for a period of two years, from soliciting any person who should, at any time during two years following termination of his employment, have been a customer of the petitioners in respect of products or services sold or supplied within any branch in which the employee had been serving the petitioners. The petitioners sought interdict in respect of an alleged contravention of the prohibition. Held that the petitioners were entitled to protect their business interests and the protection sought was reasonable: interim interdict was granted because (a) the petitioners had made out a *prima facie* case, and (b) if the interdict was not granted they would have difficulty in quantifying their loss at the end of the day, and thus the balance of convenience was in favour of interim interdict. (*Scottish Farmers' Dairy Co (Glasgow) Ltd v M'Ghee* 1933 SLT 142 at 148, and *Plowman (GW) & Son Ltd v Ash* [1964] 1 WLR 568, CA approved).

34 RANDEV v PATTAR 1985 SLT 270

Restrictive covenant Restraint of trade: period of restriction possibly too wide: balance of convenience.

The respondent, on 24 February 1983, sold the Mulberry Hotel in Glasgow to the petitioner for £400,000 of which £117,000 was for goodwill. The respondent undertook in the contract of sale not to carry on the business of an hotel, restaurant or licensed premises for five years within one mile of the Mulberry Hotel. On 14 December 1983, the respondent purchased the Shawlands Hotel which was within the prohibited area. The petitioner sought *inter alia* interdict prohibiting the respondent from carrying on business at the Shawlands Hotel. In deciding that interim interdict should be refused, Lord Wylie said that, while no objection could be taken to the area of restriction, he had serious doubts whether a period of five years was reasonably necessary to protect the petitioner's legitimate business interests. There were no specific averments as to why such a period should be necessary. If the period of restriction was too widely stated, the whole clause was open to question, notwithstanding that the respondent had accepted its terms. On the balance of convenience, his Lordship noted that here it was not a case of a seller opening up a new competitive business. The respondent was taking over an existing business already competing in custom with the Mulberry Hotel at the time of the transaction. The respondent's personal intervention in the Shawlands Hotel would have only marginal effect. The balance of convenience was against granting interim interdict.

35 AGMA CHEMICAL CO LTD v HART 1984 SLT 246

Restrictive covenant Commercial agency: circumstances in which not in restraint of trade.

The petitioners, founding upon a restrictive covenant upon the respondent, sought interdict to prevent the respondents from *inter alia* endeavouring to entice away, solicit or canvass, any persons who, in the last two years of the respondent's commercial agency with the petitioners, had been customers of their company and were in the habit of dealing with the company within the respondent's former agency area. On appeal from the Lord Ordinary, who had granted interim interdict, the court recalled the interim interdict holding that the restrictive covenant into which the respondent had entered with the petitioners was not in restraint of trade but was designed to prevent loss to the petitioners by enticement of its customers by the respondent and that provisions of this kind were easier to justify than contracts in restraint of trade. Employers and principals had a legitimate interest to preserve their business connections (see *Mulvein v Murray* 1908 SC 528). Here the period of restriction was limited to twelve months, the prohibition was against canvassing competing products only, the customers who were not to be canvassed fell within a limited class, and it was significant that during the period of restraint the respondent was to be entitled to a compensation payment.

36 GEORGE PACKMAN & SONS v YOUNG 1976 SLT (Notes) 52

Contract Validity of missives of sale of heritage: alternative remedy: availability of action of damages or action of reduction at the end of the day.

The petitioner raised an action of declarator that certain missives of sale of land formed a valid and subsisting contract, and for interdict against the respondents conveying the land to another party. Held *inter alia* that, while there may be situations in which the balance of convenience indicates interim interdict is desirable, even when decree of specific implement coud be granted (*Burn Murdoch on Interdict* para 289) the facts in the present case did not reveal such a situation. The petitioners, quite apart from a remedy of a claim for damages, would have grounds for reduction of a conveyance taken by any third party who had knowledge of the previous contract. (*Rodger (Builders) Ltd v Fawdry* 1950 SLT 345.) The interim interdict previously granted was recalled.

37 BROWN v LEE CONSTRUCTIONS LTD 1977 SLT (Notes) 61

Heritable property Trespass: tower crane swinging over neighbour's garden.

The owner of a house and garden situated next to a building site development sought interdict against a contractor who had erected a tower crane on the building site in such a position that the jib passed in an arc over virtually the whole of the petitioner's garden. Held that any intrusion upon a person's land is wrong, whether it is temporary or permanent (accepting *Miln v Mudie* (1828) 6 S 967 and rejecting *Clifton v Viscount Bury* (1887) 4 TLR 8). In the present case the operation of the crane would continue for about eight months. The operation of the crane was trespass and might expose the petitioner, his wife and children to risk of injury without the shadow of a right to do that which was being done. The balance of convenience was not argued. Interim interdict granted.

38 NICOL v BLOTT 1986 SLT 677

Heritable property Occupation of land without title: whether a case to try.

The petitioner sought interdict against the respondents using and occupying land which he claimed belonged to him and to which he alleged the respondents had no title. The respondents contended that their lack of title was due to an error in the parties' respective dispositions, but that the error could and would be rectified as soon as cll 8 and 9 of the Law Reform (Miscellaneous Provisions) (Scotland) Act 1985 became law. While accepting that there was a reasonable prospect of the Bill becoming law and that there was a prospect that the respondents might then succeed in a rectification of the error, the question was whether, at present, the interim interdict should be granted. The court held that, at this stage, the respondents did not have a statable defence and there was no case to try. In these circumstances the question of balance of convenience did not fall to be considered. Interim interdict was granted.

39 COWIE v STRATHCLYDE REGIONAL COUNCIL 1985 SLT 333

Encroachment on heritable property Inversion of status quo: balance of convenience: possibility of unlawful action by respondents: delay element.

The petitioner averred that he was the owner of land upon which he had placed a gate and bollards to prevent the passage of vehicles. He had already successfully defended an action on the merits in which members of the public had sought to establish a public right of way over the land in question. He averred he was the owner and in lawful possession of the land. The respondents averred that they intended to remove the gate and bollards. In granting interim interdict, the court took the view that the respondents were endeavouring to invert the status quo and that they intended to permit vehicles to drive over the petitioner's land apparently in pursuance of their alleged duty to the public. No good reason had been suggested why they should do this before it had been judicially decided whether the land in question was or was not a 'road' within the statutory meaning for which the respondents contended.

On the balance of convenience, if interim interdict were to be refused there was nothing to prevent the respondents taking *pendente lite,* and possibly unlawfully, the action they threatened. A further delay was unlikely to cause serious prejudice to the respondents. If the interim order were not to be granted and the petitioner succeeded on the merits in the end of the day, he would be put to the expense of re-erecting the gate and bollards. Interim interdict was granted.

40 BURTON'S TRUSTEES v SCOTTISH SPORTS COUNCIL 1983 SLT 418

Encroachment on heritable property   Canoeing on public river: interference with salmon fishings: no averment of legal grounds for interdict: lack of precision.

The petitioners, who owned salmon fishings in the River Ness (but not the land on either bank of the relevant stretch), sought interdict preventing the respondents, their servants, agents and pupils from carrying out any exercise or manoeuvre with canoes on the relevant stretch of the river, and also prohibiting the advising or instructing of any person to carry out any such exercise or manoeuvre, in so far as not necessary for the purpose of passage through the said stretch. It was alleged that the respondents' activities were disturbing the fish and causing complaints from the petitioners' tenants who were demanding (but had not so far been paid) rent rebates, and that future letting of the salmon fishings would be prejudiced. A claim by the petitioners that there was no public right of navigation in the river was not insisted upon.

In refusing interim interdict, Lord Allanbridge said the case raised novel features as to whether the petitioners had any right to prevent the respondents canoeing on the river and what was meant by navigation. These matters would require legal clarification and possibly a proof.

He was not satisfied that the petitioners had averred *prima facie* legal grounds for interim interdict. The wording of the proposed interdict was not sufficiently precise to enable the respondents to know what their rights were, and on the balance of convenience, the averments of present and future loss to the petitioners were not adequately defined. The respondents had used the river for canoeing for some years and had arranged further courses, and interim interdict would gravely disrupt their activities. The salmon fishing season, on the other hand, would be over in little more than a month. (*Wills' Trustees v Cairngorm Canoeing and Sailing School* 1976 SC (HL) 30 and *Slater v M'Lellan (A and J)* 1924 SC 854 distinguished.)

41 LEVIN v FARMERS SUPPLY ASSOCIATION OF SCOTLAND 1973 SLT (Notes) 43

Confidential information given by petitioners to respondents
Prohibition against use by defenders: interim interdict granted under conditions.

The petitioner provided to respondents, in connection with his research into production of 'Fructose', a confidential report which he had obtained from Tate & Lyle Ltd. The report was sent in response to a request by the respondents who gave assurances that the information contained in the report would not be exploited. The petitioner averred that the respondents, in the course of their own research, were making or might make use of the information in the report and that the disclosure of that information to University Departments would irreparably damage the petitioner's interest in the production of 'Fructose' in Scotland. The respondents averred, in answer, that the process referred to in the report was widely known and had been published in scientific journals. The court approved the dictum of Roxburgh J in *Terrapin Ltd v Builders Supply Co (Hayes)* 1960 RPC 128, CH that a person, who has obtained information in confidence, is not allowed to use it as a springboard for activities detrimental to the person who made the confidential communication, even when all the features have been published and can be ascertained by any member of the public. Interim interdict was granted on this basis and upon the terms of the respondents' assurance, to the extent of preventing the respondents from using the report and disclosing its terms but reserving always their right to continue their own research using only information which was public and that they should go to public sources to obtain it.

42 COWIE v COWIE (1986) 2 GWD 33

Matrimonial interdict   Interim order: exclusion order.

Where a wife obtained (a) an interim order suspending the husband's occupancy rights in the matrimonial home; (b) an interim matrimonial interdict against the husband entering the house without her permission, coupled with power of arrest; and (c) an interim matrimonial interdict against the husband entering or remaining in the matrimonial home, also coupled with the power of arrest. Held that the interim interdict under head (c) was unnecessary in view of the terms of the interim interdict under head (b). The interim exclusion order and the interim matrimonial interdict under head (b) were continued.

43 FORTH YACHT MARINA LTD v FORTH ROAD BRIDGE JOINT BOARD 1984 SLT 177

Public interest   Nuisance: work necessary and urgent: undertakings by respondents to minimise damage.

The petitioners, who operated a yacht marina near one end of the Forth Road Bridge, sought interdict prohibiting the respondents from carrying out a grit blasting operation on the bridge. This process was necessary in order to prevent the deterioration of the bridge structure and was a matter of urgency. It was averred by the petitioners that, when westerly winds blew, abrasive material was deposited on the petitioners' boats; that the material created a health hazard and that the petitioners' whole business was at risk. While accepting that the petitioners had made out a *prima facie* case of injury and damage being caused by the respondents' operations, the court refused to grant interim interdict on the grounds that there was no material health hazard occasioned by the operations; that these operations were necessary and urgent in the public interest, and that the cost impact upon the respondents of interim interdict would greatly exceed any compensation to which the petitioners might be entitled by way of damages. In any event, a claim for such damages might well be open to the petitioners at the end of the day. While refusing interim interdict, the court sought and obtained from the respondents an undertaking that they would use their best endeavours to minimise any damage or injury.

44 LAWS v FLORINPLACE LTD [1981] 1 All ER 659

Nuisance Sex shop in predominantly residential area: balance of convenience.

In August 1980, the defendants opened a 'sex shop' in an area predominantly residential but containing also shops, bars and restaurants. On 17 October, the plaintiffs, residents in the street where the shop was situated, sought an injunction against the defendants operating and advertising the shop. They moved for an interlocutory injunction. They alleged the shop would attract undesirable customers, would be an embarrassment and a possible danger to young persons, particularly young girls. The value of surrounding property would be depreciated. The operation of the shop constituted a nuisance.

The court held that there was a case to try as to whether the defendants' operations constituted a nuisance (following the principles laid down in *American Cyanamid Co v Ethicon Ltd* [1975] 1 All ER 504, HL).

On the balance of convenience, if the order were granted the defendants would not suffer loss of goodwill because it was a new business. They were experienced in the trade and would have no difficulty in estimating damages for loss of profits if they were ultimately to be successful in their defence. As to the plaintiffs, they had a natural repugnance for the trade carried on, which was at least on the border of the criminal law. The material produced might be classed as obscene. An interlocutory injunction was granted.

45 BANKS v FIFE REDSTONE QUARRY CO LTD 1954 SLT (Notes) 77

Nuisance Blasting operations: interdict adding nothing to common law.

The petitioners were owners of two houses situated 1400 feet from a quarry where large-scale blasting operations had been undertaken. In the first blast the defenders detonated 4300lbs of explosive; in the second 2800lbs; in the third 3800lbs and in the fourth 4800lbs. It was alleged that the first blast severely rocked the petitioners' houses but they did not complain. The fourth blast rocked the houses and caused damage to plasterwork. On 4 August the respondents informed the petitioners that they proposed to detonate 3500lbs of explosive. The petitioners offered to permit the blasting of 2500lbs but this was refused by the respondents as being commercially impracticable. The petitioners sought interim interdict to restrain these proposed operations from blasting in such a way as, by reason of vibration, (a) to cause a nuisance to the petitioners, and (b) to injure their property. Interim interdict was granted and the respondents appealed. The court refused to recall the interim interdict. In doing so they nevertheless criticised the form of the interim interdict granted as being useless and no real protection to the petitioners since it added nothing to the common law. Opinion on the effect of this matter reserved.

46 WRIGHT v THOMSON 1974 SLT (Notes) 15

Nuisance   Motion for caution to be found by petitioner refused: interim interdict *simpliciter* granted.

The petitioner obtained interim interdict *ex parte* prohibiting the respondents from depositing rubbish in a pond forming a contiguous boundary between the parties' properties. On a motion for recall of the interdict the respondent did not contest the interdict *simpliciter* but moved that, as a condition of continuation, caution of £7,000 should be found by the petitioners in surety of any damages subsequently found due by the petitioners to the respondents. There were no clear averments showing that any loss would fall upon the respondents in consequence of an interim interdict. Interim interdict *simpliciter* was granted and caution refused. (See also *Tasker v Tasker* 1952 SLT 152).

47 WILLIAM GRANT & SONS LTD v WILLIAM CADENHEAD LTD 1985 SLT 291

Infringement of trade mark and passing off   Undue delay: factors in deciding balance of convenience: undertaking to keep account.

The petitioners were distillers, blenders, bottlers and sellers of Scotch whisky. The respondents were *inter alia* retailers and wholesalers of wines and spirits. The petitioners had since 1909 distilled and bottled for sale a single malt whisky, 'Glenfiddoch' (being a registered trade mark) on a worldwide scale. In 1965, the respondents purchased from the petitioners twenty hogsheads of raw spirit which was, in due course, course, bottled and processed as a single malt whisky and sold in 1984, labelled as either 'Glenfiddoch-Glenlivet' or 'Glenfiddoch' at prices £6 to £7 in excess of the petitioners' product. The petitioners claimed that the action of the respondents constituted breach of trade mark and passing off and sought interdict. In considering the question of interim interdict, the Lord Ordinary (Ross) accepted that the petitioners had made out a *prima facie* case of infringement and passing off but declined to grant interim interdict. He distinguished the case from *Highland Distilleries Co plc v Speymalt Whisky Distributors Ltd* 1985 SLT 85 and *Macallan-Glenlivet plc v Speymalt Whisky Distributors Ltd* 1983 SLT 348. His reasons for refusal were (a) the quantity of whisky produced by the respondents was minute when compared with the volume of the petitioners' sales; (b) there was a difference in the whisky from each separate run; (c) the difference in price and the statement of the age on the label made it unlikely that the public (and certainly the *cognoscenti*) would be confused; (d) the label and bottle used by the respondents was quite different from the unique green triangular bottle and black and gold label used by the petitioners; (e) if interim interdict were granted the respondents would be unable to sell their quite small stocks of 'Glenfiddoch-Glenlivet' and 'Glenfiddoch'; (f) the petitioners would not suffer great loss if interim interdict were refused. The respondents were prepared to keep account of all their sales during the currency of the proceedings and the practice in infringement cases was to withhold interim interdict on an account being kept and caution found; and (g) the petitioners had known of the respondents' intentions since 1977, had taken no action on a bottling of 1979, and there had been undue delay in raising proceedings which militated against interim interdict. For all these reasons the balance of convenience was against granting interim interdict. The order refusing interim interdict was made conditional upon an accounting being kept.

48 FLAXCELL LTD v FREEDMAN 1981 SLT (Notes) 131

Passing off   Trade name: possible confusion in minds of public.

The petitioners were large retailers of 'jeans' sold from shops in London some trading under the name 'Dickie Dirts' and others to a lesser extent under 'Dirty Dicks'. They had also established a considerable market in Scotland. The respondent advertised goods for sale in the Glasgow Evening News under the trade name 'Dirty Dicks' from an address in Glasgow. The petitioners sought to interdict the respondent from trading under the name 'Dirty Dicks'. In granting interim interdict the Lord Ordinary held that two principal questions arose: (a) was there a reasonable likelihood of confusion in the minds of the public; and (b) if so, was there any likelihood of more than minute damage to the petitioners' business? They had traded under both names and this had already caused some confusion in the past. The petitioners had made out a *prima facie* case of possible confusion if the respondent was to trade under 'Dirty Dicks'. There was a likelihood of some loss of business to the petitioners by diversion of some customers to the goods of the respondent. The balance of convenience was in favour of interim interdict. The petitioners had been trading since 1976 but the respondent had only traded since September 1981. The granting of interim interdict would not disable the respondent from trading since he carried on a separate business from another address in Glasgow.

49 SCOTTISH MILK MARKETING BOARD v DRYBROUGH & CO LTD 1985 SLT 253

Passing off   Trade name: no probability of confusion in minds of the general public: speculative loss.

The petitioners were engaged in the marketing of milk, butter, cheese and other dairy products under the trade name 'Scottish Pride' and had been so since 1960. The respondents were brewers and were about to market and advertise lager under the name 'Scottish Pride'. The petitioners sought to interdict the action of the respondents whose marketing was due to commence within a few days. In refusing interim interdict the Lord Ordinary (Davidson) accepted that the use of the word 'Scottish Pride' in the petitioners' advertising campaigns had been such as to make the use of the words part of the goodwill of their products. The petitioners had however failed to satisfy him that there was a probability of confusion in the public mind which was likely to damage the petitioners' goodwill. The nature of the petitioners' products was entirely different from that of the respondents. If interim interdict were granted the respondents would suffer immediate and quantifiable loss. Their preparations for marketing were well advanced. A large number of cans had already been prepared and were due to be filled within a few days; the Christmas market could be prejudiced, and their loss could amount to £100,000. Against this, any loss the petitioners might suffer was highly speculative. It would be a simple matter for the petitioners to emphasise the link between the words 'Scottish Pride' and their dairy products. Interim interdict was refused.

50 HIGHLAND DISTILLERIES CO PLC v SPEYMALT WHISKY DISTRIBUTORS LTD 1985 SLT 85

Passing off: bottled malt whisky   Factors weighed in ascertaining the balance of convenience.

The petitioners, distillers and bottlers of a single malt whisky 'Bunnahabhain', sought interdict against the respondents selling bottled whisky prominently labelled as coming from 'Bunnahabhain Distillery' and having been distilled by the petitioners. The petitioners argued that the use of the name 'Bunnahabhain' was likely to be taken as a use of the petitioners' trade mark and that they would suffer harm in their business and in their goodwill and reputation. The respondents had undertaken to keep account of their sale of the whisky. Dealing with an application for interim interdict, Lord Ross declined to reach any final decision, at this stage, upon the complex question of infringement of trade mark and the respondents' answers to these averments of infringement. He was however satisfied that there was a case to try, and that the petitioners had put forward a *prima facie* case of infringement and passing off. On the question of the balance of convenience, the relative inconvenience to either party following the imposition of interim interdict was the dominant consideration. The respondents would suffer no loss if interim interdict were to be granted, since they could retain the whisky in barrels and use it for blending and they should be able to dispose of their stocks. If interim interdict were to be refused, the petitioners would suffer loss by loss of sales and debasement of their reputation and goodwill.

The respondents maintained that there had been undue delay on the part of the petitioners in seeking interdict (ten weeks from the expiry of the petitioners' ultimatum to the respondents). This had been due to difficulties encountered by the petitioners in consulting with counsel. The court was not satisfied that this delay was sufficient to militate against interim interdict. The balance of convenience was in favour of granting interim interdict.

51 MACALLAN-GLENLIVET PLC v SPEYMALT WHISKY DISTRIBUTORS LTD 1983 SLT 348

Passing off Immediate and irreparable harm: offer to purchase stocks: procedure.

The petitioners raised an action of interdict claiming infringement of trade mark and passing off by the respondents, in consequence of their admitted intention of marketing malt whisky under labels said to be the prerogative of the petitioners, as holders of a registered trade mark. Granting interim interdict, Lord Cameron said the petitioners had made detailed averments which set out a *prima facie* case of infringement and passing off and the intentions of the respondents were admitted. The averments of apprehended loss and the grounds for these related to matters which could bring about immediate and irreparable consequences for the petitioners. The respondents were in no such position, since the petitioners had offered to purchase their stocks. The balance of convenience therefore lay with granting interim interdict.

Lord Cameron drew attention to the need to adhere to the well-established procedure in actions of interdict and applications for interim interdict. In the present case, the petition had not been served nor intimated but, at their own hands, the parties had come into court with the writ and answers, without any order of the court. This was a clear departure from the normal and accepted procedure.

52 CHILL FOODS (SCOTLAND) LTD v COOL FOODS LTD
1977 SLT 38

Prima facie case Foundation document not produced and existence denied.
Passing off Trade names not merely descriptive: pursuers long established.

Three separate petitions sought various interdicts. In the first petition interdict was sought against alleged breach of a restrictive covenant. The document containing the covenant had disappeared but the terms of the covenant were averred by the petitioners. The respondents denied that any agreement in the terms averred by the petitioners was ever signed. Lord Maxwell, in refusing interim interdict, said that, where the right alleged to have been invaded arises from a document which is not produced, and the very existence of which is denied, if the petitioner can point to no document, admission or other *prima facie* evidence or circumstance supporting the averment of the contract, it would at least require a very strong argument on balance of convenience to justify interim interdict. This applies particularly where the document is a restrictive covenant. In such cases the precise wording of the document may be crucial to its enforceability.

In the second petition, where the petitioners sought interdict against the respondents from using confidential information obtained from a customer and supplier on cards kept for the petitioners, interim interdict was granted. The court held that the balance of convenience lay with the petitioners who had an established business which was or might be under threat. The respondents had only just started to trade in competition. If the interim interdict severely hampered their business activities, they could devote their trading energies to a different area or to a different business. The balance of convenience favoured the established business against a new interloper.

In the third petition interdict was sought against the respondents trading in frozen food stuffs under their company name, unless and until they specifically disassociated themselves from the petitioners.

This was in effect a 'passing off' interdict. The court held that the two names were not merely descriptive names (as was the case in *Office Cleaning Services Ltd v Westminster Window and General Cleaners Ltd* 1946 63 RPC 39). In the circumstances of the present case, the respondents had chosen a name so similar to that of the petitioners that they could hardly complain if, at this stage, an intention to mislead was suspected. The respondents in fact could change their name. If so, the balance of convenience would favour the petitioners, for whose long-established business change would be much more damaging.

53 AMERICAN CYANAMID CO v ETHICON LTD [1975] 1 All ER 504, HL

Patent Threatened infringement: basis for granting interlocutory injunction: action not frivolous or vexatious: maintenance of status quo.

The plaintiffs had been proprietors of a patent for absorbable surgical sutures since 1964. A rival company, the defendants, who already marketed catgut sutures, proposed to introduce their own artificial sutures. The plaintiffs sought an injunction to restrain a threatened infringement of their patent by the imminent supply of the defendants' sutures to surgeons in the UK. The plaintiffs moved for an interlocutory injunction. At first instance, the patent judge, having considered a large volume of affidavit evidence, held that the plaintiffs had made out a strong *prima facie* case and that, on the balance of convenience, an interlocutory injunction should be granted to maintain the status quo pending trial. On appeal, the Court of Appeal reversed this decision on the ground that there was a well-established rule of law that the court was precluded from making such an order, or from considering the balance of convenience, unless the evidence adduced satisfied the court that, on the balance of probabilities, the plaintiffs would ultimately succeed in obtaining a permanent injunction.

On appeal by the plaintiffs to the House of Lords, the court held (a) that there was no rule of law to the above effect; (b) all that was necessary was that the court should be satisfied the claim was not frivolous or vexatious, that is, that there was a case to try. On balance of convenience the factors were that the defendants had not yet put their sutures on the market, whereas, the plaintiffs were already establishing a growing market for their absorbable sutures in competition with the defendants' catgut sutures. Giving judgment and allowing the appeal Lord Diplock said, 'What the Court of Appeal was doing was trying the issue of infringement on the conflicting affidavit evidence as it stood, without oral testimony or cross examination.'

There was, he said, now no distinction in the principles governing interlocutory injunctions in patent cases as opposed to any other form of action (overruling *Smith v Grigg Ltd* [1924] 1 KB 655). So, unless the material available at the hearing failed to disclose that the plantiff had any real prospect of ultimately obtaining a permanent injunction, the court should, in the application for interlocutory injunction, go on to consider the balance of convenience.

As to the balance of convenience in the present case, where the factors were evenly balanced, it was a counsel of prudence to take such measures as would maintain the status quo. The patent judge at first instance had properly assessed the balance of convenience and the interlocutory injunction would be granted.[1]

54 McDAID v CLYDEBANK DISTRICT COUNCIL 1984 SLT 162

Town and Country Planning Acts Enforcement Notices defective and a nullity: jurisdiction of the Court of Session not displaced by statute.

The respondents, as planning authority, served enforcement notices upon the occupier of a yard and garage requiring him to cease using the yard for a scrap metal business and to restore the garage to its previous dimensions. Section 84(5) of the Town and Country Planning (Scotland) Act 1972 requires that enforcement notices must be served upon the owner of the land in question, in addition to service upon the occupier thereof. No such service was effected upon the owner (the petitioner in this case) although the respondents were aware of his identity. The occupier failed to appeal to the Secretary of State against the enforcement notices. The petitioner did not become aware of the service of the notices upon the occupier until long after the time for lodging an appeal had expired. The petitioner sought suspension of the enforcement notices and interdict against the respondents relying upon the same. The Lord Ordinary refused the petition on the ground that it was barred by s 85(10) of the Town and Country Planning (Scotland) Act 1972, which provides that the validity of an enforcement notice shall not (except by way of appeal to the Secretary of State) be questioned in any proceedings. On appeal to the Inner House, the court held that the appellate jurisdiction of the Court of Sessions was not excluded by s 85(10), where, for reasons beyond the control of the persons seeking to challenge the planning authority, the procedure provided by the statute

---

1 See, however, Lord Fraser in *NWL v Woods* (1979) 3 All ER 614 at 628 as to Scottish practice of weighing strengths of parties' averments.

could not be used. The enforcement notices, not having been properly served in the manner required by the Act, were a nullity. Exclusion of the jurisdiction of the Court of Session could only be effected by the clearest legislative provision in direct and most unambiguous terms. No such legislative intention could be derived from s 85(10) of the Act and the petitioner's right to invoke the jurisdiction had not been displaced. The interim interdict sought should be granted.

55 EARL CAR SALES (EDINBURGH) LTD v CITY OF EDINBURGH DISTRICT COUNCIL 1984 SLT 8

Town and country planning Court cannot prohibit issue of stop notice when within the legal powers of the planning authority.

The petitioners sought suspension of a 'stop notice' issued under s 84 of the Town and Country Planning (Scotland) Act 1972, as amended by s 4 of the Town and Country Planning (Scotland) Act 1977, and interdict *ad interim* against its enforcement. The petitioners, who were tenants of garage premises, had applied for planning permission to use ground at the rear of the garage for open parking and storage of vehicles. The application was refused, but the petitioners proceeded to use the ground for the said purposes. The respondents, as planning authority, issued an enforcement notice, against which the petitioners appealed to the Secretary of State. Interim interdict against issue of a stop notice was granted in the Outer House, on the ground that the question of whether the issue of the stop notice was *ultra vires* did not require to be decided at that stage and the balance of convenience favoured interim interdict. The respondents appealed. Giving judgment and referring to *Central Regional Council v Clackmannan District Council* 1983 SLT 666, the Lord President (Emslie) said that the court had no power to prohibit a planning authority from exercising their legal right to issue a stop notice, and the court would not interfere, unless it appeared *prima facie* at least that the planning authority had gone beyond its powers. In the present case the petitioners' averments (which were that the use made of the strip of land was not an 'activity of the land' within the meaning of the Town and Country Planning (Scotland) Act 1972, and that the issue of a stop notice was on that ground *ultra vires*) were plainly irrelevant. The judge of first instance had erred in not deciding this question of relevancy.

56 CENTRAL REGIONAL COUNCIL v CLACKMANNAN DISTRICT COUNCIL 1983 SLT 666

Town and country planning Enforcement notice not in issue but interdict sought against issue of stop notice.

The petitioners, as highway and education authority, obtained from the respondents as planning authority, a planning permission to construct a road, the line of which encroached upon a school playground. It was a condition of the planning permission that work would not start until such time as adequate alternative educational provision had been made. A dispute arose between the parties as to this and the respondents issued an enforcement notice in terms of ss 84(1) and 84(3) of the Town and Country Planning (Scotland) Act 1972. The petitioners appealed to the Secretary of State under s 85(1) of the Act. They also presented a petition craving interdict prohibiting the respondents, as planning authority, from issuing a stop notice under s 87 of the Act which would prevent encroachment on the playground. The cessation of work necessary under a stop notice would, said the petitioners, cause substantial loss and damage to the public.

In refusing, on appeal, the grant of interim interdict, the court held that, since the validity of the enforcement notice was not in issue, the service of a stop notice was *intra vires* of the respondents as planning authority, and the court had no power to restrain the exercise by the respondents of their statutory right to issue the stop notice. It was irrelevant to plead that the exercise of that statutory right would result in loss or damage. In any case, if the enforcement notice were ultimately to be quashed by the Secretary of State, the petitioners would have their remedy in a claim for compensation for any loss suffered by the service of a stop notice under s 166 of the Act. (Followed in *Earl Car Sales (Edinburgh) Ltd v City of Edinburgh District Council* 1984 SLT 8.)

Index

Abortion
 right of wife to have, 122
Abuse of power
 education, 172-174
 exclusion from meetings, 160
 local authority, by, 160
 public bodies, 117-119
Abuse of process
 action persisted in, 20-21
Access agreements
 trespass, 54
 water and streams, 50
Acquiesence
 defence to action, as, 19
Actio popularis
 title and interest to sue, 14
Action of reduction
 arbitration proceedings, 24
 public bodies, against, 115
 wrongful interdict, 123
Affadavit evidence
 exclusion orders, 95
 interim interdict, 141-142
Agents
 defenders, as, 7
Air
 pollution of, 33
Air space
 trespass in, 54
Aircraft
 nuisance, as, 31
 trespass in air space, 54
Alternative remedies. *See*
  EXCLUSION OF THE REMEDY
Amendment
 crave, of, 1
Animals
 nuisance by, 30
 trespass by, 53
Appeals
 interdict, against, 123
  enforcement restrained pending
    appeal, 21

Apprehension of wrong
 anticipated nuisance, 29-30
 continuing wrongs, 3
 evidence required, 1
 objectionable works, 2
 planning matters, 2
Arbitration
 action of reduction, 24
 interdict as alternative, 159
 stay of proceedings, 23-24
Arrest, powers of
 matrimonial interdicts, 96-98
Arrestment
 wrongful use of, 25
Assault
 threat of, 120

Bias
 disciplinary committee, 162
Boats
 mooring of, 47
Breach of interdict. *See under*
  ENFORCEMENT OF INTERDICT
Burial grounds
 encroachment upon, 41-42
Business names
 protection of, 64-65

Caution
 interim interdict refused where
  caution sufficient, 137, 146
 juratory caution, 150
 petitioner for interim interdict to
  lodge, 136-137
 procedure
  Court of Session, 149-150
  Sheriff Court, 154
 repetition of breach of interdict,
  against, 136, 138
Caveats
 procedure, 149, 154
Children
 "child of the family' defined, 91

Children—*continued*
　marriage of parties below certain
　　age, 120-122
　removal from jurisdiction, 122, 151
Coal mining
　rights of support, 42-45
Cohabiting couples
　interdicts and exclusion orders, 89,
　　98-99
Collective liability
　jurisdiction, 8
Common law interdict
　matrimonial homes, 96
Companies
　conduct of internal affairs, 168-169
　directors
　　appointment and removal, 57
　　fiduciary duty, 55-56
　liquidation proceedings, 25, 58
　majority and minority shareholders'
　　rights, 55-56
　'seat' as domicile of, 6
　transfer of shares, 57-58
　ultra vires actings, 56-57
　winding up, 25, 58
Completed wrongs
　availability of interdict, 3
Computer programs
　copyright in, 71, 73-74
Confidential information
　breach of confidence, 132-134, 185
Continuing wrongs
　availability of interdict, 3
Contracts
　breach of confidence, 132-134
　breach of contract
　　agreement to delay or to refrain
　　　from decree, 23
　　generally, 126
　　miscellaneous contracts, 131-132
　　third party's inducement of, 13,
　　　132, 161-162
　negative obligations, 126
　restraint of trade or employment
　　balance of convenience, 176, 177,
　　　178, 180
　　duration and nature of restraint,
　　　130, 179, 181
　　employment and trading
　　　restraints, distinguished,
　　　127-128
　　examples of, 176-182
　　general principles, 126, 127
　　geographical area of restraint,
　　　128-130, 179-180

Contracts—*continued*
　restraint of trade or
　　employment—*continued*
　　manufacturers and distributors,
　　　128
　　public interest, 127, 131
　　pursuer's interest to sue, 13
　　reasonableness, 127
　　severable restraints, 127, 175
　　title to sue arising under, 13
Copyright
　artistic works, 74-75
　broadcasting, 79
　cable transmission, 79
　cinematograph films, 78-79
　commissioned works, 75
　computer programs, 71, 73-74
　Crown copyright, 80
　designs, 76, 81-82
　exemptions from copyright, 75-76
　fair dealing exclusion, 75, 76
　future copyrights, breach of, 74
　infringement generally, 72
　　proceedings for, 79-80
　literary, dramatic and musical
　　works, 72-73, 168
　nature of, 71-72
　performance in public, 73, 77-78
　period of, 71-72
　proceedings for infringement, 79-80
　proof of facts, 80
　public policy exclusion, 75-76
　published editions, 77
　satellite broadcasting, 79
　sound recordings, 77-78, 167-168
　television and sound broadcasts, 79
　video taping, 79
Corporate bodies. *See also* COMPANIES
　interdict against, 8
Corporeal moveables
　title to sue, 12
Court of Session
　control of inferior courts and
　　administrative bodies, 21, 114
　judicial review, 114-116
　jurisdiction, 5
　patents jurisdiction, 85
　procedure in interdict actions,
　　147-152
　supervisory jurisdiction, 4, 114-115,
　　116
Crave
　amendment of, 1

Criminal proceedings
  availabiity of interdict, 16
  breach of interdict, 135
  matrimonial interdict
    powers of arrest, 96-98
  prevention of prosecution, by
    interdict, 20
  quasi-criminal nature of interdict, 1
  trespass, 51
Crown
  copyright, 80
  declaratory order against, 113-114,
    115
  foreshore, 48
  immunity, 19
  interdict against, 113-114, 115
  judicial review, 114-116
  ministers and officers of, 113-114,
    115
  Queen's Award for Industry, 66
  Royal Warrant or Arms, 65-66

Damages
  wrongful interdict, for, 123-125
Defamation
  availability of interdict, 120
  interim interdict, 120, 140-141,
    169-171
Delay
  bar to action, whether, 18
Designs
  protection of, 76, 81-82
Diligence
  ex parte statements, founded on, 26
  interdict against wrongful use of,
    24-27
  periculo petentis, grant of, 26
Dismissal of petition
  preliminary stage, at, 1
Divorce. *See also* MATRIMONIAL
    HOMES
  removal of property, 122
Documentary evidence
  interim interdict, 141
Domestic violence
  exclusion orders, 91-95
Domicile
  basis of jurisdiction, as, 6
  defenders to interdict actions, of, 5-6

Education
  interim interdict, 171-175
EEC member state
  defender domiciled in, 5-6

Elections
  returning officer's duty, 165-166
Employees
  defenders, as, 7-8
  implied obligation of confidence,
    132-134
  restraint clauses. *See under*
    CONTRACTS
Employers
  defenders, as, 7-8
Encroachment
  heritable property, 40-42, 183-185
  water rights and the foreshore,
    upon, 47-50
Enforcement of interdict
  breach of interdict
    caution against repetition of
      breach, 136, 138
    complaint of, 135
    defended cases, 137
    fines on trade union, 138
    imprisonment, 135, 138
    induciae, 136
    interim interdict, 152
    liability for criminal prosecution,
      135
    measure of proof required, 135
    misnomer of defendent, 135-136
    non-appearance of defender,
      137-138
    penalties for, 1, 135
    procedure where breach admitted
      or proved, 137
    wilful disregard of order, 138
  change of circumstances, 139
  defect in jurisdiction, 136
  duration of enforcement, 136
  postponement of interdict, 137
  undertaking by defender, 137
England
  defender domiciled in, 5
Entry upon land or premises
  statutory powers of, 53-54
Evidence
  affidavit evidence
    exclusion orders, 95
    interim interdict, 141-142
  interim interdict
    affidavit evidence, 141-142
    documentary evidence, 141
  required for grant of interdict, 1
Exclusion of the remedy
  acquiescence as defence, 19
  common law remedies available as
    alternatives, 15-16

Exclusion of the remedy—*continued*
  criminal proceedings, 16
  Crown immunity, 19
  delay as bar to action, 18
  interdict not a replacement for competent diligence, 15
  legal proceedings, prevention of, 20
  matter already subject of legal proceedings, 15
  mora and taciturnity as bar, 18
  planning matters, 17
  res judicata plea, 18-19
  statutory remedies, by, 16-17, 23, 166
Exclusion orders
  matrimonial homes, 91-95
    cohabiting couples, 98-99

Feu charter
  title to sue to prevent breach, 13
Feuing restriction
  title to sue, 9
Fishing
  trespass, as, 52
  water rights, 47-50
Foreign courts
  restraint of proceedings in, 22
Foreshore
  Crown rights, 48
  public right to use, 34, 48

Games
  playing of, as nuisance, 35
Goods
  suspension and interdict of poinding, 26-27
Goodwill
  protection of, 59
Government acts
  interdict against, 113-114
  judicial review, 114-116

Heritable property
  competing rights, 141
  encroachment upon, 40-42, 183-185
  interim interdict, 183
  proprietor's title to sue, 9-10
  trespass. *See* TRESPASS

Imprisonment
  breach of interdict, for, 135, 138
Increase in actions
  interdict, of, 3
Industrial disputes
  acts in furtherance of trade disputes, 104-106

Industrial disputes—*continued*
  ballots, 111-112
    action without ballots, 103
  compulsion to work restricted, 112
  employment protection legislation, 101
  ex parte interdicts, 112
  historical background, 100-101
  picketing
    criminal acts, 107
    peaceful, 103-104
    primary, 107-108
    restraint of operations by interdict, 109
    rights of non-striking workers, 108-109
    secondary action, 109-111
  political ends, 107
  secondary industrial action, 109-111
  'sit-ins' and 'work-ins', 104-106, 109
  strike, defined, 111
  trade dispute, defined, 106-107
  trade unions
    immunity from legal proceedings, 100-102, 104
    vicarious liability of, 102-103, 138
  worker in dispute, defined, 106
Inhibition
  wrongful use of, 25
Inspection of documents
  court's powers extended, 7
Intellectual property
  business and professional names and designations, 64-65
  copyright. *See* COPYRIGHT
  definition, 88
  disclosure of information ordered, 88
  goodwill, 59
  interim interdict, 88
  passing off. *See* PASSING OFF
  patents. *See* PATENTS
  registered designs, 76, 81-82
  Royal Warrant, 65-66
  self-incrimination in proceedings, 87
  trade marks. *See* TRADE MARKS
Interest to sue. *See* TITLE TO SUE
Interim exclusion orders
  availability and grounds, 93-95
Interim interdict
  affidavit evidence, 141-142
  alternative remedy available, 137, 146, 180, 182
  balance of convenience, 146
  basic requirements, 145
  breach of, 152

Interim interdict—*continued*
caution required of petitioner, 136-137
caveats against, 149, 154
change of circumstances, 142
competency of interdict questioned, 142
competing titles to heritage, 141
damages for wrongful interdict, 125
defender's entitlement to damages for loss, 142
discretion of court, 140, 143
documentary evidence, 141
duration, 142
end of principal action by, 143
examples
  digest of cases, 159-196
  grant of, 143-145
  refusal of, 145-146
intellectual property actions, 88
inversion of present position as result of, 125
nature of remedy, 140
periculo petentis, grant of, 142
prima facie case on declaratory judgment, 141
procedure
  Court of Session, 148-149
  Sheriff Court, 153-154
refusal where caution sufficient to satisfy loss, 137, 146
relevant factors, 142-143

Joint proprietors
title to sue, 11-12
Judicial review
interdict in, 114-116
statutory functions, of, 4
Jurisdiction
arbitration proceedings, 23-24
collective liability, 8
company, partnership or unincorporated body, 6
control of inferior courts by Court of Session, 21
corporate bodies, 8
courts with, 5
defect in, 136
domicile as basis of, 6
domicile of defender, 5-6
employer and employees, 7-8
principals and agents, 7
proceedings commenced elsewhere in U.K. or E.E.C., 6-7

Jurisdiction—*continued*
protective measures where proceedings commenced elsewhere, 6-7
supervisory jurisdiction, 4, 114-115, 116

Leases
interdict against assignee, 4
irritancy clauses unenforceable by interdict, 15-16
title to sue of landlord or tenant, 10-11
Legal proceedings
diligence, wrongful use of, 24-27
interdict unavailable to suspend anticipated adverse decision, 21
prevention of, by interdict, 20-24
publication of proceedings, 21-22
restraint of proceedings in foreign courts, 22
restraint of statutory bodies, 22-23
Liquidation of companies
availability of interdict, 58
stay of proceedings, 25
Local authorities
abuse of power, 160
breach of statutory duty, 163
remedies available against, 4
ultra vires actions, 165

Malicious actions
interdict against, 20
Marriage
prevention of, by interdict, 120-122
Matrimonial homes
'child of the family', defined, 91
cohabiting couples, 89, 98-99
common law interdict, 96
court orders available, 90-91
definition, 90
exclusion orders, 91-95
  cohabiting couples, 98-99
furniture and plenishing, 90, 92, 96
legislative reforms, 89
matrimonial interdicts, 95-97, 186
molestation interdict, 95
occupancy rights of spouses, 89-91
Members of the public
title to sue, 14
Mining operations
rights of support, 42-45
Misnomer of defender
proceedings for breach, 135-136

202   Index

Molestation
  matrimonial molestation interdict, 95
  threat of, 120
Mora
  plea to bar action, as, 18

Natural justice
  bias, 162-163
Nature of interdict
  general principles, and scope, 1-4
Negative interdict
  incompetency of, 2-3
Negative servitude
  enforcement of, 9
Noise
  nuisance by, 30-31, 166-167
Northern Ireland
  defender domiciled in, 5
Notice of interdict
  essential in breach proceedings, 135, 152
Nuisance
  animals, by, 30
  anticipated nuisance, 29-30
  balance of convenience, 187
  categories, 28
  common law nuisance, 28-29
  conventional nuisance, 35-36
  defences
    acquiescence, 36-37
    coming to the nuisance, 38
    licence, 37-38
    normal and familiar use of property, 39
    prescription, 36
    public interest, 38-39
    remedial measures possible, 39-40
    statutory authority, 37-38
    undertakings to modify nuisance, 40
  interim interdict, 186-188
  miscellaneous common law nuisances, 34
  misuse of highway or foreshore, 33-34
  nature of, 28
  noise and vibration, 30-31
  objectionable works, 29
  playing of games, 35
  pollution
    air, of, 33
    water, 31-33, 49
  public interest, 186
  statutory nuisance, 35

Nuisance—*continued*
  undertakings to modify, 40
Partnerships
  breach of partnership agreement, 13
  'seat' as domicile of, 6
Passing off
  class actions, 63-64
  damages combined with interdict, 61
  descriptive names for goods, 60-61
  examples of, 62-63, 188-193
  fraud and fraudulent intent, 61-62
  'get-up' of goods, 61
  nature of, 59-60
  trade mark infringed, 62
Patents
  assignation of, 86
  Comptroller of Patents referred to, 85
  definition, 83
  exclusions, 83
  infringement, 83-85
    nature of interdict sought, 85
    procedure, 151-152
    threatened, 86, 193-194
    threats of proceedings for, 87
  international conventions, 86
  jurisdiction, 85
  licences, 86
  partial validity, 85
Patrimonial interest
  title to sue, 12-13
Personal nature
  interdict, of, 3-4
Picketing. *See under* INDUSTRIAL DISPUTES
Pipe lines
  operation and maintenance of, 45-46
  support of, 45
Planning matters
  availability of interdict, 17, 23, 194-196
  nuisance in implementation of permission, 37
  scope of interdict, 2
Poinding
  suspension and interdict of, 26-27
Police
  powers of arrest for matrimonial interdict, 96-98
  powers of entry, 54
Pollution
  air, of, 33
  noise, 30-31, 166-167
  water, of, 31-33, 49

Positive obligations
  enforcement by interdict, 3
Postponement
  order of interdict, of, 137
Principals
  defenders, as, 7
Procedure
  Court of Session
    appointment to adjustment roll, 150-151
    breach of interdict, 152
    caution generally, 149-150
    caveats, 149
    certificates of refusal, 150
    commencement of action, 147
    decrees in absence, 151
    further procedure, 148
    induciae for service of petition, 147
    infringement of patents and registered designs, 151-152
    interim interdict, 148-149
    juratory caution, 150
    no appearance, no answer by defender, 151
    productions in interim orders, 150
    removal of children, 151
  Sheriff Court
    caution, 154
    caveats, 154
    commencement of action, 152
    further procedure, 153
    induciae, 152-153
    interim interdict, 153-154
    production of documents, 154
Professional names and designations
  protection of, 64-65
Public authorities and bodies
  abuse of power, 117-119, 160-161
  action of reduction, 115
  breach of statutory duty, 164
  discretion, exercise of, 117-118
  interim interdict and balance of convenience, 146
  judicial review, 114-116
  statutory remedy against infringement of powers, 118
  ultra vires acts, 116-117
Public highway
  misuse of, 33-34
  use interfered with, 13
Public interest
  nuisance proceedings, 38-39
  postponement of order, 137

Public interest—*continued*
  restraint of trade or employment, 127, 131
Public rights
  actio popularis, 14
  foreshore, 48
  interference with, 13, 14
  navigation, of, 47
  private individuals unable to protect, 14
Publication of proceedings
  interdict against, 21-22
Pursuer
  liability for truth of averments, 125

Queen's Award for Industry
  use of device, 66

Ratepayers
  title to sue, 12-13
Recall of interdict
  wrongful interdict, 124-125
Reduction, action of
  arbitration decree, 24
  public bodies, against, 115
  wrongful interdict, 123
Registered designs
  protection of, 76, 81-82
    infringement procedure, 151-152
Reinstatement of rights
  interdict, by, 4
Repetition of wrong
  threat of, 3
Res judicata
  plea, as bar to action, 18-19
Restraint clauses. *See under* CONTRACTS
Restrictive covenants. *See* restraint clauses *under* CONTRACTS
Rights of support. *See* SUPPORT, RIGHTS OF
Rivers
  encroachment upon water rights, 47-50
Royal Warrant
  protection of, 65-66

Scope of interdict
  preventative process, as, 2
Self-incrimination
  intellectual property proceedings, 87
Sequestration
  wrongful use of, 25
Service marks
  protection of, 70

Servitudes
  title to sue, 10, 12
Shareholders
  'fraud on the minority', 55-56
Sheriff Courts
  jurisdiction, 5
    procedure in interdict actions, 152-154
Specific implement
  interdict unavailable, 2
Specific performance
  statutory duty, of, 4
Statutory bodies
  restraint of, by interdict, 22-23
  ultra vires acts, 116-117
Statutory powers of entry
  land or premises, on, 53-54
Subsidence
  rights of support, 42-45
Supervisory jurisdiction
  Court of Session, 4, 114-115, 116
Support, rights of
  adjacent buildings, 46-47
  landowner's general right, 42
  mining operations, 42-45
  pipe lines, 45-46
  prescription or acquiescence do not extinguish, 45

Taciturnity
  plea to bar action, as, 18
Terms of interdict
  precision required, 1-2
Title to sue
  contractual interest, 13
  corporeal moveables, 12
  heritable and possessory titles, 9-11
  interest to maintain action, and, 9
  joint proprietors, 11-12
  landlord and tenant, 10-11
  legal relationship required, 9
  members of the public, 14
  patrimonial interest held, 12-13
  ratepayers, 12-13
  servitudes, 10, 12
  teachers' remuneration, 171-172
Trade designs
  protection of, 76, 81-82
Trade disputes. *See* INDUSTRIAL DISPUTES
Trade marks
  general principles, 66-67
  infringement
    arising out of contract, 69

Trade marks—*continued*
  infringement—*continued*
    delay in proceedings, 188-189
    nature of, 67-69
    threatened, 69
    threats against, 69
  passing off actions, 62
  service marks, 70
Trade names
  protection of, 64-65
Trade secrets
  protection of, 130-131, 132-134
Trade unions. *See also* INDUSTRIAL DISPUTES
  'closed shop' agreement, 176
  expulsion from, 177-178
  fines for beach of interdict, 138
  ultra vires acts, 119
Trespass
  access rights, 54
  air space, in, 54
  animals, by, 53
  apprehension of repetition, 51
  competency of interdict, 51-52
  criminal proceedings, 51
  damages claimed, 52
  encroachment, distinguished, 40
  evidence required, 1
  examples, 52, 182-183
  interim interdict, 183
  nature of, 51
  no damage caused, 51-52
  statutory authority to enter, 53-54
  trivial incidents, 51-52

Ultra vires acts
  companies, 56-58
  elections, 165-166
  local authorities, 165
  statutory bodies, 116-117
  trade unions, 119
Undertaking
  defender, by, to remedy, 137, 146
  modification of nuisance, 40
Unincorporated associations
  'seat' as domicile of, 6

Vexatious actions
  legislation against, 20
Vibration
  nuisance by, 30-31

Wales
   defender domiciled in, 5

Water rights
   access rights, 50
   foreshore, 48

Water rights—*continued*
   navigable rivers, 47-48
   non-navigable rivers, 49-50
   pollution of water, 31-33, 49

Wrongful interdict
   damages for, 123-125